IMAGES
of America

LAKE MARY

On the Cover: Pictured is the house of Dr. William Harrison Evans and his family. The Evans family has been pivotal to the development of Lake Mary, including Dr. Evans's charismatic son Frank, standing on the far right with his baby daughter and wife. Close-knit families like this have given Lake Mary the character it has today. (Courtesy of the Lake Mary Historical Society.)

IMAGES
of America

LAKE MARY

John Hope

ARCADIA
PUBLISHING

ISBN 978-1-4671-1305-2

Published by Arcadia Publishing
Charleston, South Carolina

Printed in the United States of America

Library of Congress Control Number: 2014941638

For all general information, please contact Arcadia Publishing:
Telephone 843-853-2070
Fax 843-853-0044
E-mail sales@arcadiapublishing.com
For customer service and orders:
Toll-Free 1-888-313-2665

Visit us on the Internet at www.arcadiapublishing.com

To Lake Mary city commissioner Allan Plank, who not only believed in this book but also gave everything to help make Lake Mary the best town to live in.

Contents

ACKNOWLEDGMENTS

This book could not have been made without the hard work and dedication of the Lake Mary Historical Society and the residents of Lake Mary, who provided photographs and many stories to help share the community's history. Special thanks to Jane Kenovich, president of the Lake Mary Historical Society, for her hard work collecting photographs and stories, verifying information, and generally being the heart and soul of this book. And thank you to all the honest, down-to-Earth people who have made Lake Mary one of the best places to live and work in America.

All images are courtesy of the Lake Mary Historical Society.

Introduction

Starting as two small villages, Belle Fontaine and Bents Station, to the south and north of Lake Mary, respectively, the area began as a citrus-based agricultural community. Beaches along Crystal Lake and Lake Mary and other attractions provided opportunities for residents and vacationers to relax and enjoy time off with family and friends. Early settlers included lumbermen, turpentine workers, and families from Fort Reed (Sanford), who mainly worked in orange groves. As the railroad expanded into central Florida, railroad workers and winter visitors from the north helped to grow the villages.

Swedish-born Axel Evald "A.E." Sjoblom left Henry Sanford's employment in the mid-1880s, moved to the Lake Mary area, and later acquired work in nearby Snowville (later named Altamonte Springs) splitting rails for a new rail line that connected the city of Sanford with the relatively new town of Orlando, formerly known as Jernigan. By 1886, he had bought 30 acres and a house on Crystal Lake close to the new rail line. Sjoblom saw a great opportunity for Belle Fontaine and Bents Station. The area had beautiful lakes, a strong sense of community, and a new train stop. He wisely bought and sold land over the coming years and later built homes and stores, all of which formed the heart of the early villages.

Steam engines became a vital link to draw people and supplies into central Florida, fueling the development in surrounding areas. When Henry Plant later purchased Henry S. Sanford's railroad and completed a link from Jacksonville to Tampa, a focus on tourism brought even more rail passengers to Lake Mary for a pleasurable dip in its waters. The completion of the railroad between Belle Fontaine and Bents Station brought the two communities together. In the late 1890s, Judge David Pulling and Dr. William Harrison Evans merged the two and renamed the area Lake Mary. The first time the town of Lake Mary officially appeared on a map was in 1899.

In 1882, Dr. Evans moved his family from Indiana to the south shores of Lake Mary to recover from an illness. Dr. Evans practiced medicine in Sanford and planted orange trees on his property. His son Frank was hardworking and incredibly charismatic. In his youth and into his adulthood, he starred in local shows, played music using a saw and violin bow, performed magic tricks, and acted in minstrel shows. Frank grew in prominence in the community and was key to the town's growth.

By 1923, Frank Evans had founded the Lake Mary Chamber of Commerce, whose goals included good roads, schools, lighting, civil government, telephone infrastructure, city beautification, publicity, and a volunteer fire department. Frank built the Lake Mary elementary school, garage, commercial buildings, and community center. As isolated as the town might have seemed to outsiders, it had the same range of amenities as any town in America. Lake Mary had its own orchestra, Boy Scout and Girl Scout programs, and of course, there were the lakes. Both Lake Mary and Crystal Lake were not only playgrounds for residents, but also centers for tourism, attracting big-city folks from surrounding areas and from far away, thanks to the ever-growing railroad. In 1925, town leaders first attempted to incorporate the city but residents turned it down, fearing possible "rigid rules" that may have resulted.

World War II affected Lake Mary as it did the rest of America. Residents participated in recycling drives and Victory Gardens while many of their young men and women shipped off to the war. Children showed their support by wearing a "V" for victory on their sleeves. Everyone rationed, which meant things like sugar, coffee, and chocolate were difficult to come by. The growth of a military presence in Sanford's new naval air station and Orlando's McCoy Air Base drew more and more people closer to the small town. Following the war, the community attempted to return to small-town life.

In 1956, Lake Mary's volunteer fire department was established. A local resident donated a non-functioning flatbed truck, the City of Altamonte Springs donated a 500-gallon tank with four sections of hose, and the City of Sanford donated an extension ladder. Then in 1960, the town was uprooted when Hurricane Donna's eye wall passed through Lake Mary, destroying crops and buildings and ultimately becoming one of America's costliest natural disasters.

A distinctive feature of Lake Mary is its city planners' careful preparation for growth while always being mindful to maintain its small-town feel. This is ever present in the city's ingenious zoning. Balanced residential and commercial areas have allowed various prominent corporations to build offices within and near the city, while providing space for people to call Lake Mary home. The city commission has embraced "total quality of life," providing homes and work opportunities in close proximity to reduce daily commutes and solidify the sense of community. This led the way to a 2007 *Money* magazine article naming Lake Mary the fourth best place to live and work in the United States.

Two key foundations to this planning included the paving of roads and the building of an Interstate 4 interchange. Both have been vital conduits for growth that have given the community a substantial foothold to establish itself with the surrounding cities. By the early 1970s, Lake Mary residents saw the expansion of surrounding cities and came to the realization that the only way to keep the community from being swallowed by its neighbors was to incorporate. This led to the official incorporation of the City of Lake Mary in 1973, which opened the city to further opportunities to grow. It also ushered in a new wave of residents who helped shape the city into what it is today.

One

Building Lake Mary

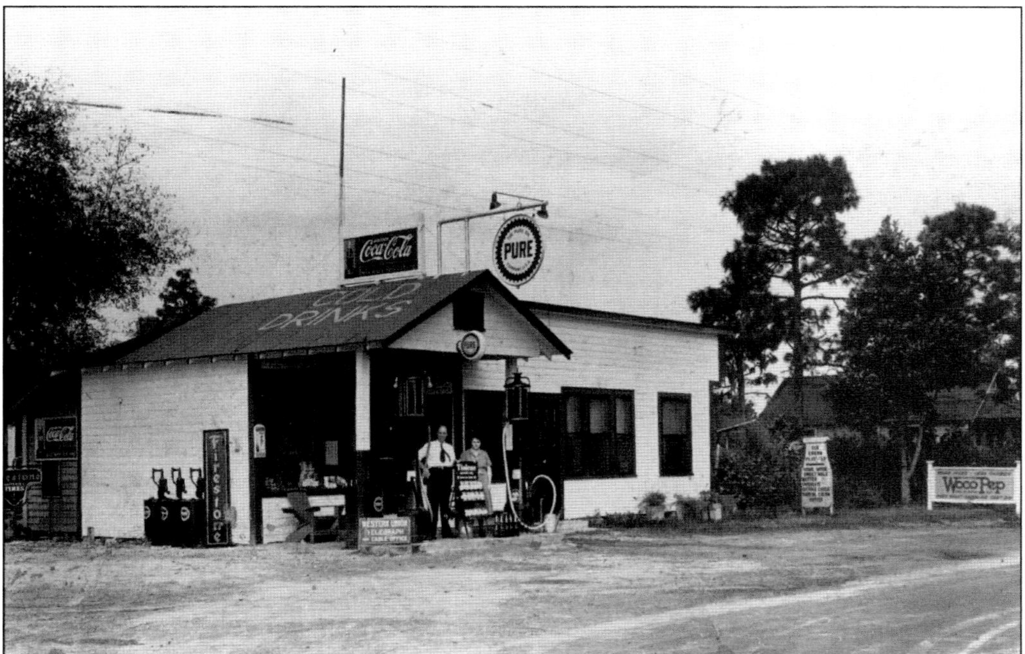

This chapter touches upon the beginnings of the area that was eventually known as Lake Mary. Piece by piece, building by building, Lake Mary emerged from the dense forests of central Florida. The early structures depicted in this chapter established the foundations of the original town.

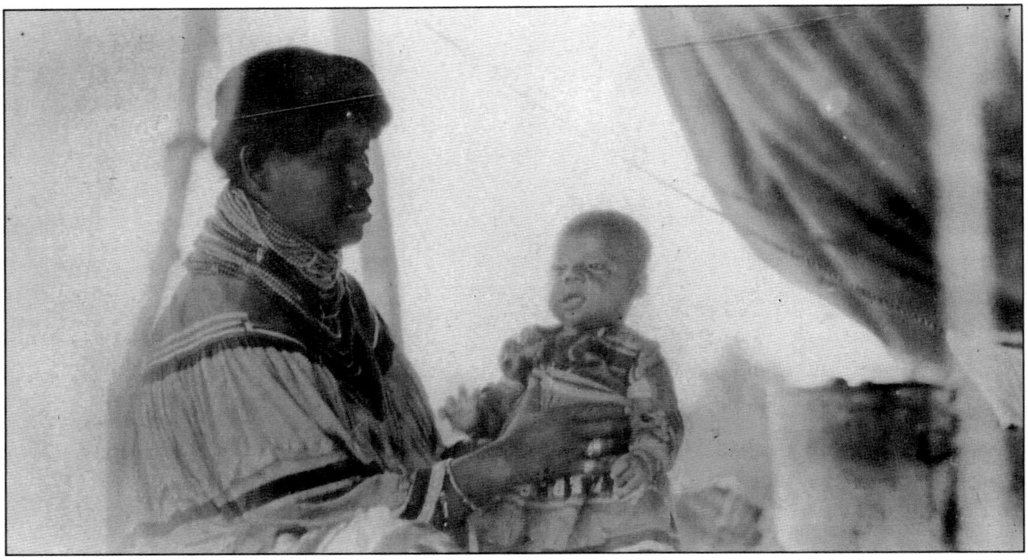

When Europeans first "discovered" Florida in the early 1500s, the area had close to 200,000 aboriginal people in hundreds of tribes, generally all members of the Maskókî linguistic family. By the time Lake Mary was settled by Americans in the 1800s, many of these original residents had been killed by disease, starvation, or warfare. Americans referred to all of these people as Seminoles. The name Seminole comes from a Spanish name, *cimarrones* (meaning free people), because they would not allow themselves to be dominated by the Europeans. In the top photograph, a mother sits with her child. The photograph below depicts aged drawings on rock found near Lake Mary, believed to be from these original Florida settlers.

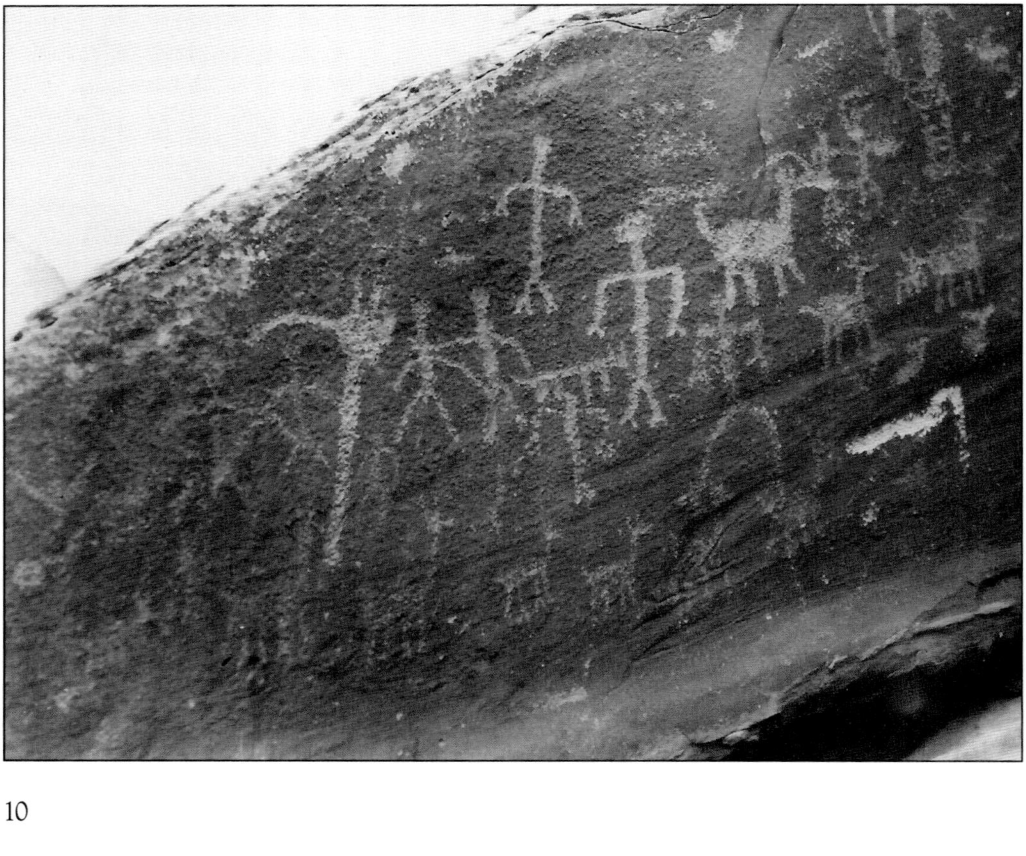

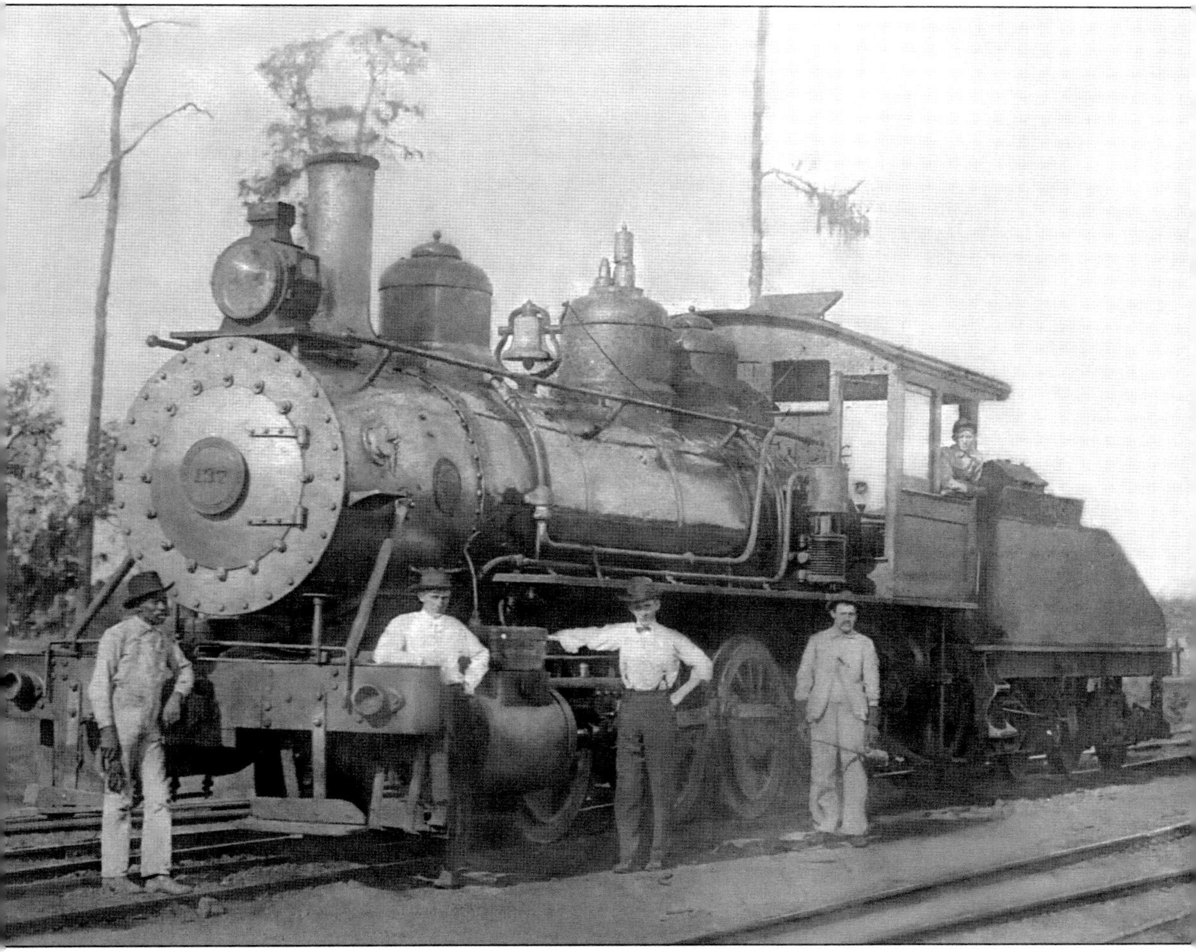

Pictured is an 0-6-0-steam switcher, so named for its wheel configuration. Switchers were used to assemble and disassemble trains so that larger engines could haul passengers and freight with minimal delay. The men pictured, from left to right, include the fireman, who kept the boilers running; the flagman, who threw the yard switches; the conductor, who was responsible for the train; the brakeman, who had the dangerous job of setting and releasing brakes car by car; and the engineer in the cab, who controlled the throttle. These men needed to work as a team to operate the trains safely and get passengers and products in and out in a timely manner.

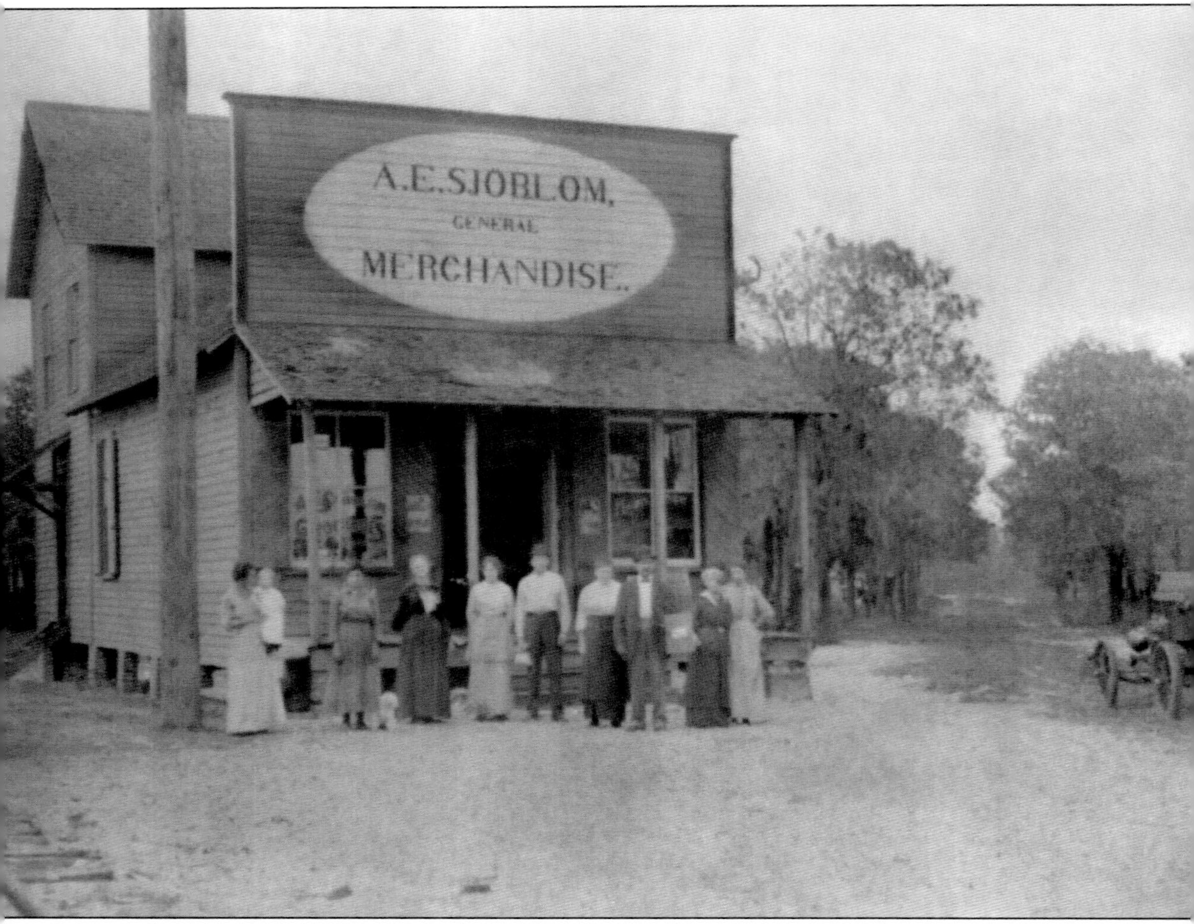

In this photograph taken around 1900, residents gather at A.E. Sjoblom's general store. Barely visible on the left is the railroad where goods and mail were delivered to the store, which was often a meeting place for residents. The villagers came to Sjoblom's to cash checks, post letters, and buy goods such as lumber, groceries, shoes, cemetery plots, and real estate. A.E. Sjoblom notarized documents and performed marriages and funerals. This general store stood near where the Florida Department of Transportation now operates its SunRail commuter train station, once again acting as a key gateway for the community.

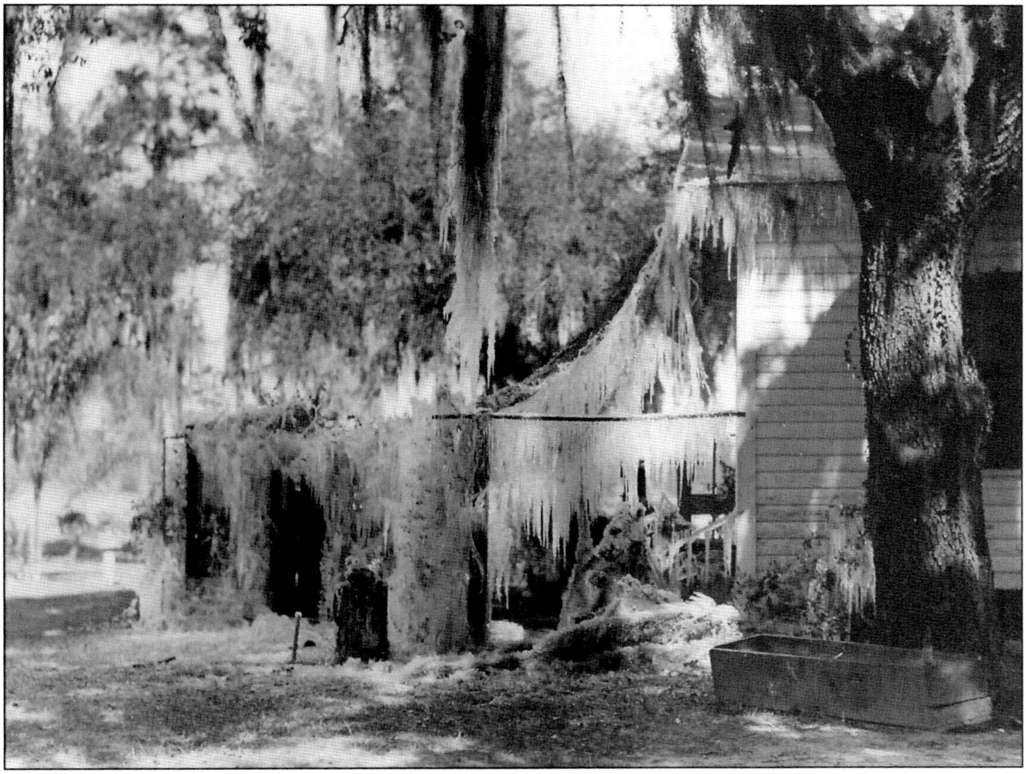

Though uncommon in Florida, freezes have had devastating effects on farming. Eight years after A.E. Sjoblom bought 30 acres of land near Crystal Lake and established his crops, the freezes of 1894 and 1895 killed many of his and other area farmers' trees, forcing them to start again.

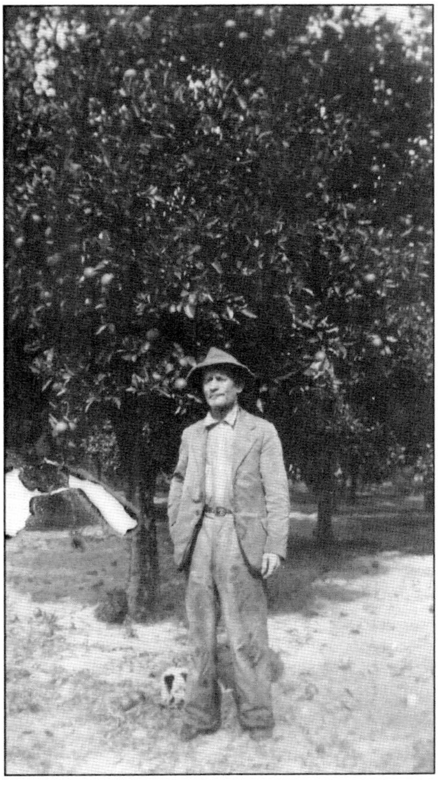

Pictured is a fairly common look for a Florida farmer in the early 1900s, with his family dog close behind. Small farming families laid the foundations of towns across America. Their sheer will and tenacity to overcome freezes, floods, droughts, insects, and other challenges formed the early personality of towns like Lake Mary.

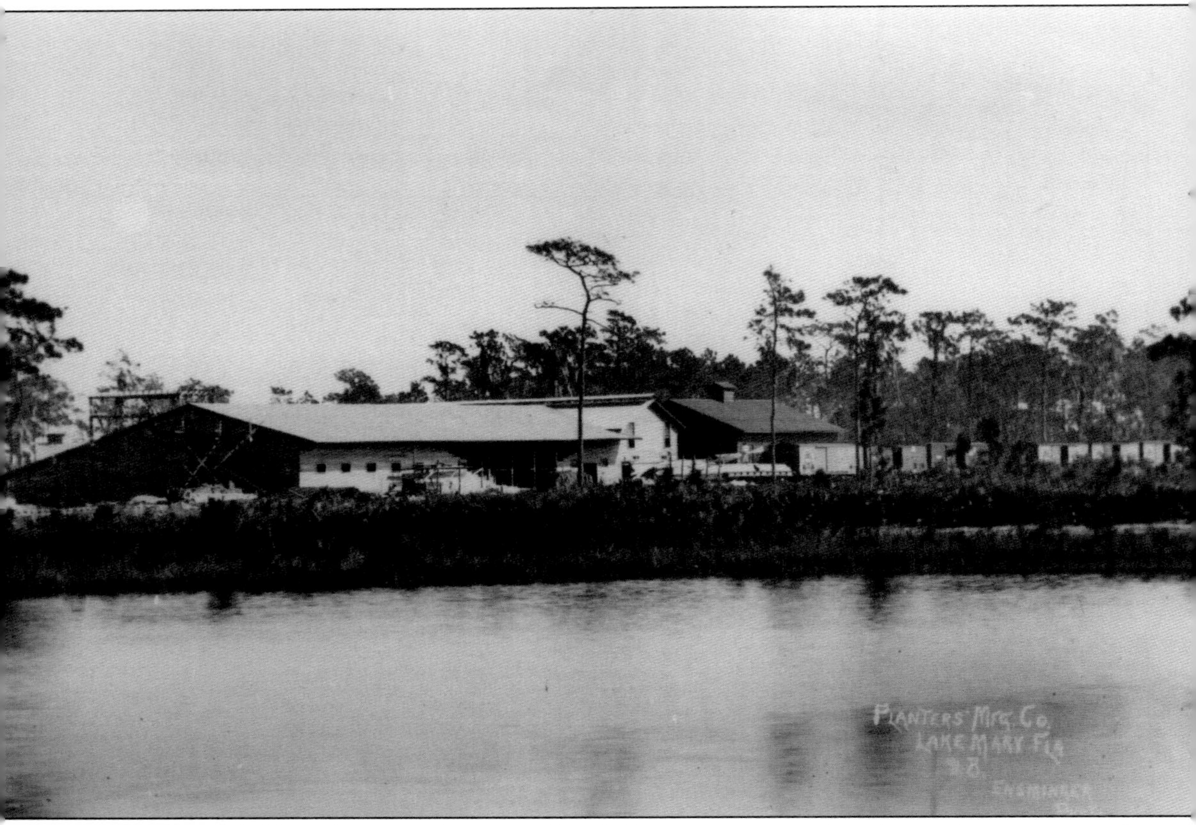

The Planter's Manufacturing Company Starch Factory once stood at the northwest corner of Crystal Lake Avenue and Fifth Street. After the disastrous freezes of 1894 and 1895, many of those who chose not to leave found jobs with Planters. It produced starches, dextrins, farina, and tapioca from the cassava, an exotic-looking plant with an edible root. The plant had been a staple in the diet of tribes living in Central Florida before the arrival of the Spaniards. The factory was built in 1901 and thrived as a major employer until the need to import additional cassavas made the operation uneconomical in 1909. The factory was sold to Overstreet Turpentine Company in 1911, then to A.E. Sjoblom in 1916. Later, it housed Perkin's Glue Factory.

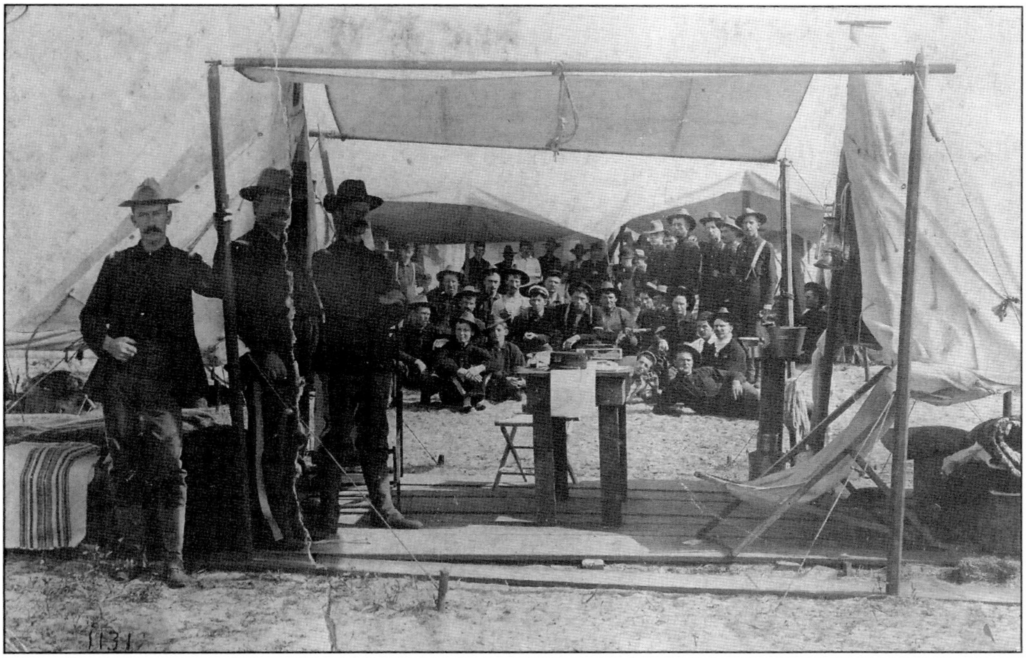

Pictured are American troops, some from Lake Mary, assembling in preparation for the Spanish-American War. The war had an impact on Lake Mary. Not only did key members of the community serve in the military, but trains packed full of soldiers en route to Tampa for their departure to Cuban often passed through the small town. Sometimes Lake Mary's cool waters were the last taste of personal freedom these boys had before shipping off to war. The tipi-like tent in the photograph at right, called a sibley, was used throughout the war and could sleep six men.

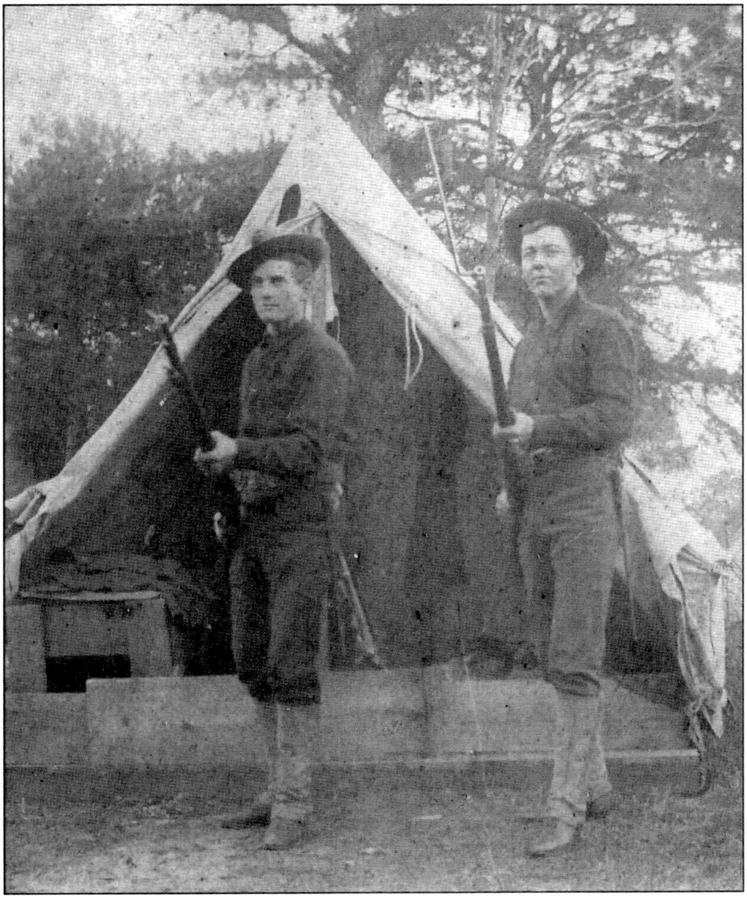

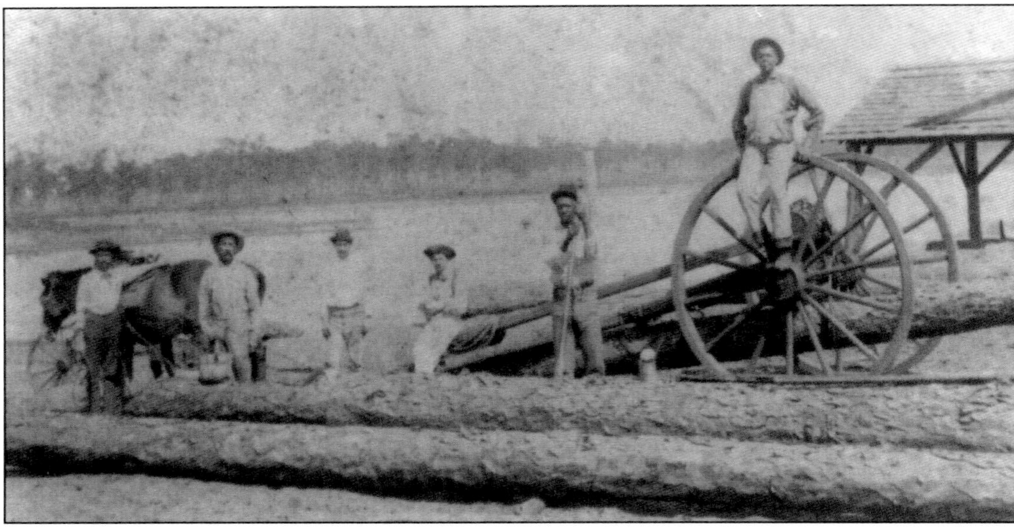

A.E. Sjoblom's sawmill drew men of various skills and backgrounds to the area. Here, men use horses and specialized lumber-hauling wagons to transport freshly cut lumber to Lake Mary's waters. Once in the lake, the lumber floated across to the sawmill on the other side for processing.

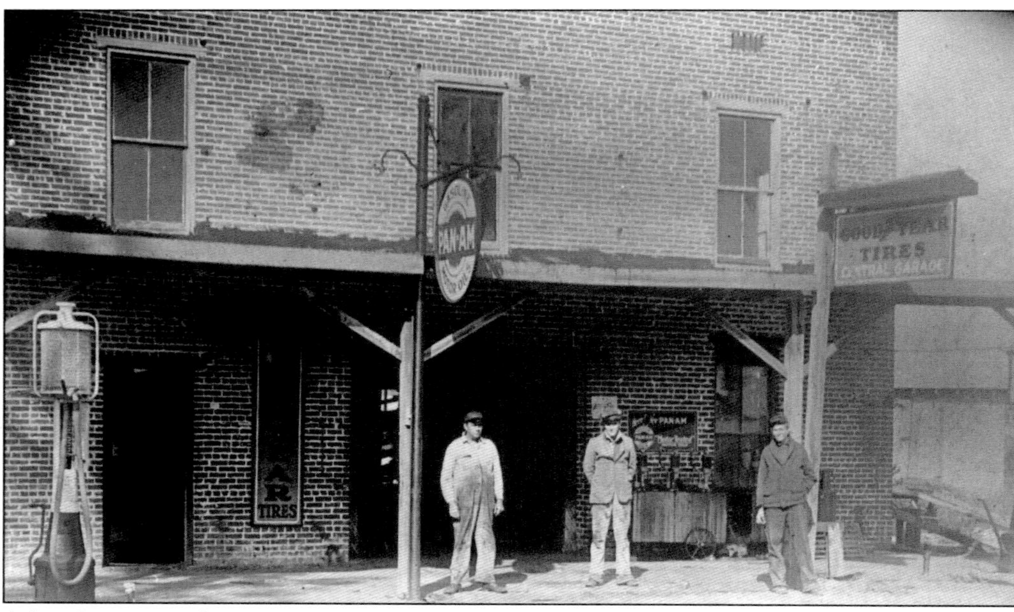

A local garage and station provided skilled mechanics to repair and maintain automobiles and other equipment, which were often problematic in Florida's violent weather. Being a farming community, residents brought their farm equipment to this garage.

Pictured is Frank Evans standing next to the building known as the Old Schoolhouse, a one-room school that served the Lake Mary area for years before a much larger school could be built in response to the growing young population. The school was on the northwest corner of Country Club Road and Lake Mary Boulevard.

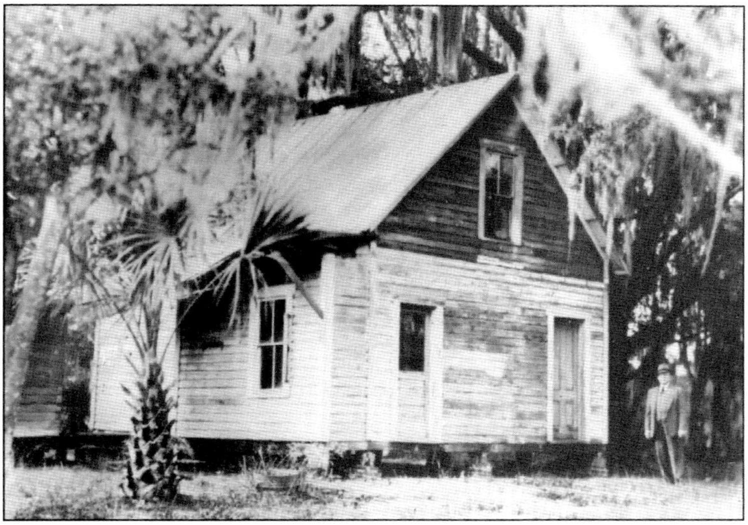

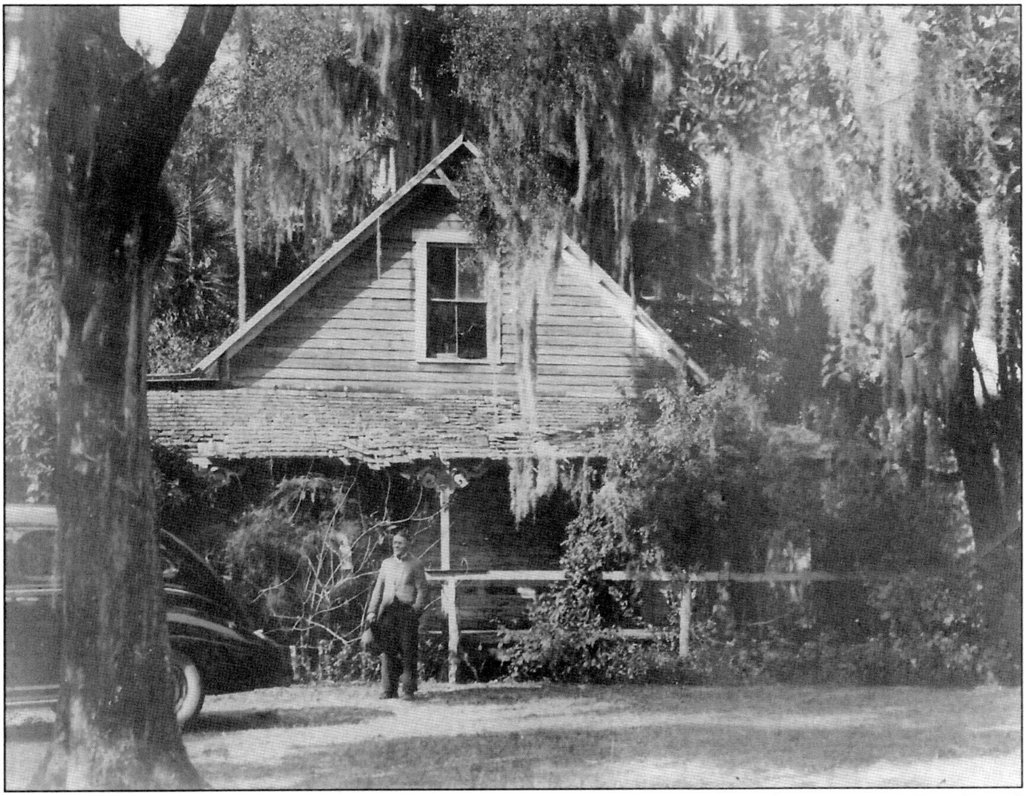

Jonnie Evans stands in front of Dr. William Harrison Evans and Mrs. Melissa Evans's abandoned family home in February 1940, just before it was torn down. Spanish moss and vines drape over the wooden house. Such natural invasiveness was common in a Florida home and accelerated deterioration of the structure. In this image, a few droopy shingles are likely the result of Florida's harsh environment. Though the roof may have been a headache to constantly repair, the greenery contributed to Lake Mary's relaxed, laid-back atmosphere and made coming home a pleasant experience.

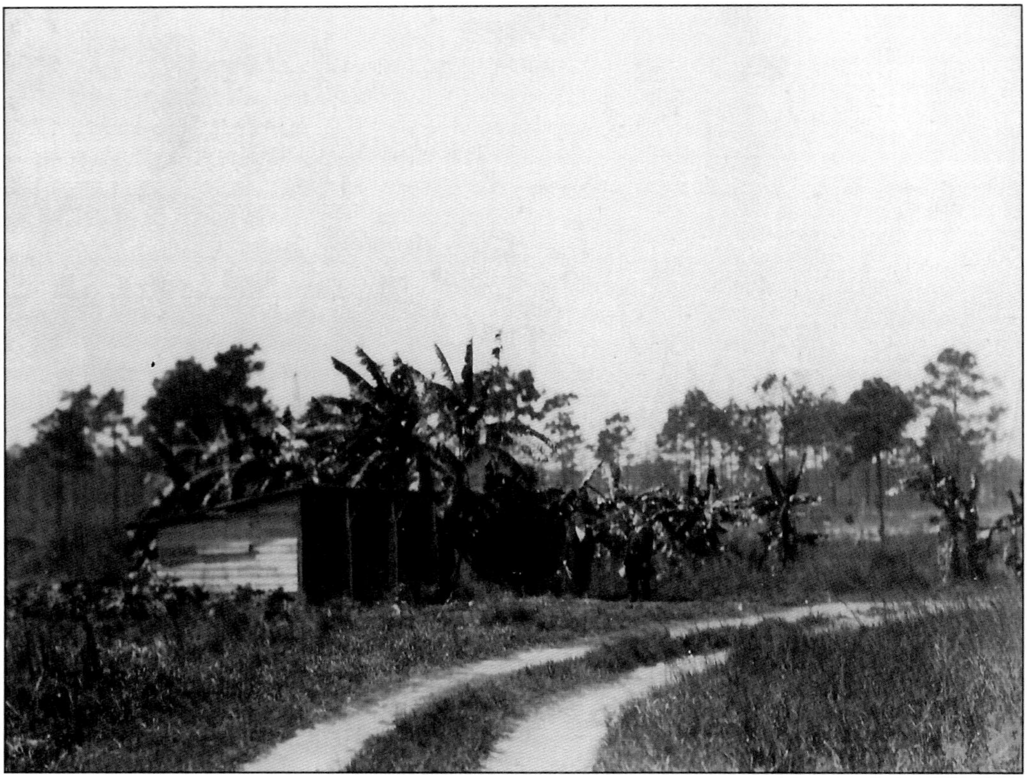

Frank and Claire Evans stand near a crop of banana trees at the southeast end of Lake Mary on Evansdale Road. Other Evans family members built homes along this road.

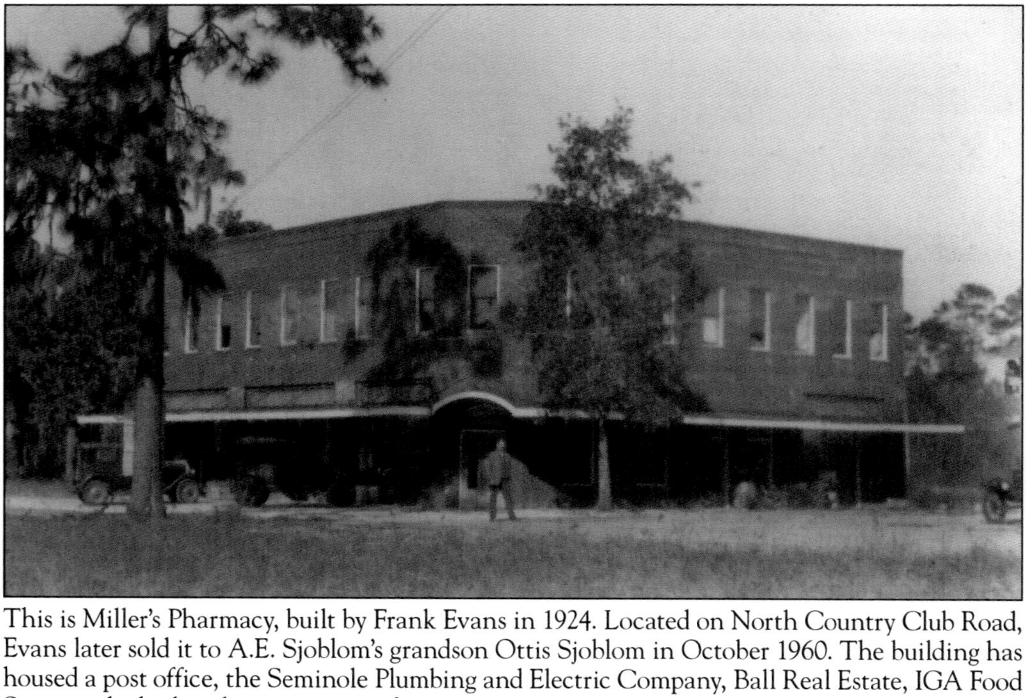

This is Miller's Pharmacy, built by Frank Evans in 1924. Located on North Country Club Road, Evans later sold it to A.E. Sjoblom's grandson Ottis Sjoblom in October 1960. The building has housed a post office, the Seminole Plumbing and Electric Company, Ball Real Estate, IGA Food Store, and a barber shop, to name a few.

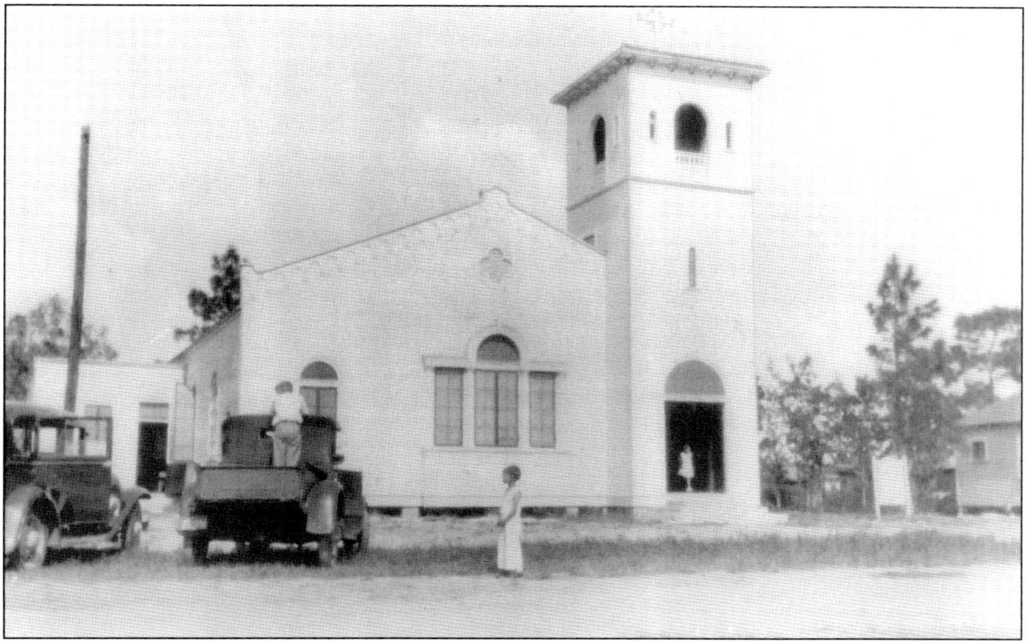

Just off of Country Club Road on Wilbur Avenue stands the First Presbyterian Church of Lake Mary. When it was built, it was known simply as The Community Church. Services started within the first year of its construction, but due to a fire in 1926 (below), the building was not completed and dedicated until March 30, 1930. Architect J.L. Snoddy volunteered his time to prepare the building plans, which were used by the leading workmen, Leon Pickering and Walter Flanders. Frank Evans was on the building committee and established credit and assisted in acquiring materials.

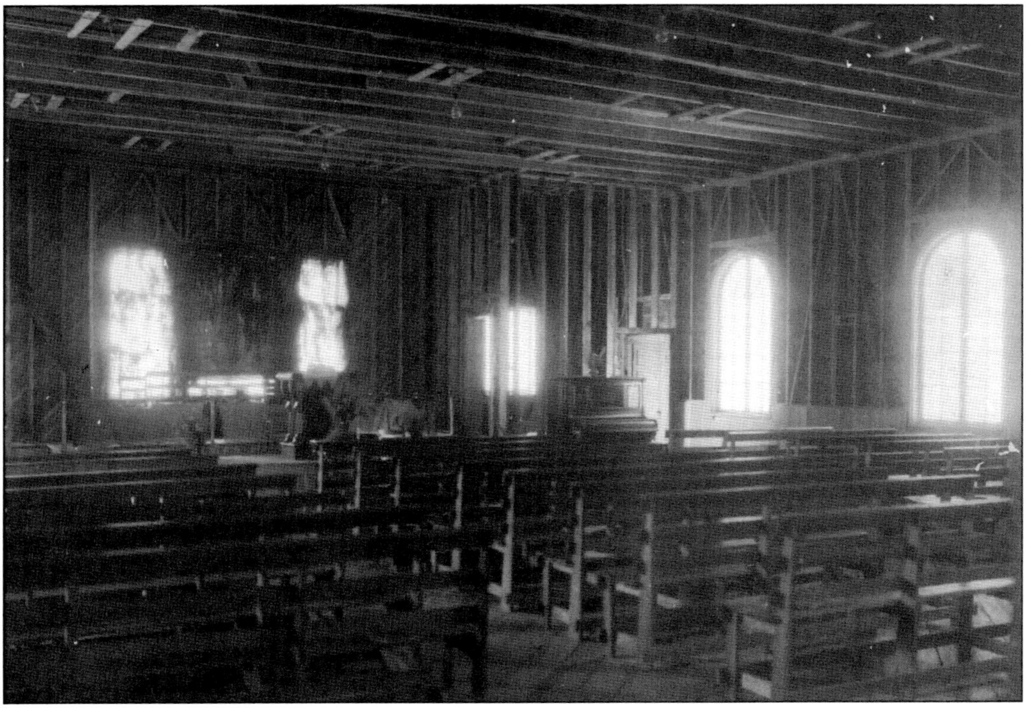

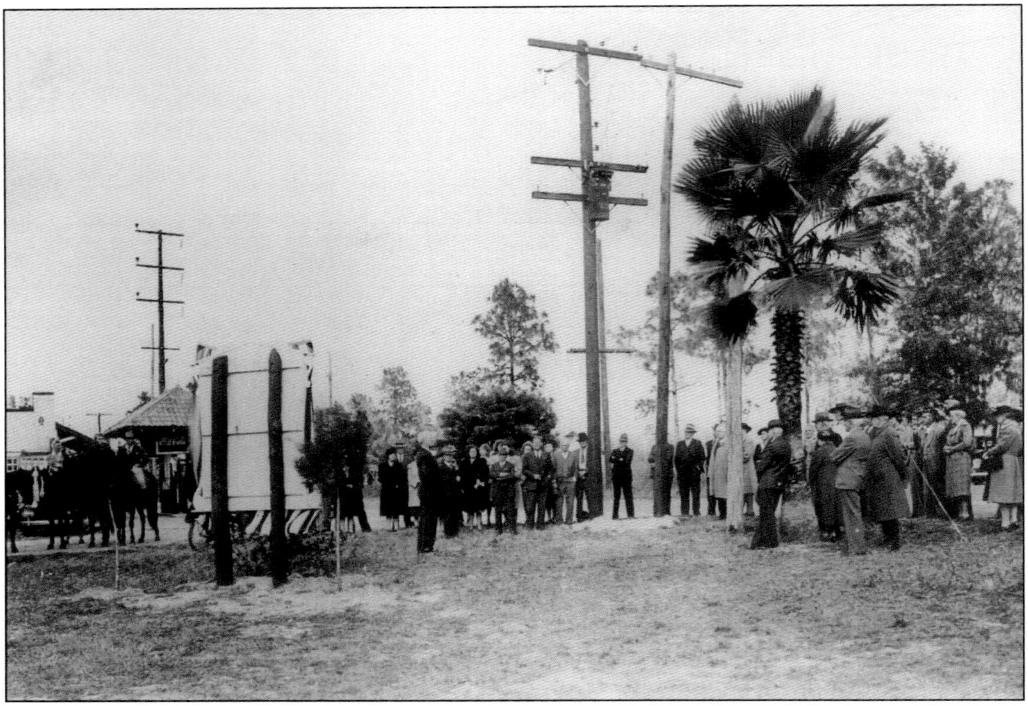

Taken in the late 1940s, this photograph shows a vacant lot on the east side of North Country Club Road with residents dedicating the military honor roll of those from Lake Mary who served in World War II. A replica of the original dedication is housed in the Lake Mary Museum.

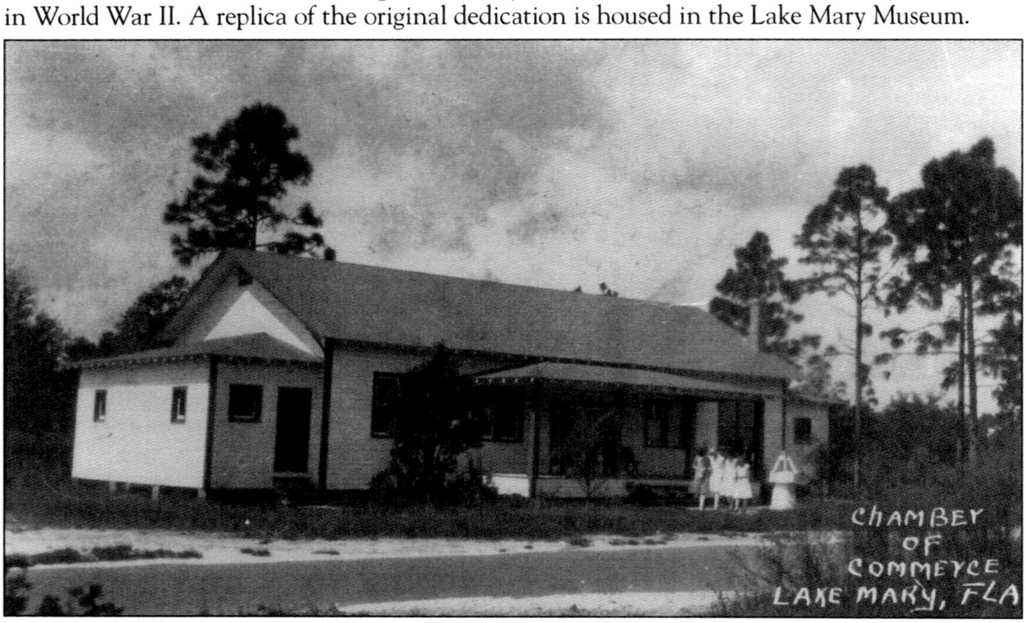

The Chamber of Commerce Building, also known as the Community Center, is seen here in 1926, the year it was completed. It has had multiple uses over the years, including hosting meetings for various town organizations, banquets, school dances, weddings, and even the Lake Mary Orchestra. It was used as the city hall from 1973 until 1990, when the current city hall was completed. The building is still in use today, housing the Lake Mary Historical Museum, and is listed in the National Register of Historic Places.

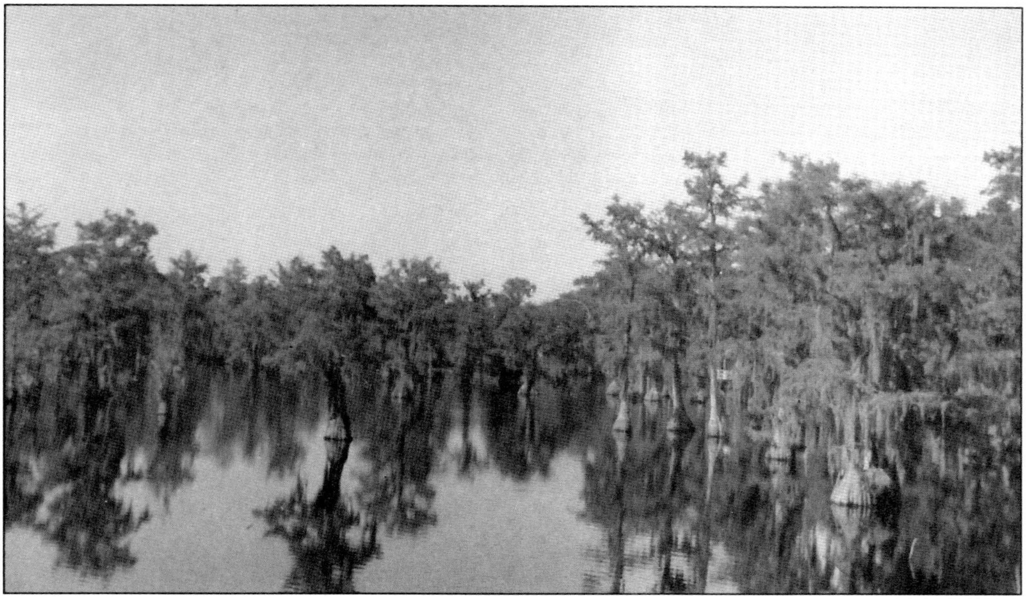

What did the first settlers of Lake Mary see when they first saw their homestead? Pictured here is the answer. The top photograph shows a field of cypress trees draped with Spanish moss growing out of Lake Mary. The photograph below shows a variety of palmetto trees interspersed with conifers and the occasional oak. These forests were so densely packed with drooping greenery that even the most experienced could easily get lost. Machetes were common implements to help with the simplest chores, like fetching water from the lake.

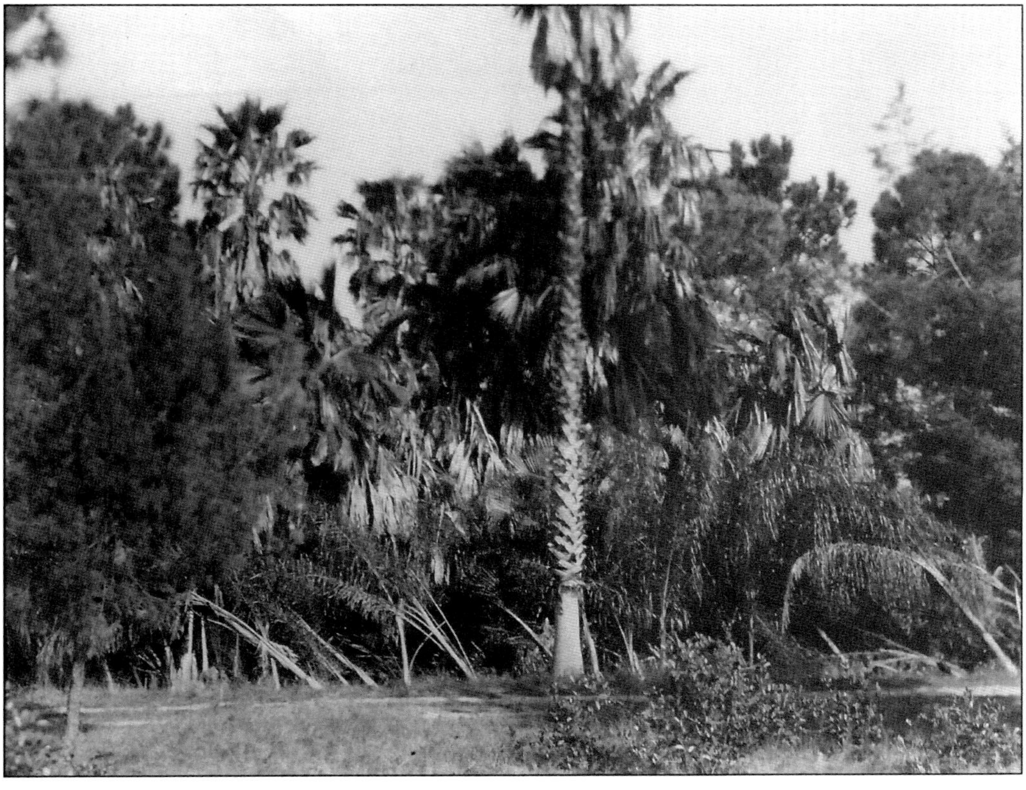

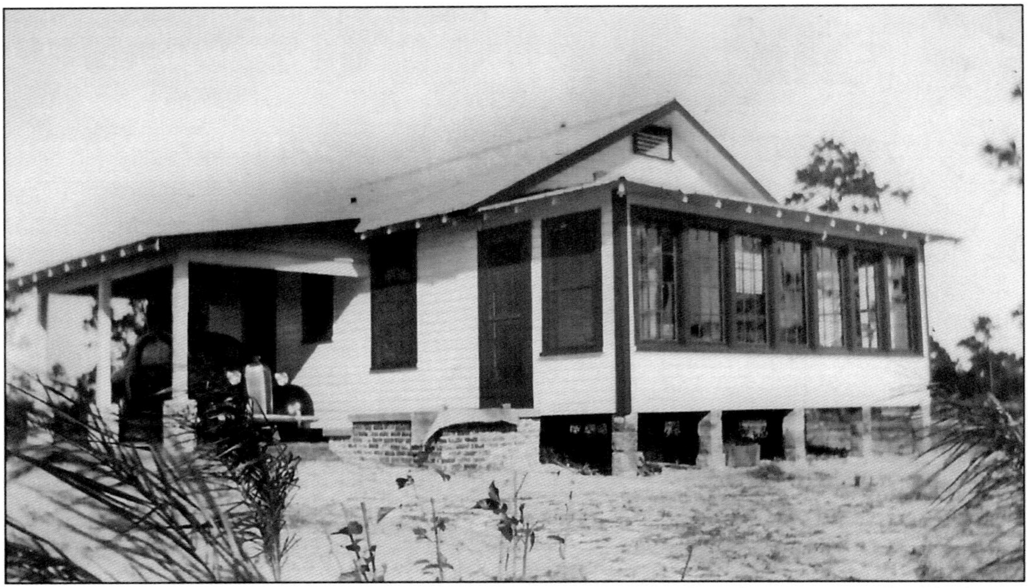

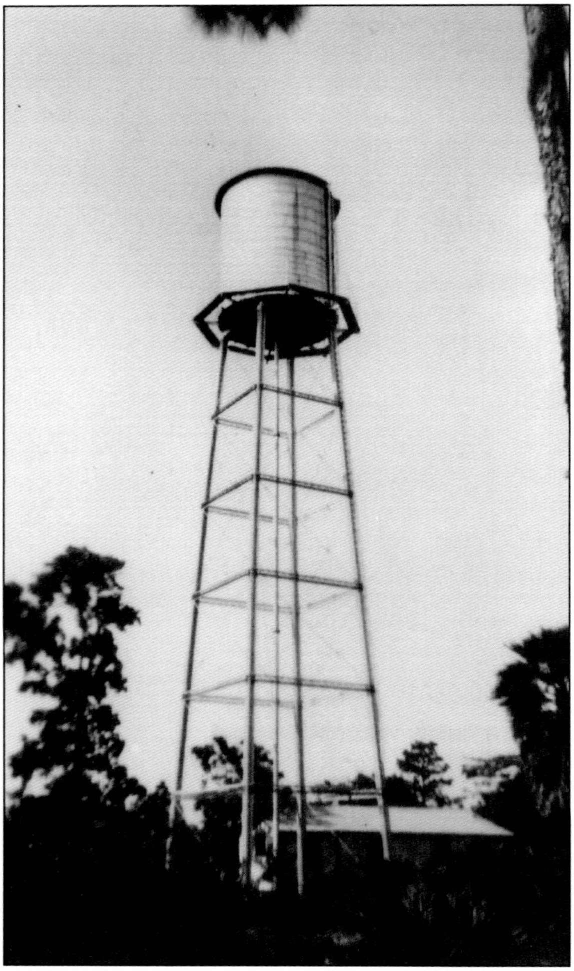

Pictured is a house on cinder blocks on Christmas Day 1936. Elevating houses on blocks was a common design for residential buildings throughout Florida at this time. The gap below the house kept the wooden structures away from Florida's corrosive rainwater during the wet summers, though often these shaded areas provided a cool haven for snakes and various other pests.

The Lake Mary water tower, located near the town's center, helped to provide running water to residents. With a relatively flat landscape throughout the town, the tower stood as the highest structure in Lake Mary for many years. Today, a much larger tower stands southwest of this one, colorfully painted and aptly labeled "Lake Mary, City of Lakes."

Two

Founding Families

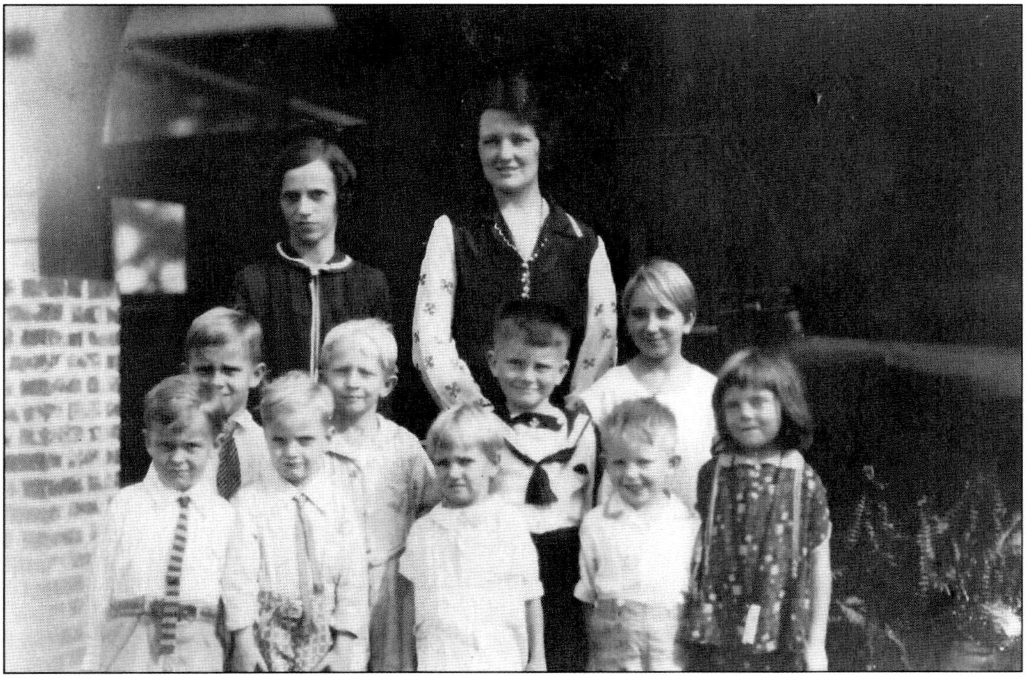

This chapter focuses on the families that founded the Lake Mary community. The warm kinship built between these people gave the town a distinct atmosphere. At the same time, they dedicated their blood, sweat, and tears into laying the architecture for a thriving Lake Mary community.

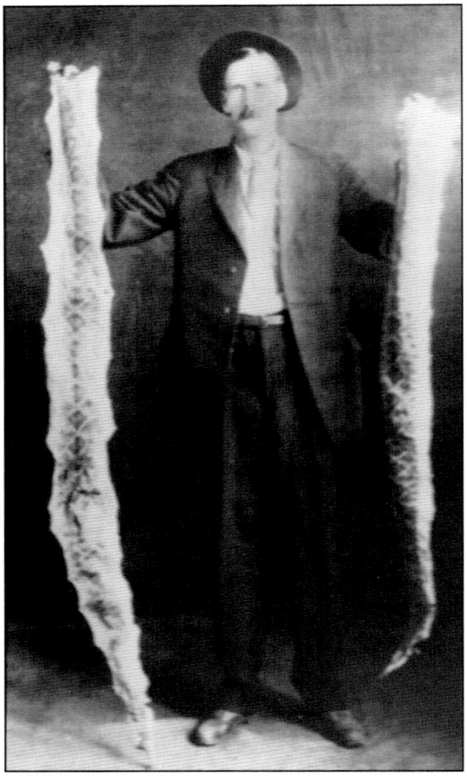

In the mid- and late 1800s, Henry Sanford traveled to Sweden in search of workers for his 12,535 acres of orange groves near Lake Monroe. In 1882, young A.E. Sjoblom joined fellow Swedes and sailed across the Atlantic with the promise of a new and exciting future in America. Sanford paid for their passage in exchange for one year of work. When Sjoblom arrived, however, he discovered Sanford's drive toward a booming citrus business and prominent hotel left little freedom for new Americans like him. During a workers' strike for better food, Sanford jailed those involved. Sjoblom was even jailed when he simply tried to quit Sanford's job. On the left, a man shows off two sizable snakeskins. Below are Sjoblom and his wife Tilda in the 1920s.

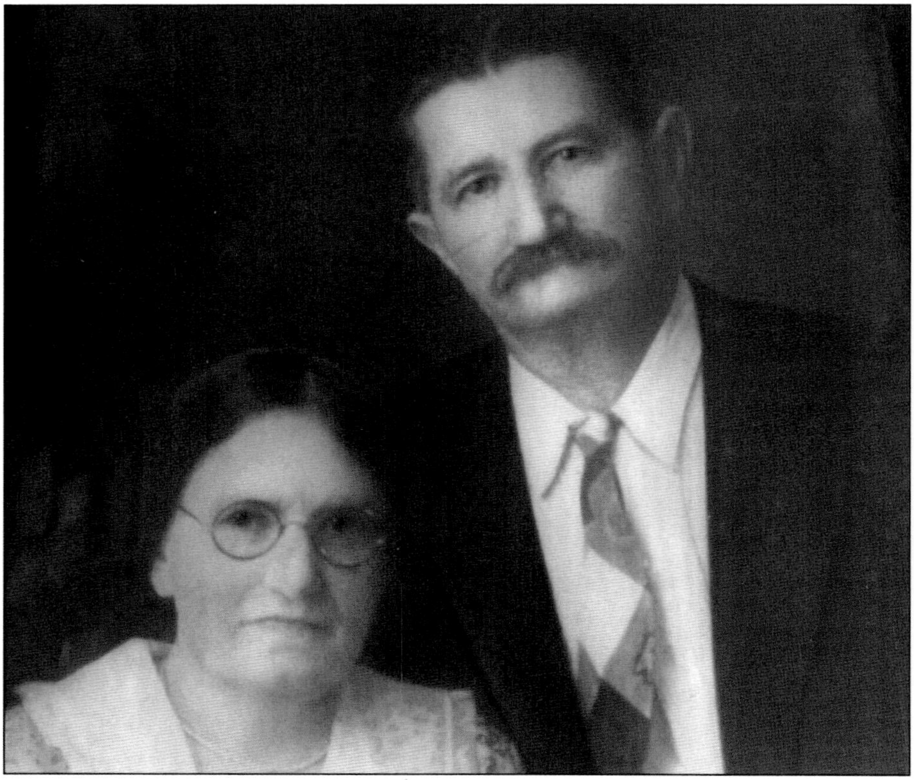

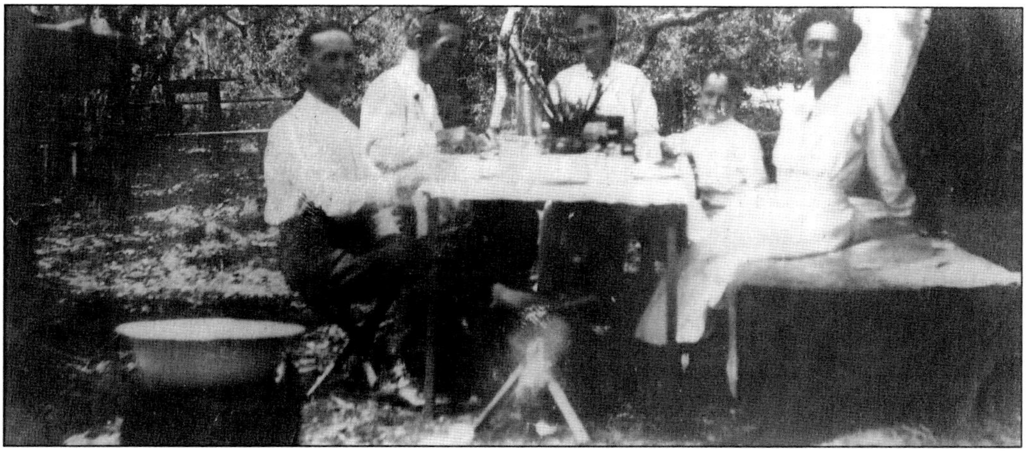

Early residents of Lake Mary sit and enjoy a quiet evening dinner in a common setting. A tent can be seen on the right. Before building homes, people lived out of tents. Their kitchen and bath consisted of the white bowl seen at lower left.

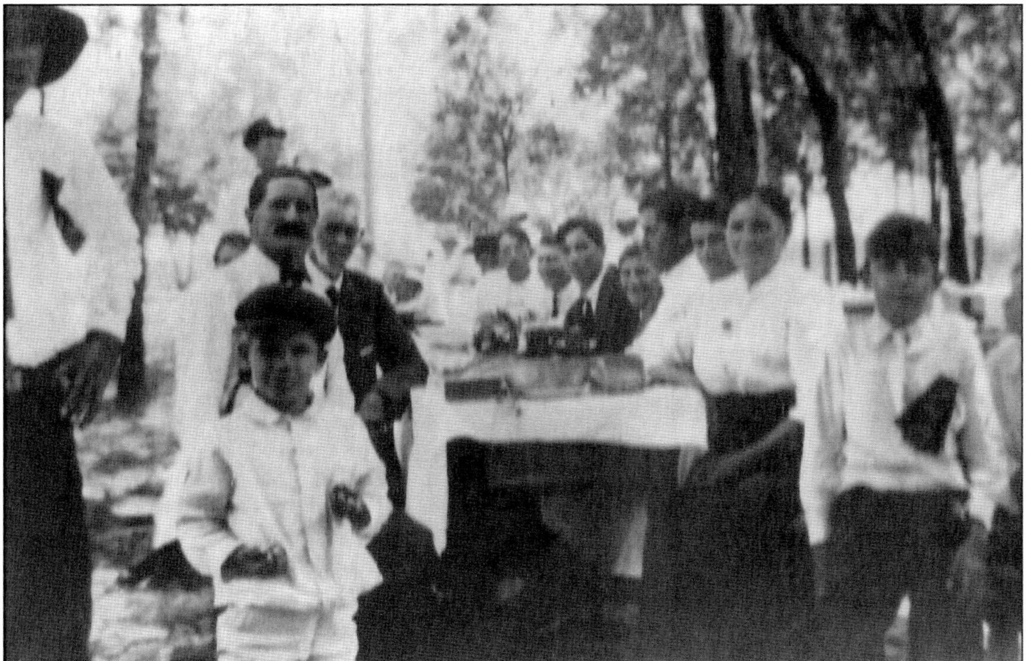

When they could, families met and feasted on the crops they grew and prepared. In this gathering, kids and adults are dressed in their best clothes. Often, these dinners were held following a church service.

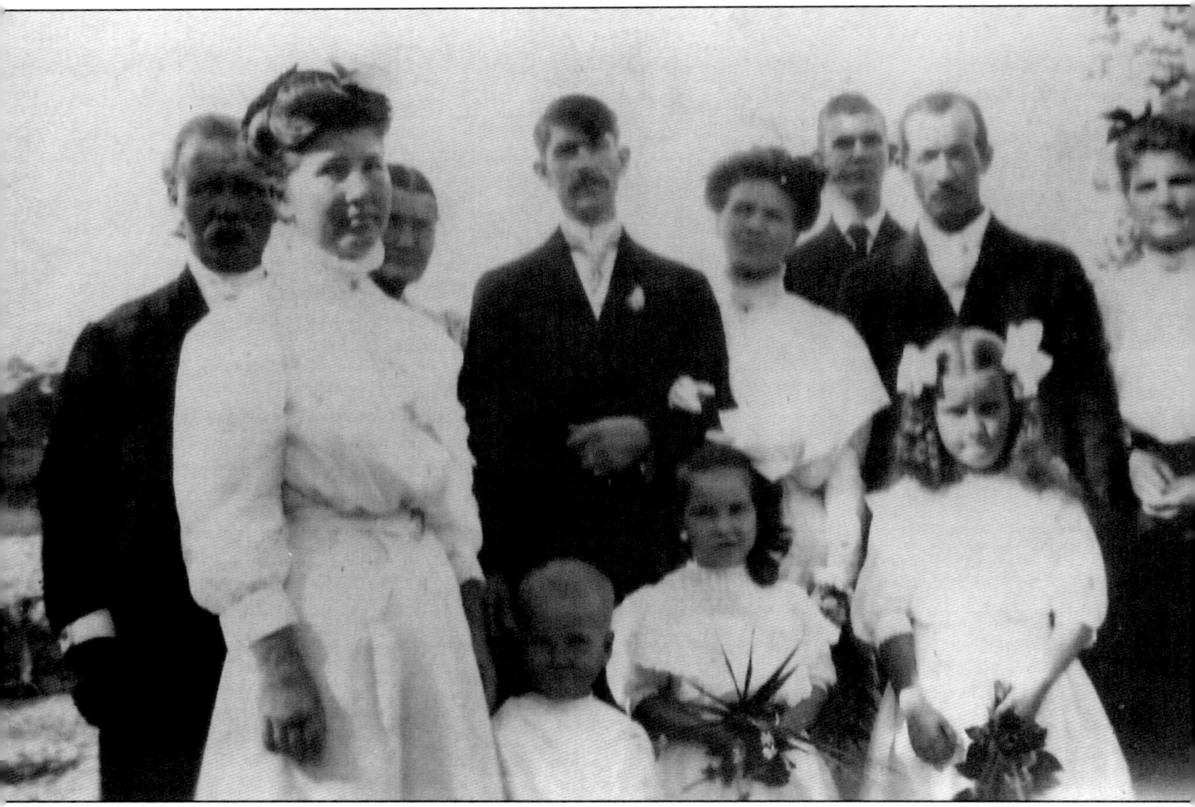

Pictured is the Sundell family wedding. Samuel McBride stands arm-in-arm with his bride, Lillie Sundell. Rev. John Frederick Sundell, on the far left, likely officiated the wedding. Note the flower girls in the front carrying Florida-style greenery, with palm leaves accenting a collection of Florida wildflowers.

Taken around 1910, the photograph at right shows Reverend Sundell and Mary Amelia Sundell on the right posing next to their daughter and son-in-law Lillie and Samuel McBride. Reverend Sundell emigrated from Sweden and was a reverend at Upsala Presbyterian Church in the nearby community of New Upsala. He later helped to establish the Lake Mary Presbyterian Church. The lake that gave Lake Mary its name was itself named after his wife, who settled on its northern shores. The photograph below shows John and Mary's joint tombstone, which sits in the Lake Mary Cemetery today, not far from their former Lake Mary home.

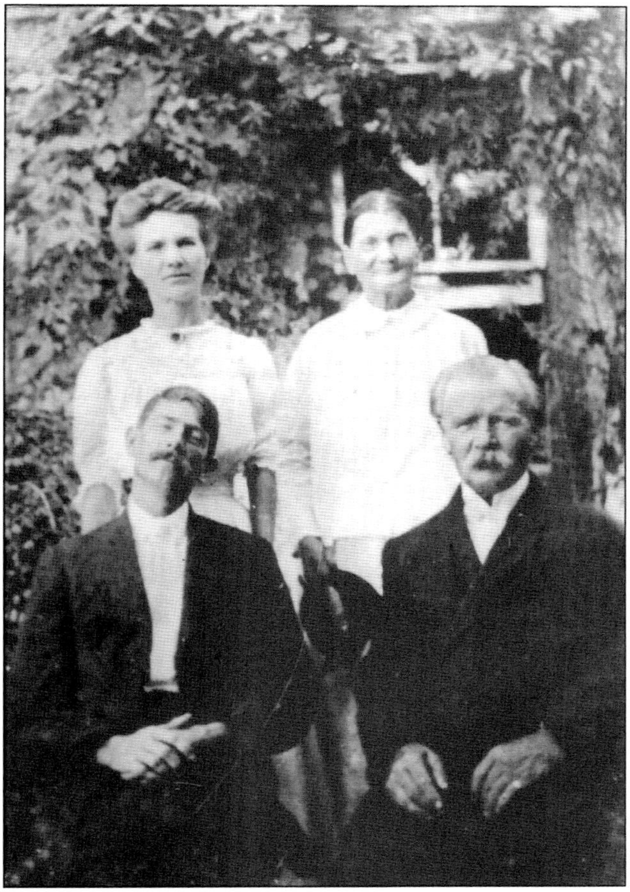

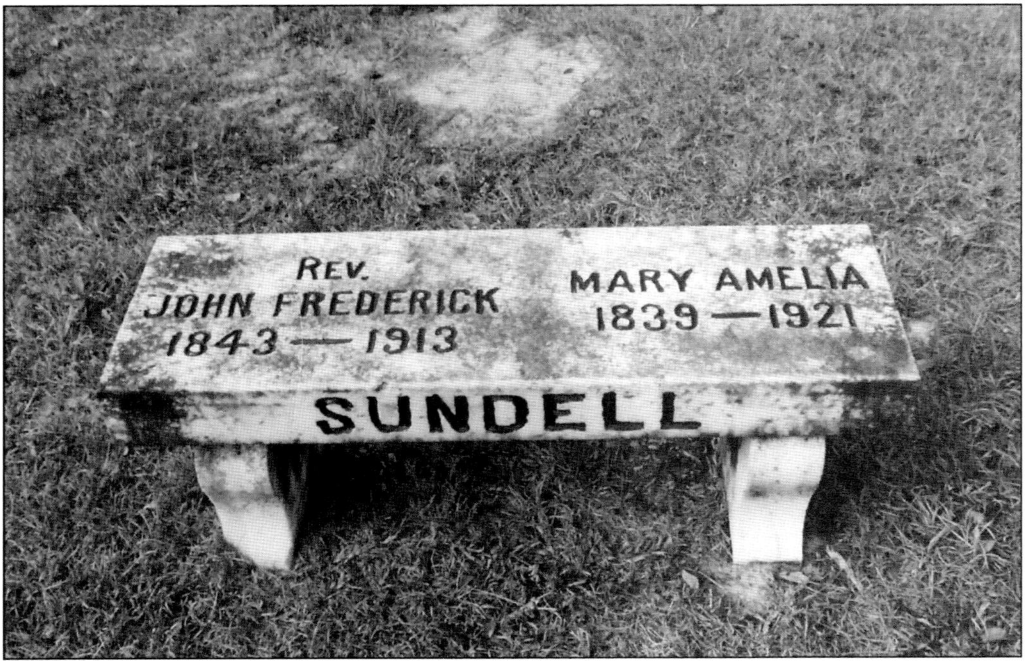

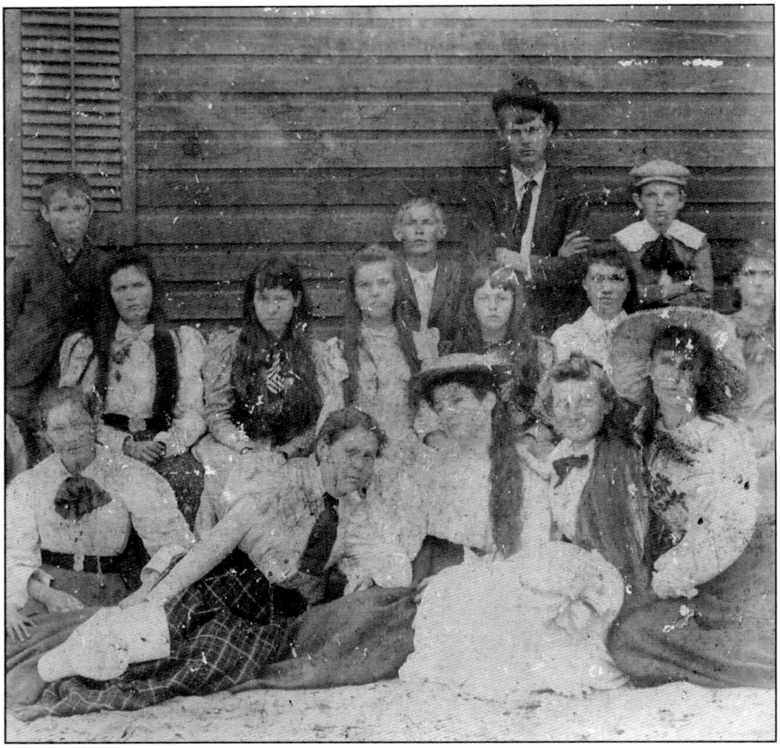

Pictured are Tom and Frankie Fourte, Max Maye, Charlie Glass, Rose Lord, Etta Hester, Herrietta Hester Evans, Lulia Nollen, Josey Kerell, a couple of Stenstrum children, and a few other unknown kids outside the Old Schoolhouse. Children of varying ages learned reading, writing, and arithmetic in the same one-room class.

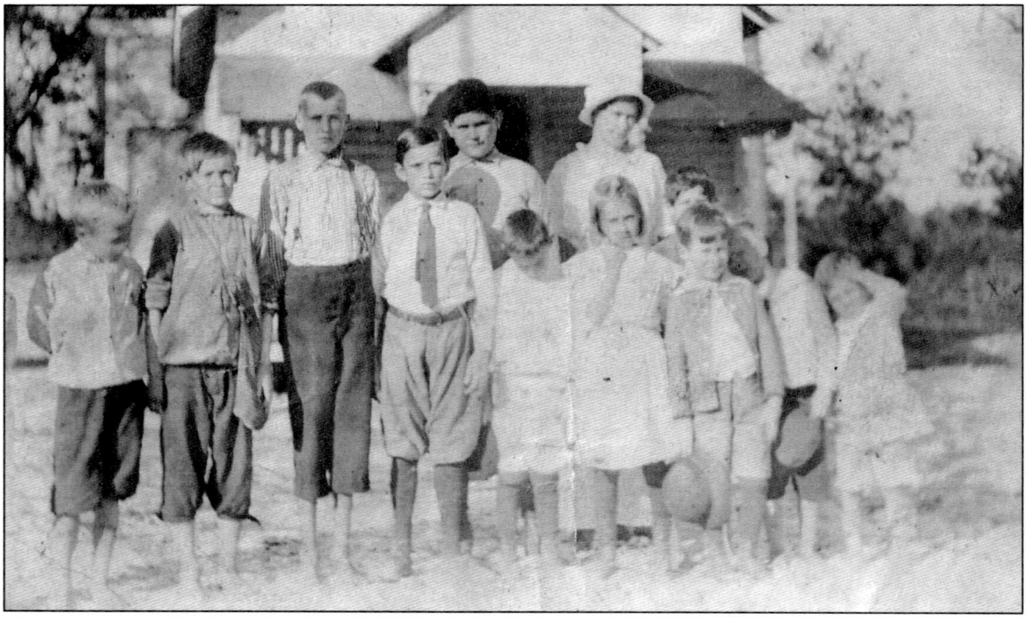

This photograph of early resident kids shows that they are likely dressed for school. Though many families were drawn to Lake Mary from common themes of opportunity and a pleasant environment, they came from different socioeconomic backgrounds. Some of their children—like the boy in the middle—had a tie, belt, and shoes, while others—like the boys on the left—were shoeless with simple clothing.

Pictured at right is Dr. David Sander Evans, and below is his son Dr. William Harrison Evans. Dr. William Harrison Evans not only practiced medicine and operated a drugstore in Sanford, but also tended to his 50 acres of orange groves on the south shore of Lake Mary. He moved to central Florida with his wife, Mellissa Victoria, and their sons in 1882. He was so well connected with the people of the area that in 1889, Sanford residents elected him mayor. He served for three terms. Judge David Pulling and Dr. Evans officially named the town Lake Mary, and by 1899, the name started appearing on Florida state maps.

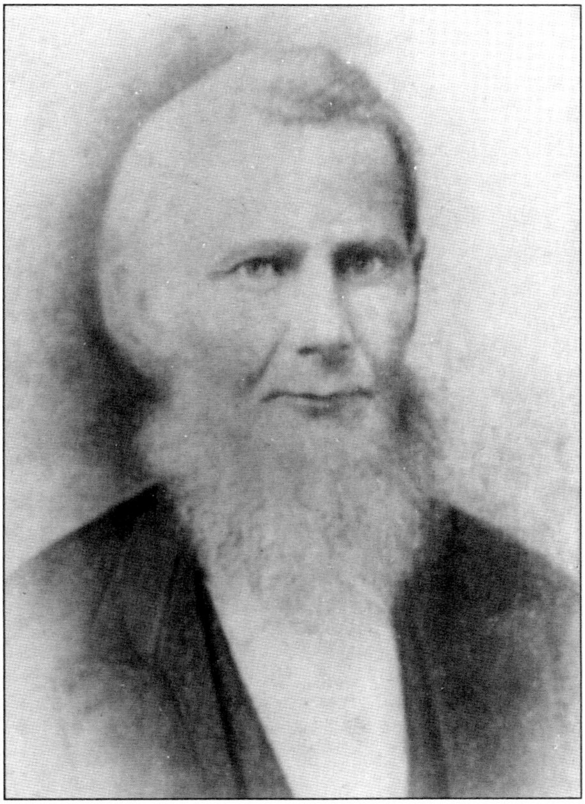

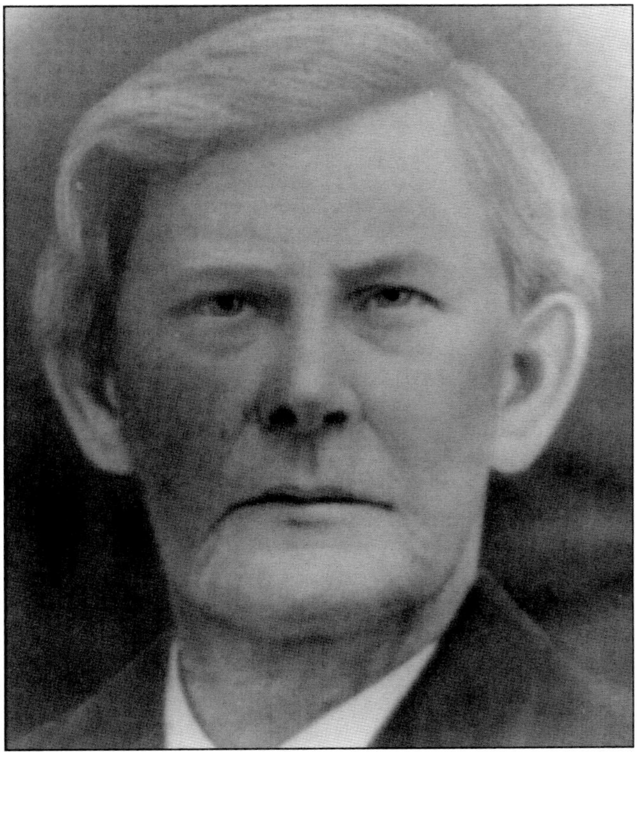

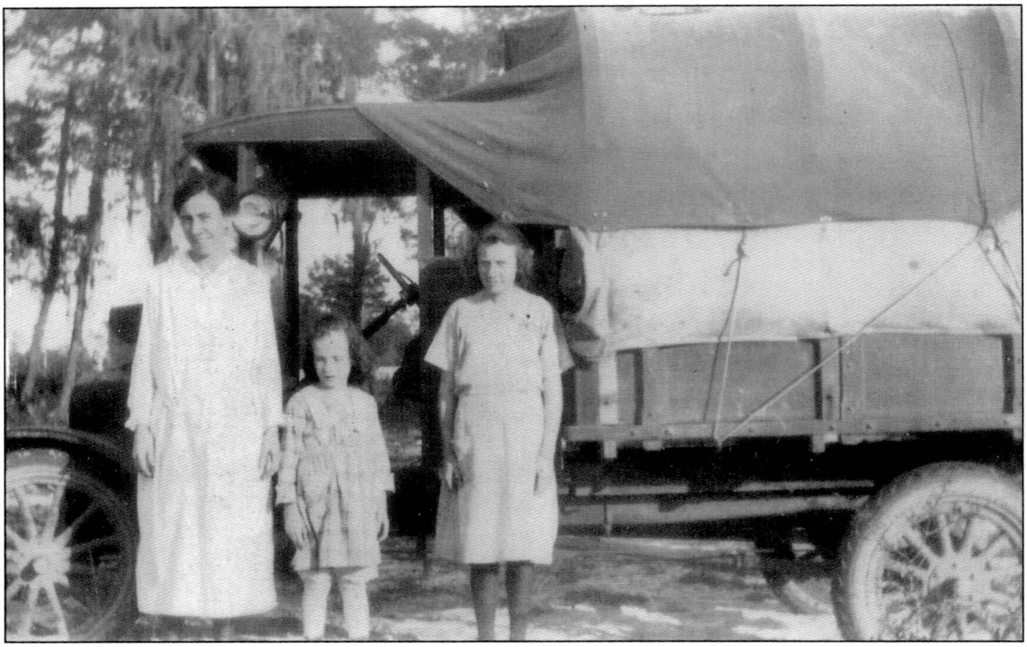

Pictured is the Snow family in Lake Mary during the mid-1920s. The top photograph was taken shortly after arriving—their truck still packed with their belongings. Many families found opportunities in Lake Mary during this time. With good weather and no pollution, a family could buy land, plant crops, and raise children. As a result of their hard work, the Snows were able to buy the bicycle Norman Snow is shown sitting on below. Often, kids used bicycles for additional income delivering packages, messages, or other small items.

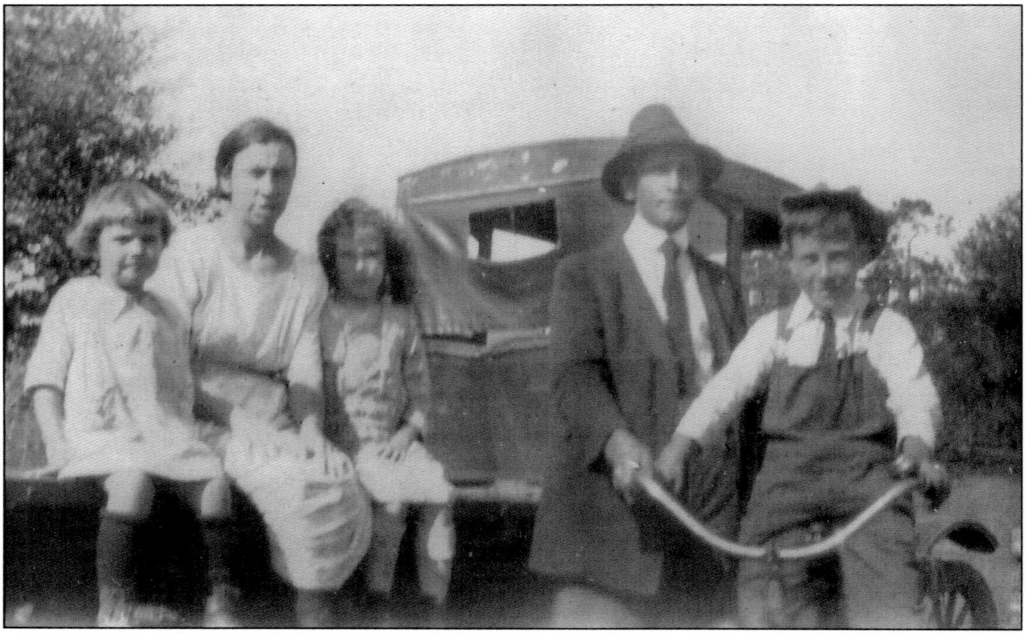

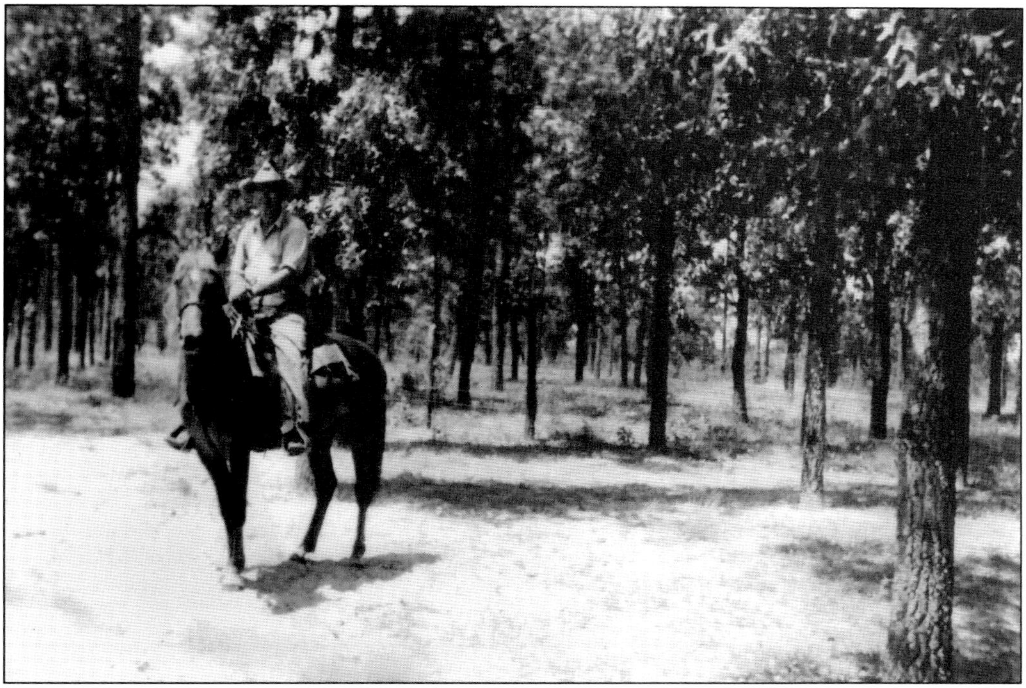

Pictured is Ross Humphrey, son of William T. and Lula Nola Humphrey. A true cowboy and early settler of Lake Mary, he rode on the primary mode of transportation at the time, a horse. Behind him, barbed wire fencing marks off land where the Humphreys raised various animals on their Lake Mary ranch.

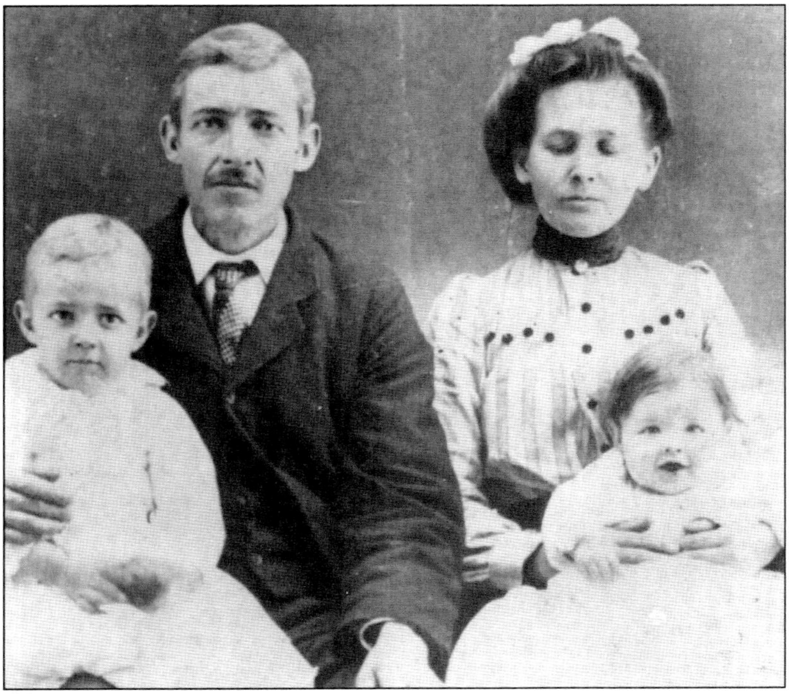

Pictured are William and Meriam Melvin-Dunn with their boys William Jr. and Donald. The Dunns were one of the early Lake Mary families, with their descendants still living in the city.

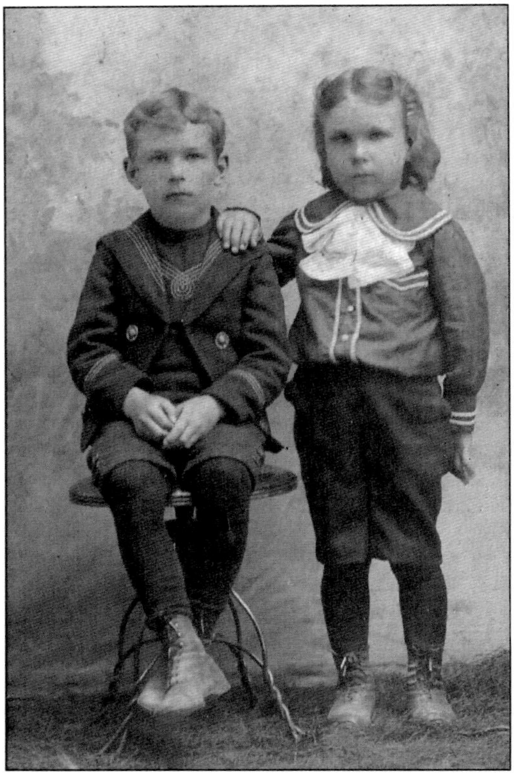

In these two photographs, siblings pose dressed in period-specific clothing. Note that none of these kids are smiling. Many think people did not smile in photographs during this period because of poor dental care, but this is a myth. At the time, smiling in photos was associated with indecent living and drunkenness. Consequently, not smiling was a sign of good character. Though these photo sessions may not have been fun for the kids, having to bathe and dress up in uncomfortable clothes, they were undoubtedly instructed not to smile.

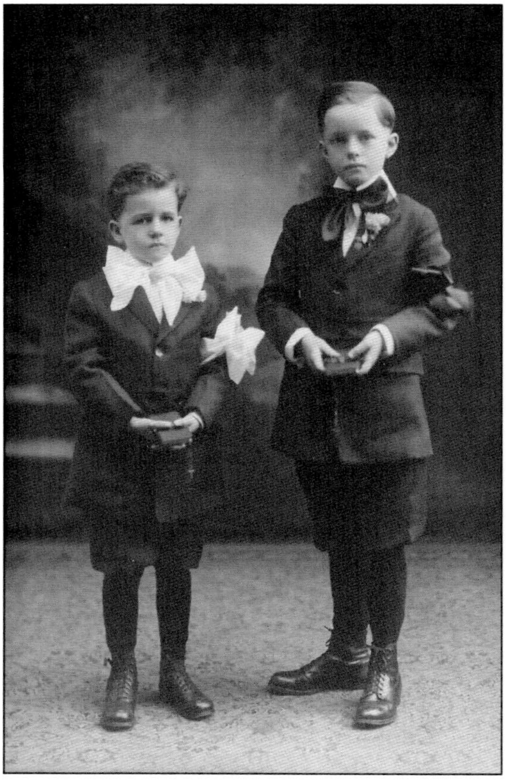

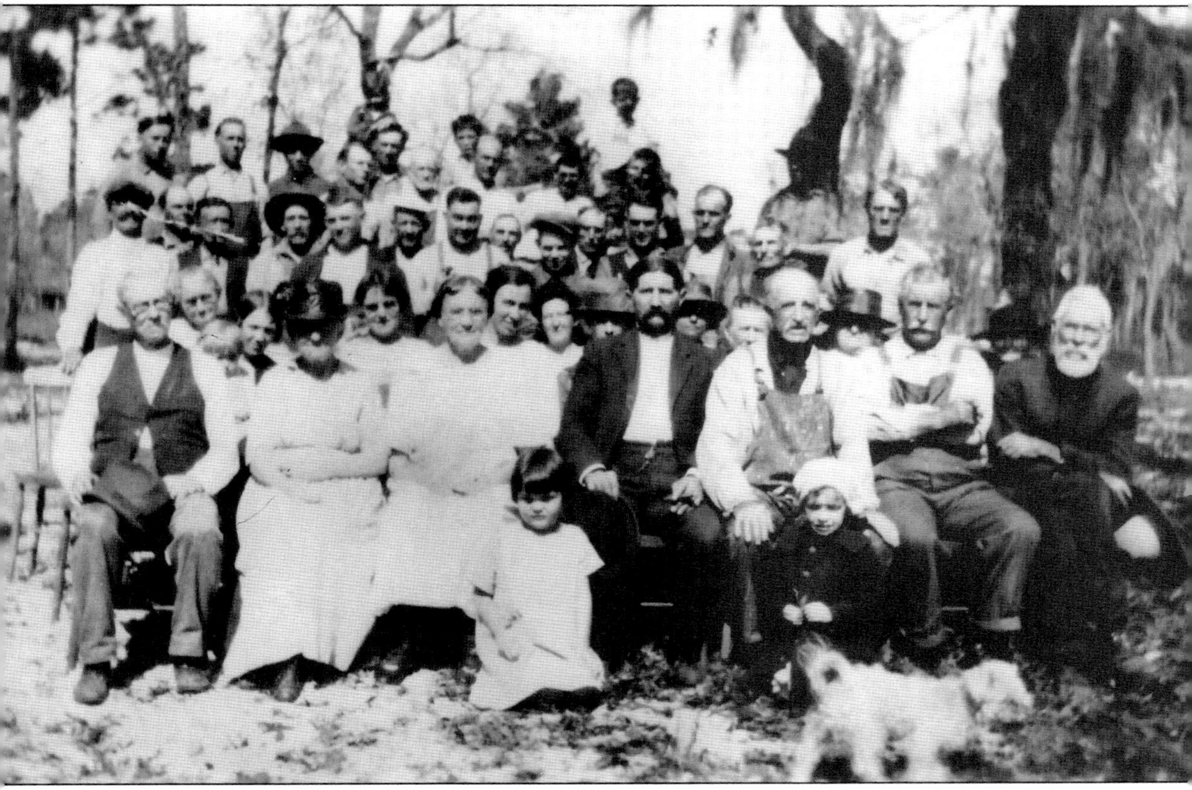

Posed here is the bulk of Lake Mary's residents in the early 1900s. Seated in the front with his rich Scandinavian mustache is A.E. Sjoblom with his wife, Tilda, on his right. The residents during this time were almost entirely citrus growers and/or railroad workers. Most were Swedish immigrants like Sjoblom, who were drawn to Florida as a result of General Sanford's vigorous recruitment efforts. Living together, residents were able to bring their Scandinavian traditions, farming techniques, and culture to the area.

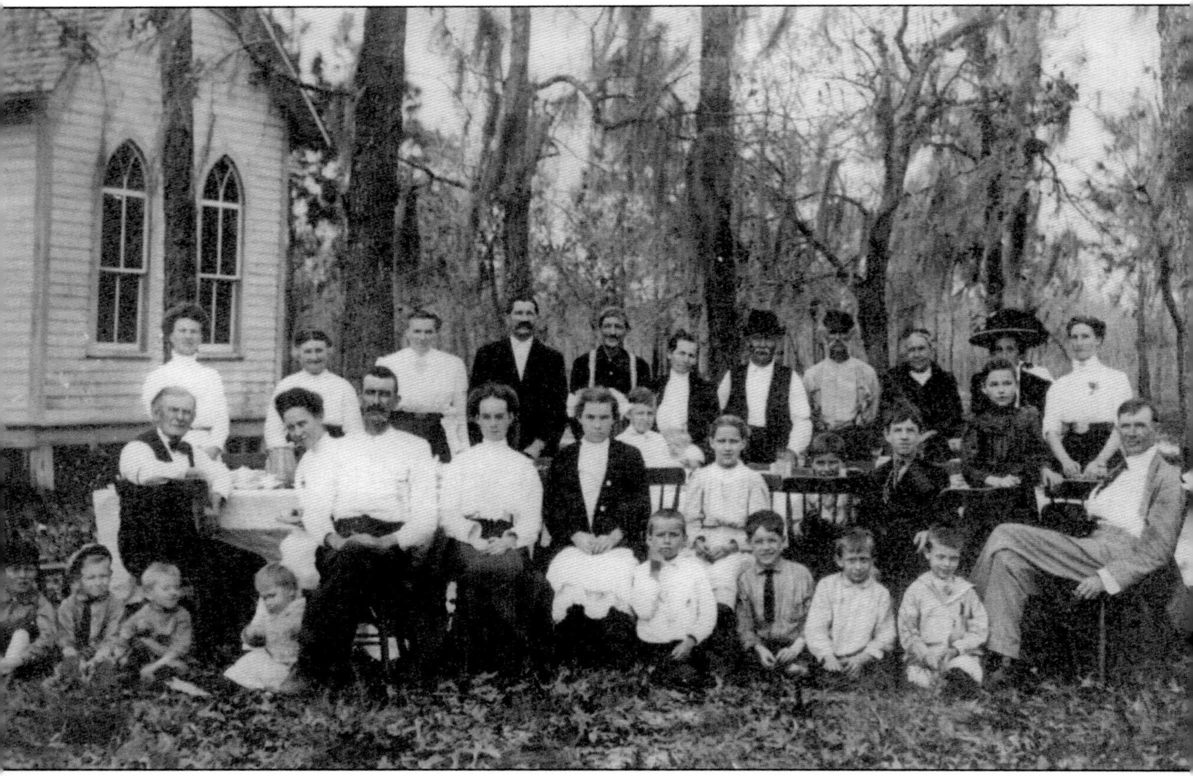

This is a rare photograph of a church picnic with both the Sjoblom and Evans families in the late 1800s. The two families worked side by side to build the foundations of Lake Mary. Occasionally, they found time to spend a peaceful afternoon together to eat, talk, and enjoy the day.

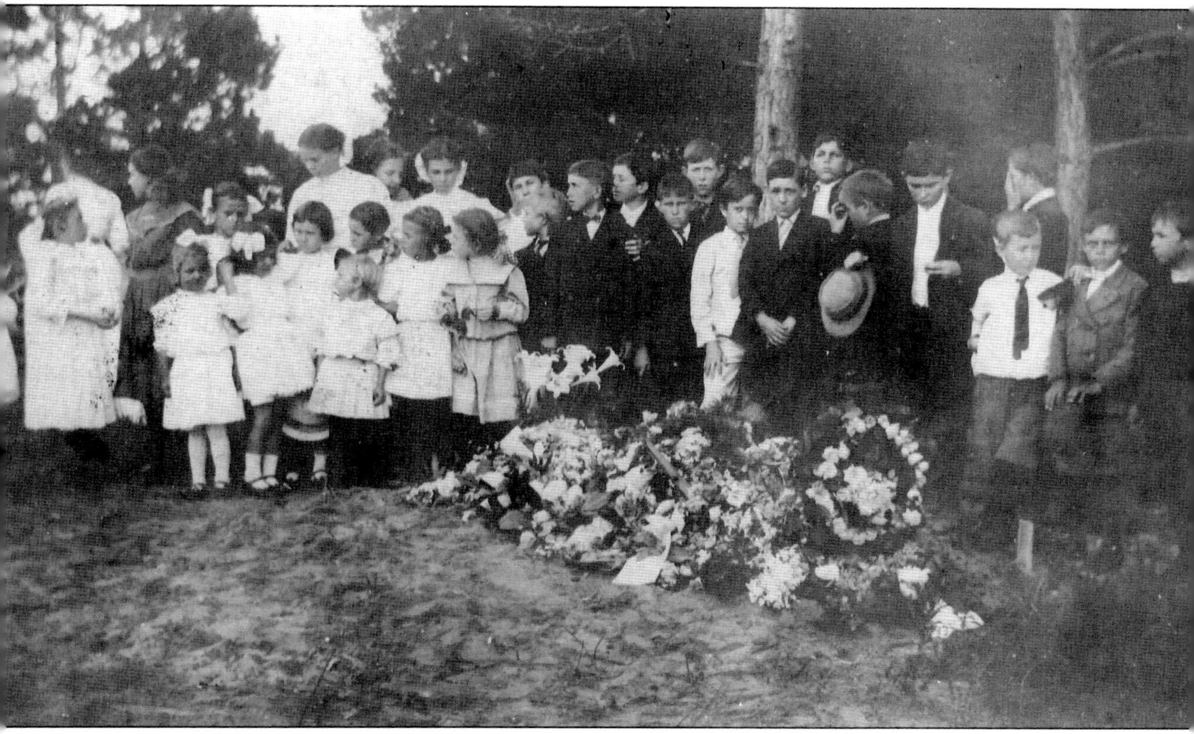

An unfortunate common event in Lake Mary included funerals. Here, the entire town meets to pay their respects to a now-unknown lost loved one. In the early 1900s, the leading causes of death in the United States were influenza and tuberculosis. In 1918, a worldwide outbreak of influenza killed at least 50 million people, more than the causalities of World War I.

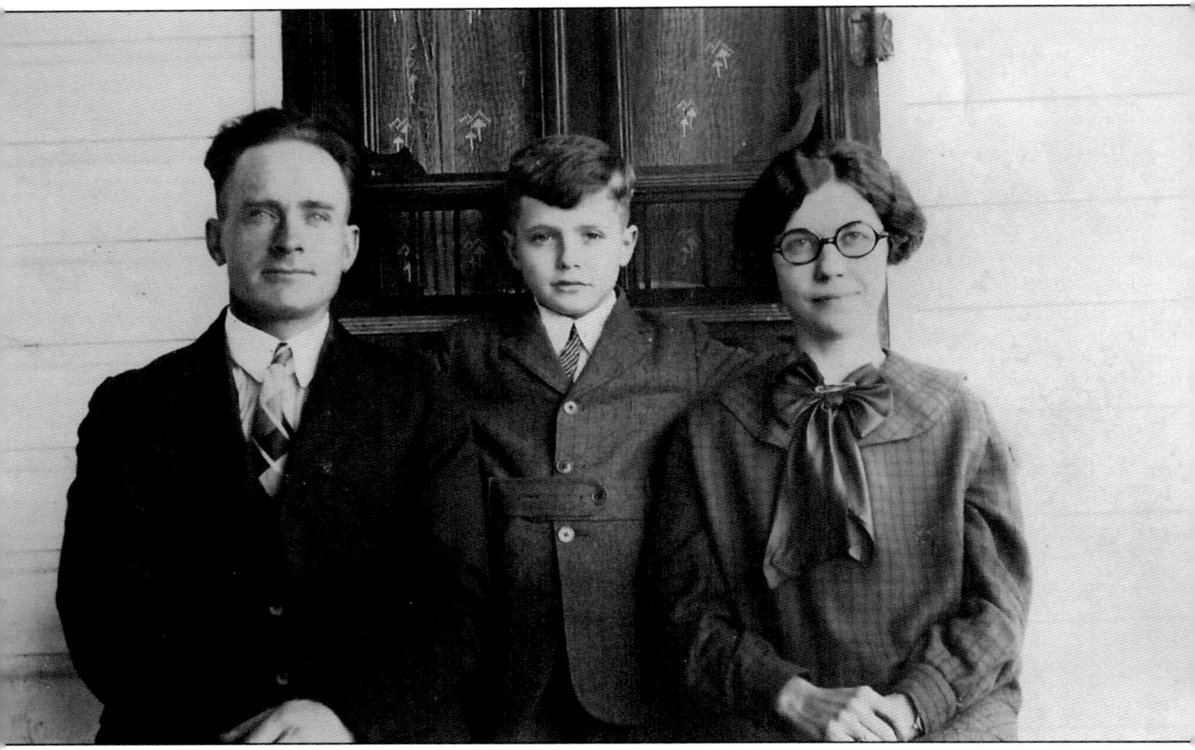

Pictured is an early Lake Mary family of three from the beginning of the 1900s. Relatively small families like this were somewhat uncommon during this time due to the high child mortality rate. In 1900, about 16.5 percent of all children in America died before their first birthday. A hundred years later, the rate was about 0.7 percent.

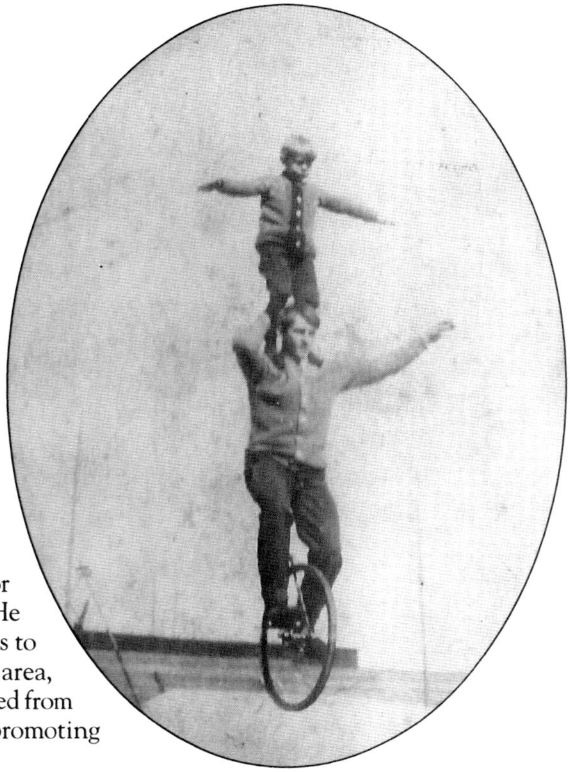

The picture on the right shows an unknown boy standing on the shoulders of Frank Evans as he rides a unicycle in the early 1900s. Frank was always known for his charismatic showmanship, often performing in front of large crowds. Below, he plays a violin while riding a unicycle. At the time, some long-time Lake Mary residents viewed his antics as a bit too ostentatious for small-town life. Frank thought otherwise. He enthusiastically performed these flashy acts to draw in tourists and other business to the area, helping the community to grow as it benefited from the crowds. In his later life, he continued promoting the town using less dangerous stunts.

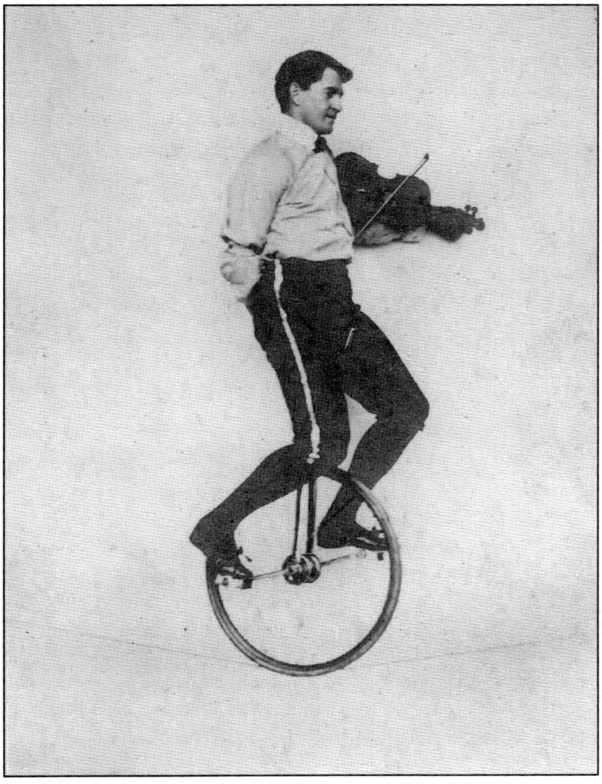

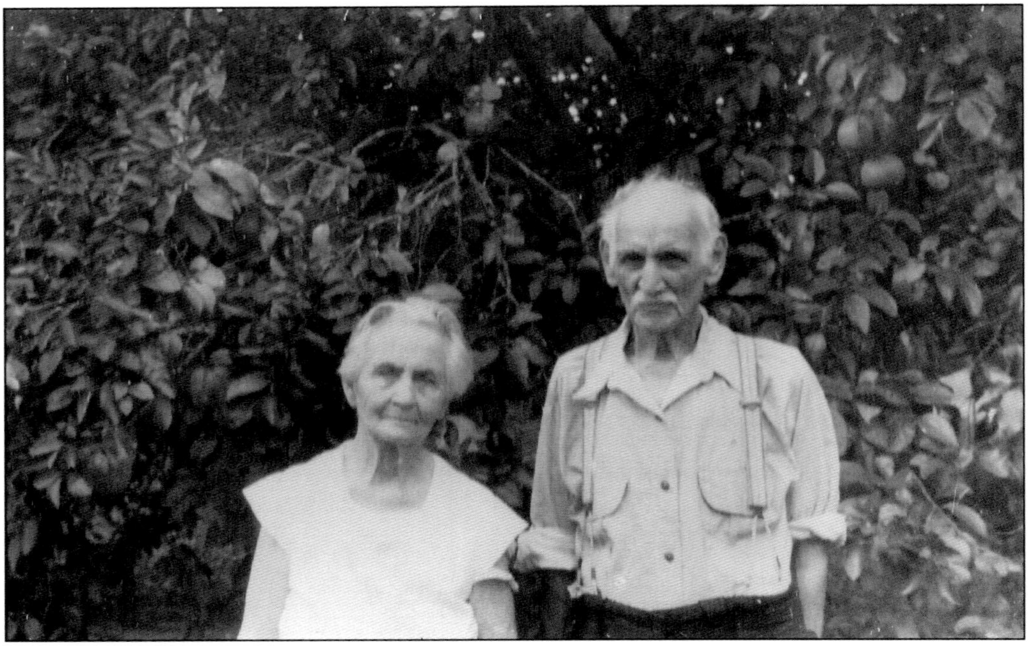

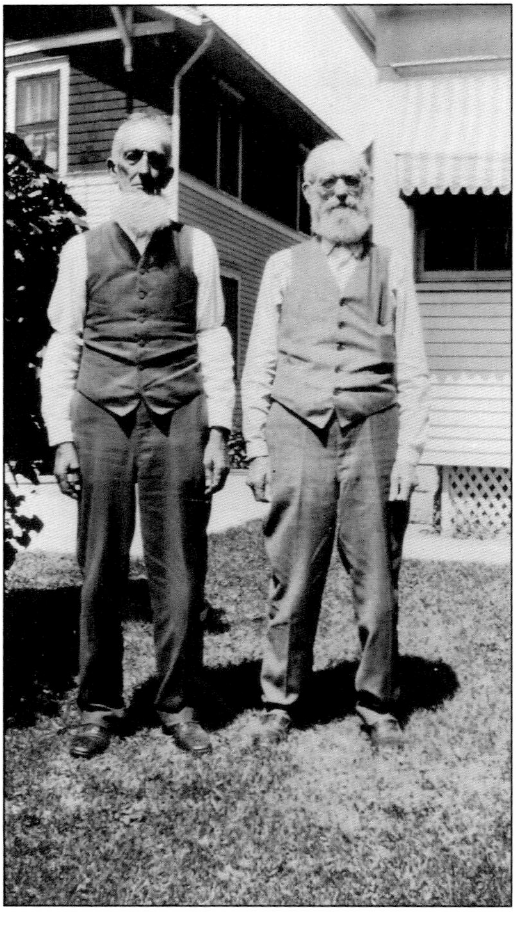

Shown are Swedish farmers living in Lake Mary in the early 1940s. In the early 1890s, A.E. Sjoblom chronicled his journey from Sweden to central Florida, his hard life working on Henry S. Sanford's citrus farms, and his experiences in jail when trying to escape Sanford's hold on poor immigrants like him. His eventual settlement on the shores of Lake Mary and his entrepreneurial spirit laid the foundations of the village of Lake Mary, and attracted other Swedish immigrants like him to the area.

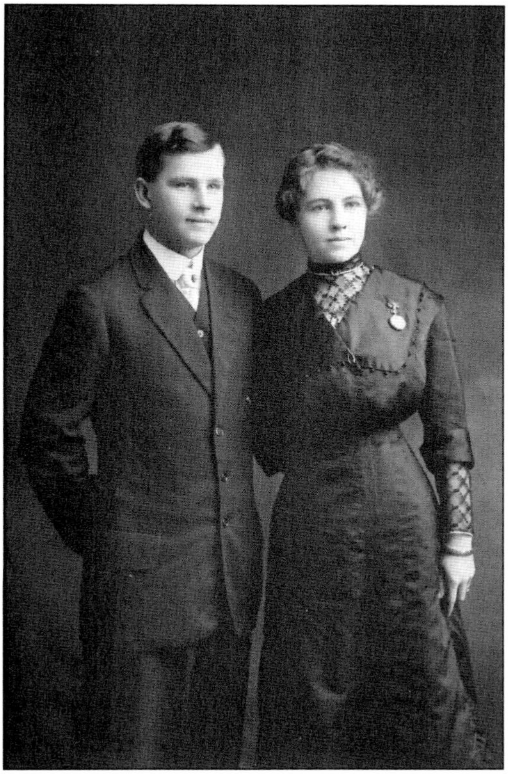

These photographs show Frank Evans and his first wife, Mina Lewis, and their first son. Frank and Mina were married when Frank was only 17 years old.

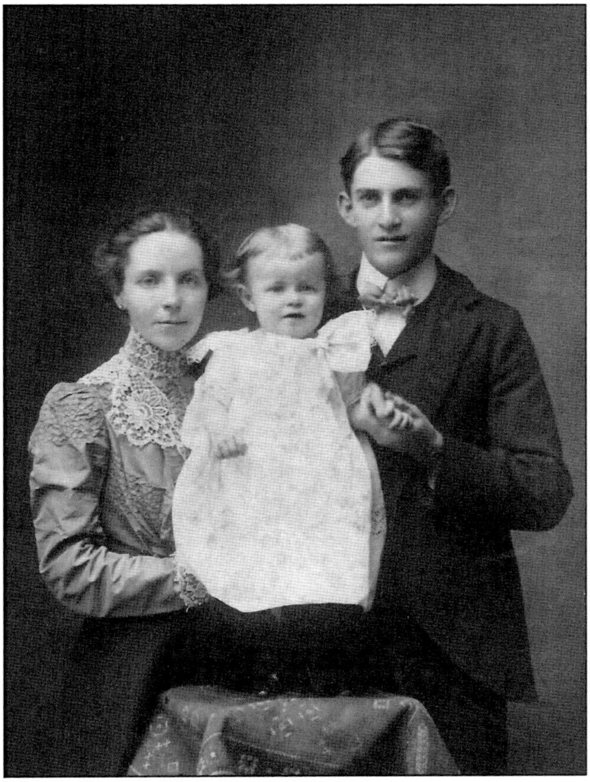

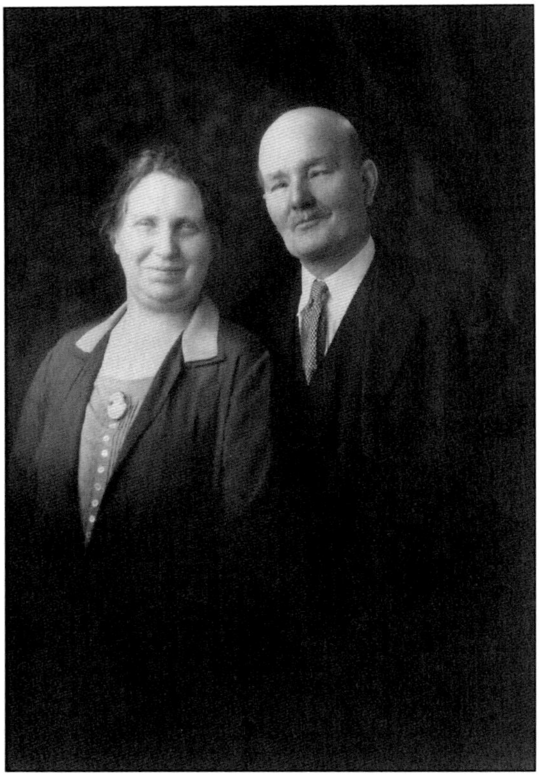

Pictured are George and Benneth "Green" Pelley. Frank Evans married two of their daughters. After Evans's first wife Mina Lewis died, he married George and Green's daughter Stella. After Stella died, he married her sister, Claire.

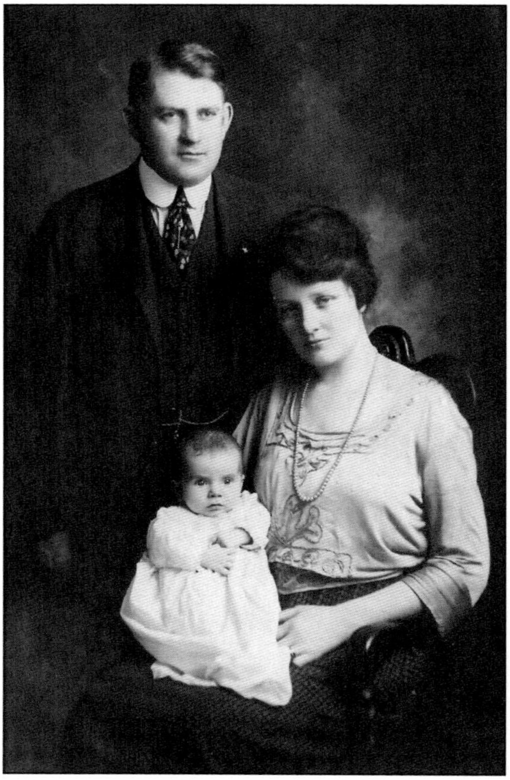

Pictured are Frank Evans and his second wife, Stella Pelley Evans. In 1926, Florida governor John W. Martin appointed Frank the county commissioner, and voters re-elected him twice.

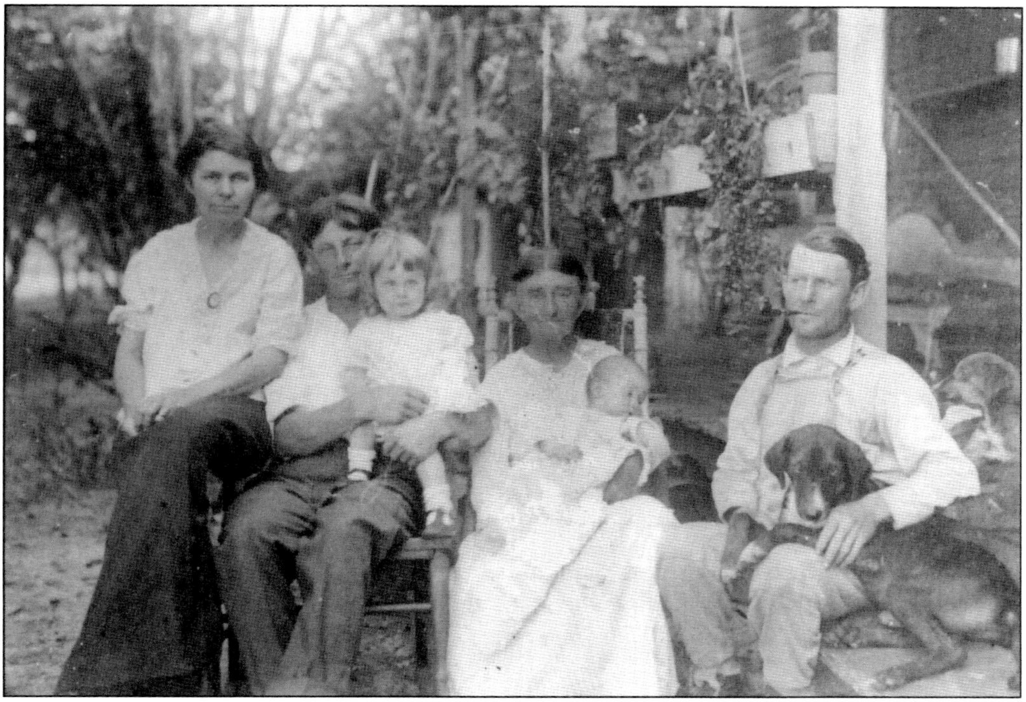

In the top photograph, from left to right are Mitty, Will, Rebecca, Melissa Victoria, Billy, and Jonnie Evans. In the photograph below, Melissa Victoria Evans holds her grandson Billy Evans during a pleasant canoe ride on Lake Mary.

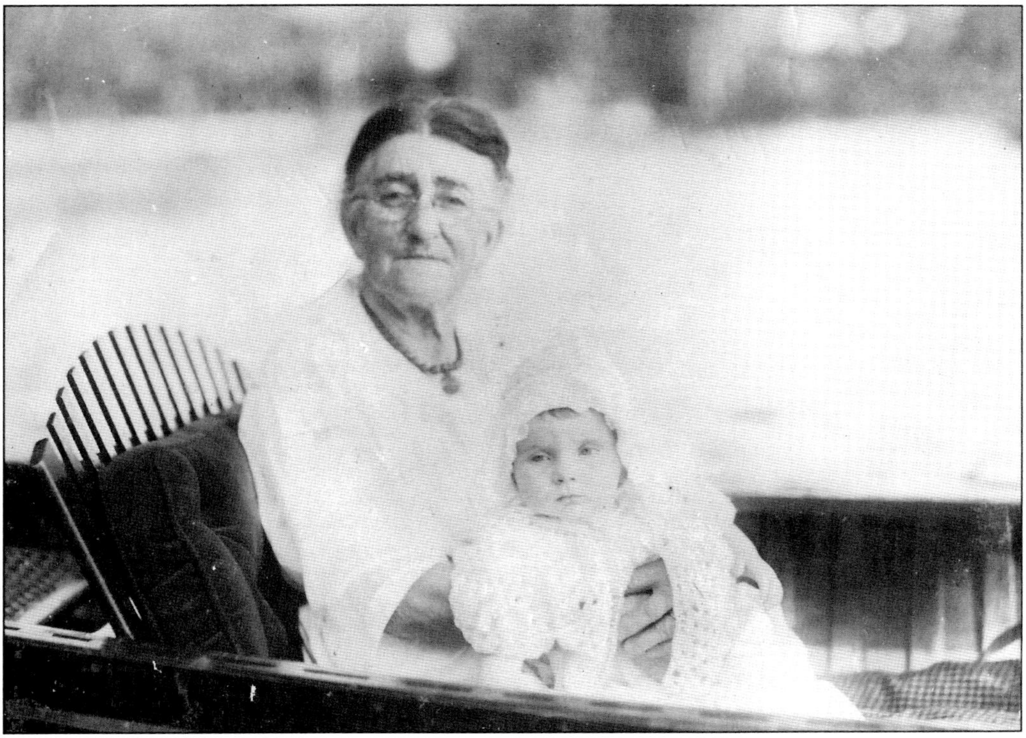

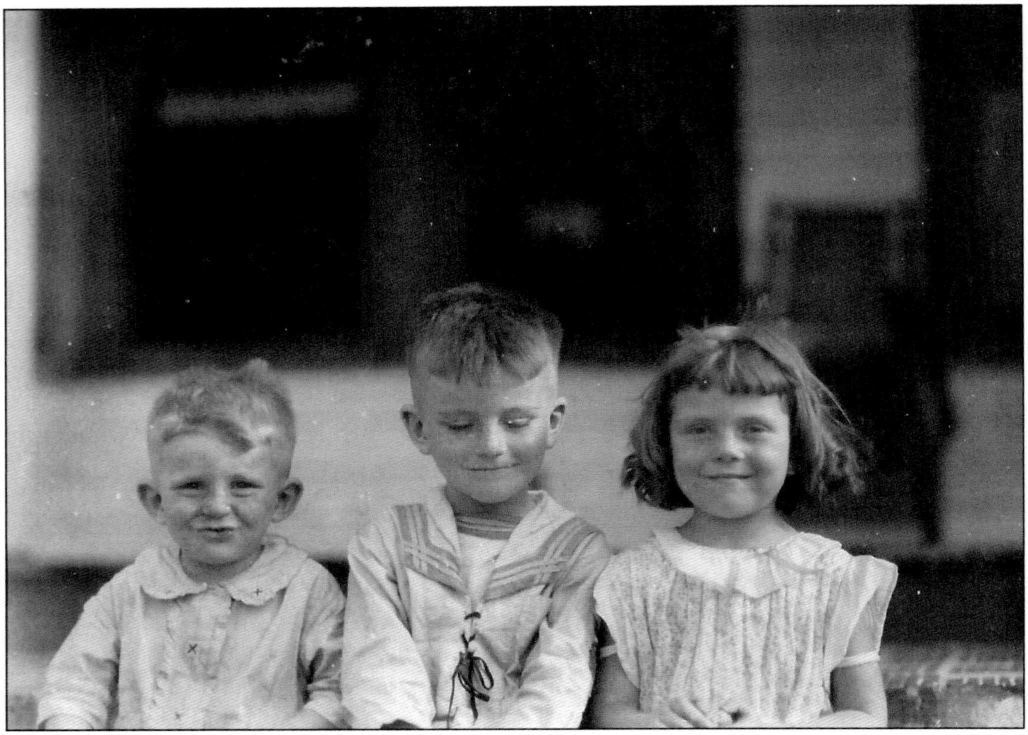

Both photographs are of Bill, Claire, and Jackie Evans, children of Frank Evans. Growing up in a small town has its ups and downs. Everyone knows everyone. The same was true about the Evans family. But family ties were strong in Lake Mary and siblings like them grew up to be friends, always looking out for each other and doing things together.

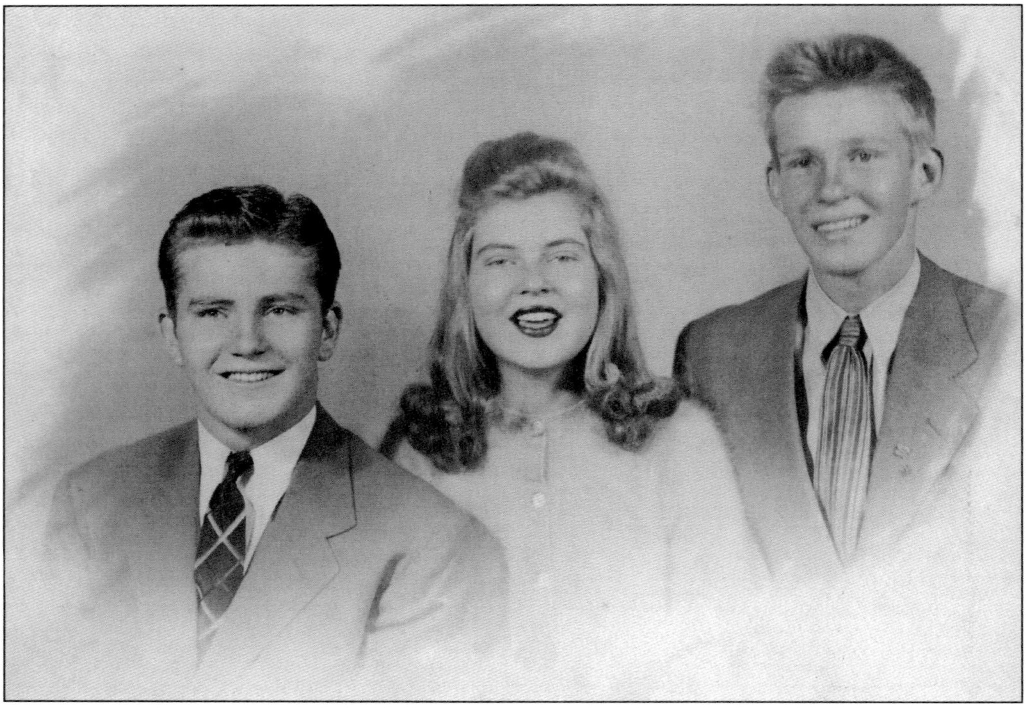

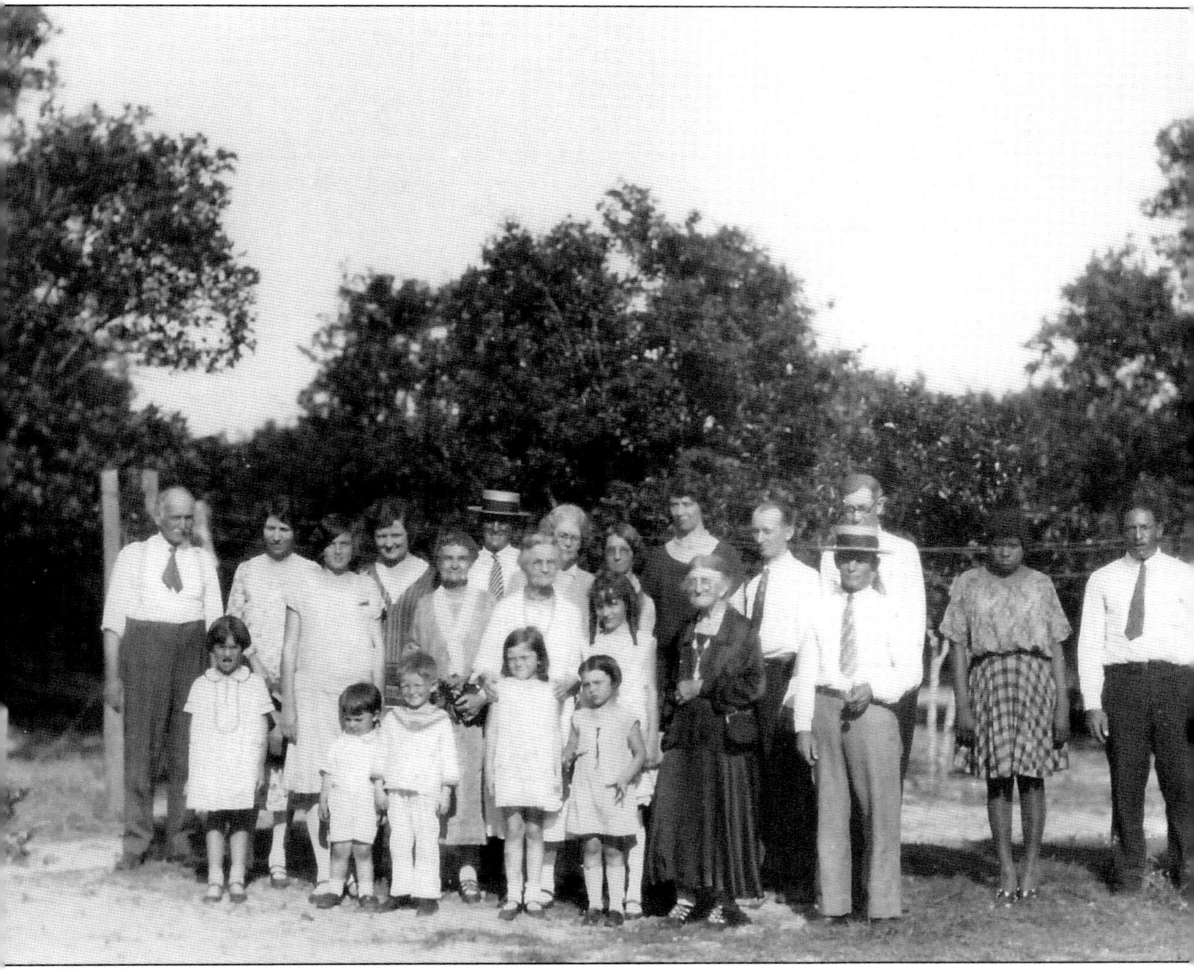

Pictured are the Evans and Thompson families and a few other friends. On the right are Oscar and his wife Victoria, two descendants of slave families who worked for the Evanses. Oscar and Victoria lived with the Evanses and were treated like part of the family.

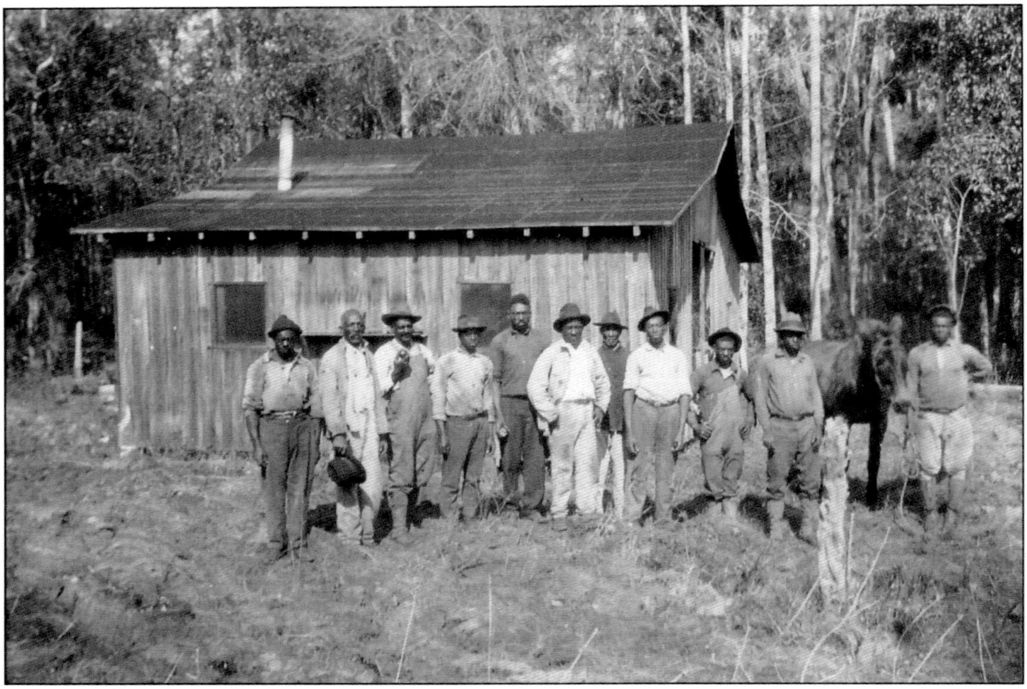

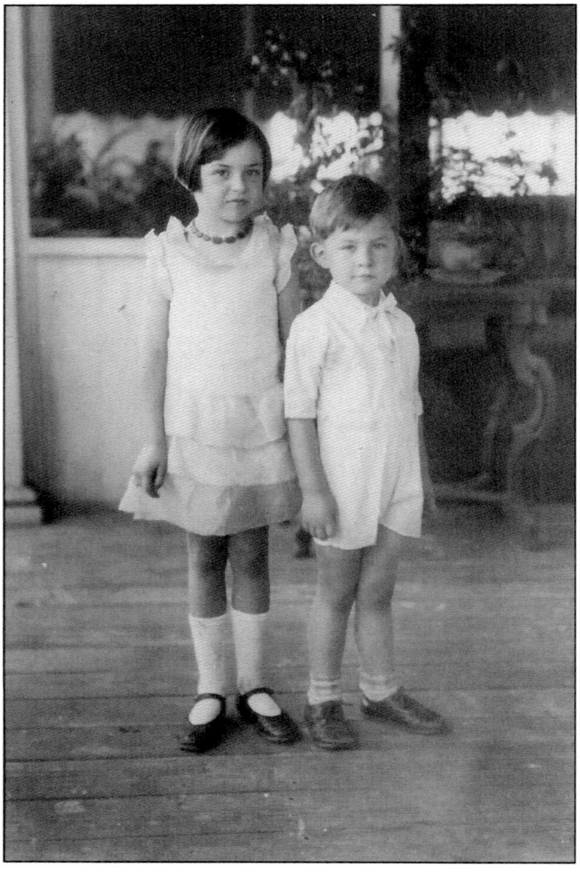

Often, the only opportunities for black workers were manual, backbreaking jobs. Although most of Lake Mary's founding families worked the fields themselves, these men tended the animals and farm fields for the white families who could afford to pay their wages, which was not much. Some were hired short term to handle planting or harvesting crops, forcing them to bounce from farm to farm wherever there was work.

Frances Mary and her younger brother James Booth, children of Rev. James Moore Thompson and Isabelle Booth, are pictured around 1930. The reverend preached at the Community Church from 1927 to 1937. Their great uncle William Booth founded the Salvation Army in 1878, and their mother's twin brother, Cameron Booth, is a renowned artist.

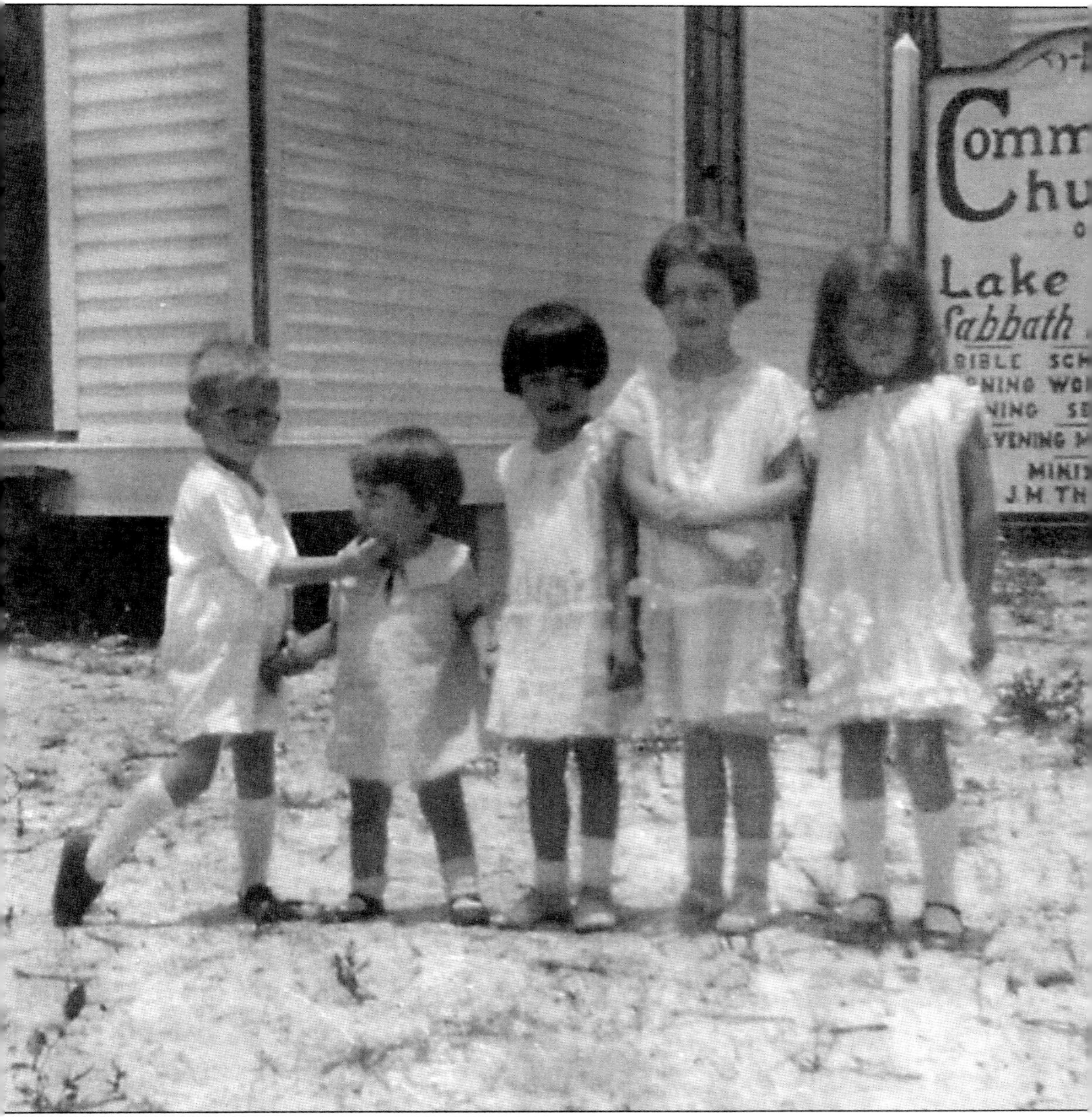

"Stop pinching my chin!" The mischievous Jack Evans on the left picks on little James Thompson while getting their picture taken outside the Community Church. In 2014, Thompson still remembers this moment. In the early 1930s when this photograph was taken, his family needed to be so careful with their money that little James wore handed-down clothes from his sister, such as the dress he wears here.

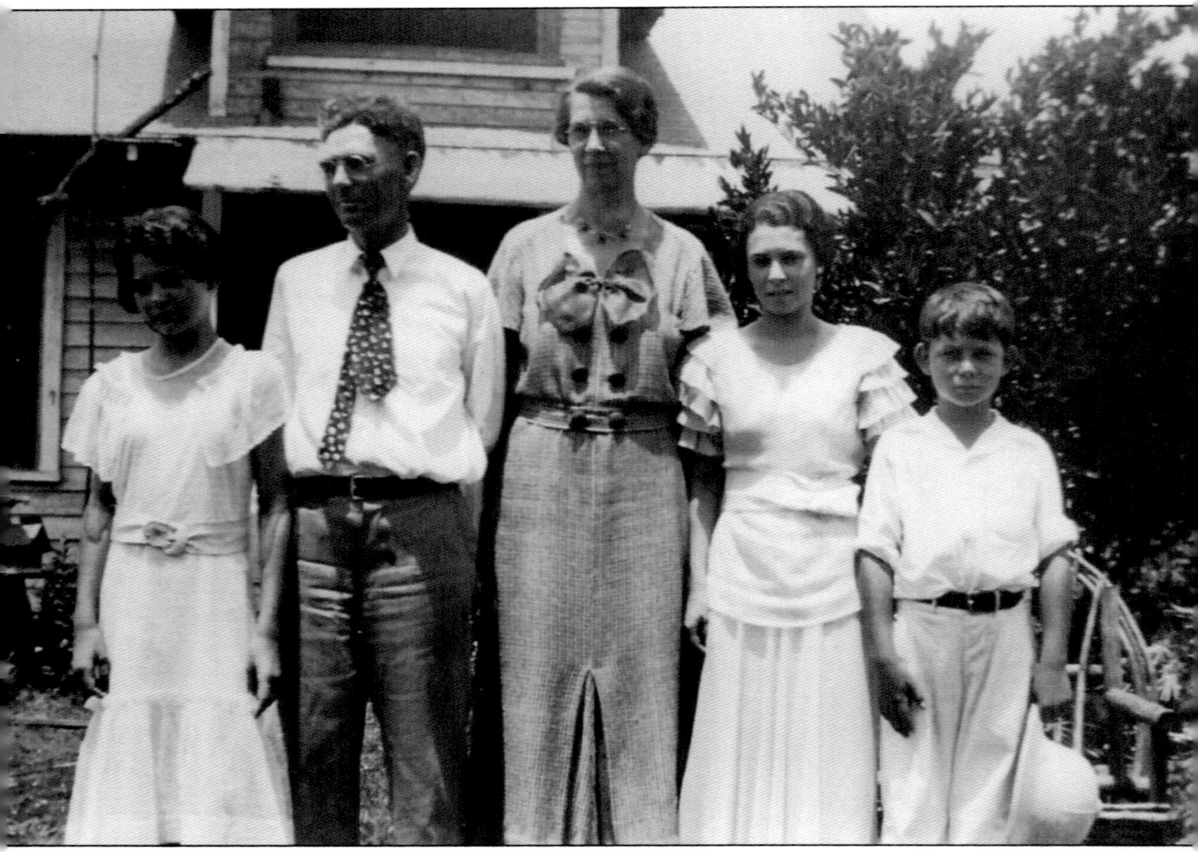

In 1935, Reverend Thompson's niece Elizabeth, second from the right, came from Pennsylvania to visit. She liked Lake Mary so much that she stayed and eventually her mother and father traveled south. The boy on the right, James Thompson, is dressed ready to work on his home garden. Home gardens were very common in Lake Mary and maintaining them was a job often shared by the whole family. James and his sister Fran, on the far left, grew up in the house behind them. Their father furnished the attic, giving the kids a spacious bedroom and playroom upstairs. The house was located on Lakeview Avenue, the only paved road at the time. Lakeview was originally named Sjoblom Avenue but was changed because it was hard to pronounce.

Pictured is Ettie Jane Gleason, daughter of Homer and Lena Gleason, at seven months keeping cool from the Florida heat and nodding off in the middle of an outdoor bath. The Gleasons owned and operated a general store and gas station commonly known as Gleason's Store.

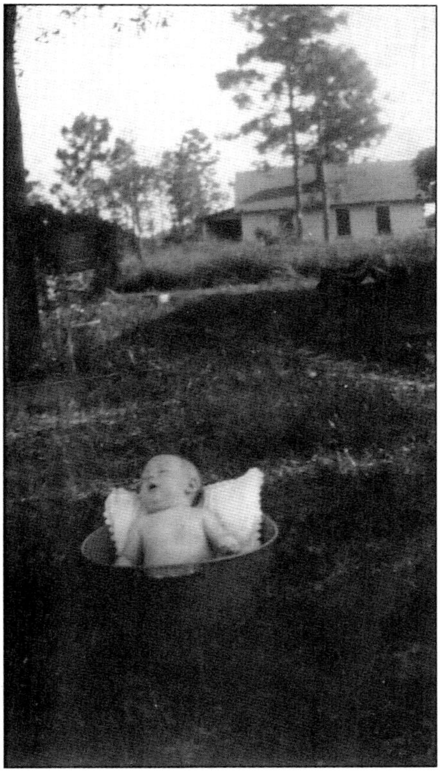

Young girls and a few boys line up outside church on Easter Sunday in 1936. They are all dressed in their clean, white Easter clothes, most of which were handmade.

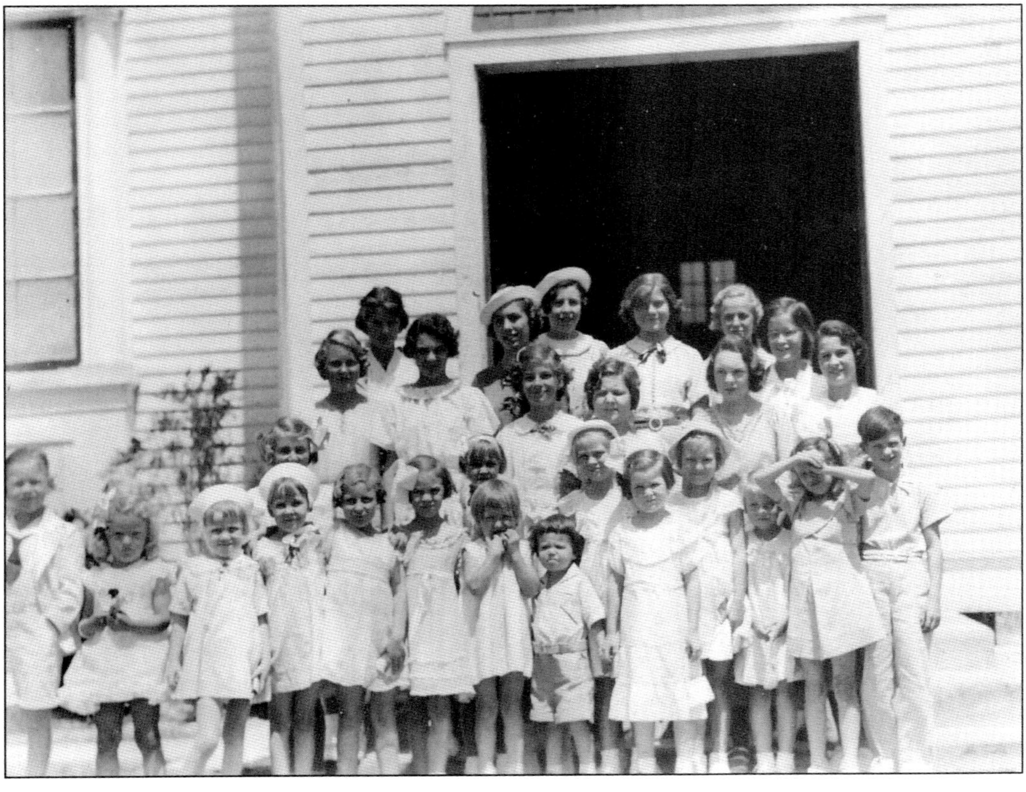

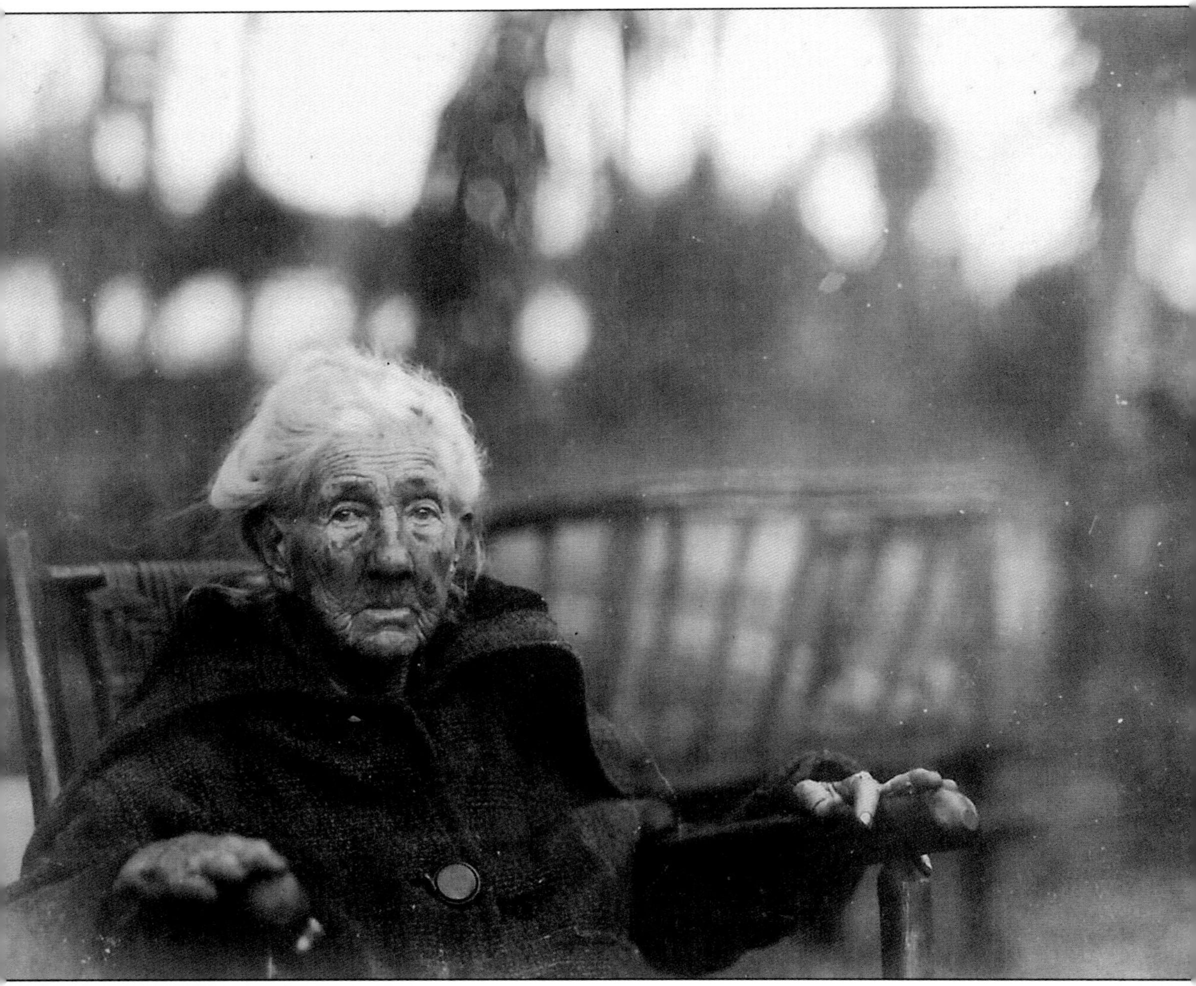

Pictured is Mrs. Hillard at 103 years old in April 1936. She had seen Lake Mary grow from a pair of small train stops to a bustling town. When she was born, Andrew Jackson—once Florida's military governor—was president of the United States. She was on the cusp of entering her teenage years when Florida became a state in 1845. By the time A.E. Sjoblom started buying land near Crystal Lake in the early 1900s, she was in her seventies. In her lifetime, she endured not only the American Civil War and Spanish-American War, but also the Great War, later known as World War I.

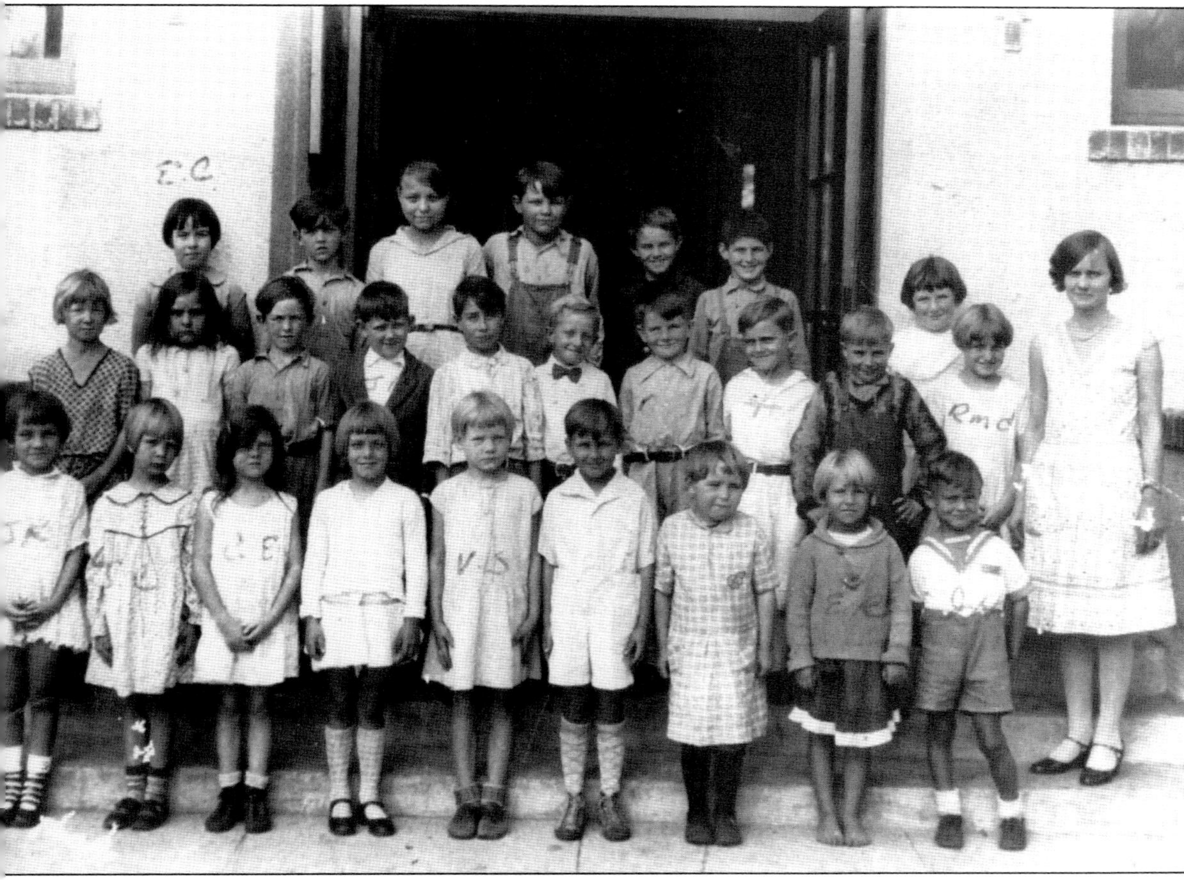

Pictured are kids and their teacher from the Lake Mary Elementary School in the 1930s. Organized education in the state started with the formation of the Florida Education Society in 1831, fourteen years before Florida was admitted as a state. Consisting of parents and volunteers, the society laid the foundations of the state's education system.

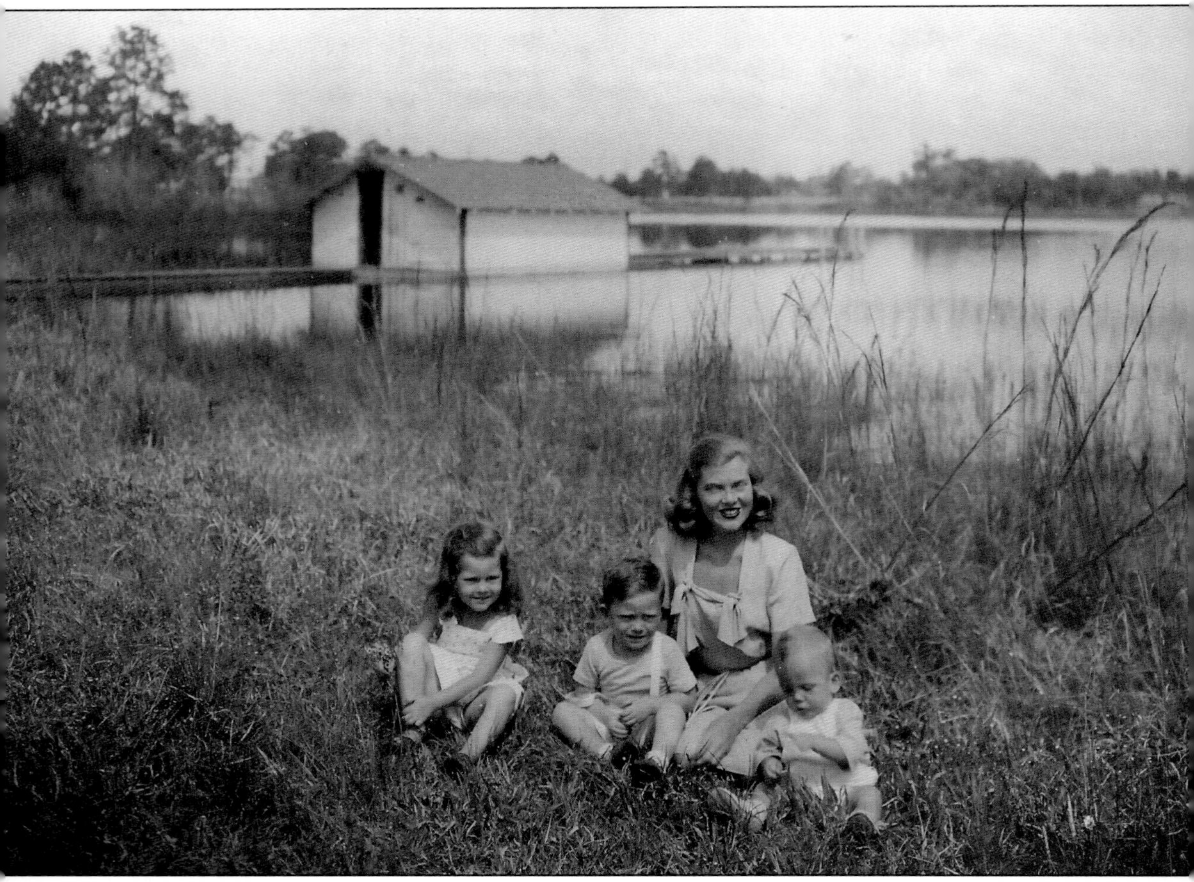

In this photograph, a young family sits on the shore of Lake Mary, with a boathouse in the background. Surrounding the family are straggly stalks of saw grass. Saw grass is common to Florida's fresh and brackish water. It provides both food and shelter for birds and small wildlife. Sitting or playing in this grass was not pleasant for kids, with its sharp, saw-like spikes.

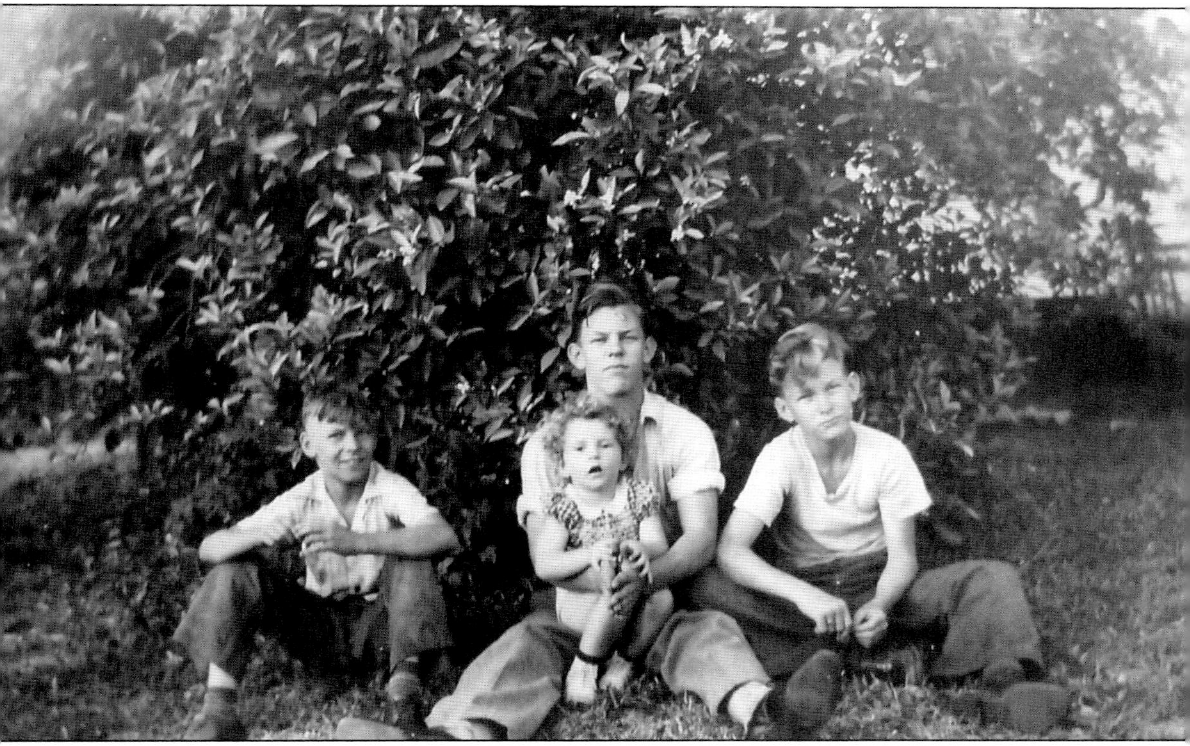

In 1900, kids had a one-in-three chance of losing a sibling and thousands worked 40 (or more) hours a week on farms or in mines and factories. In the years following, the Great War and the Depression brought even more heartache to children and their families. As the nation moved into the 1940s, a continued push for further limiting child labor, increased attention on children's health, and the rise of suburbia set the stage for the baby boom following World War II and a much more pleasant childhood for kids.

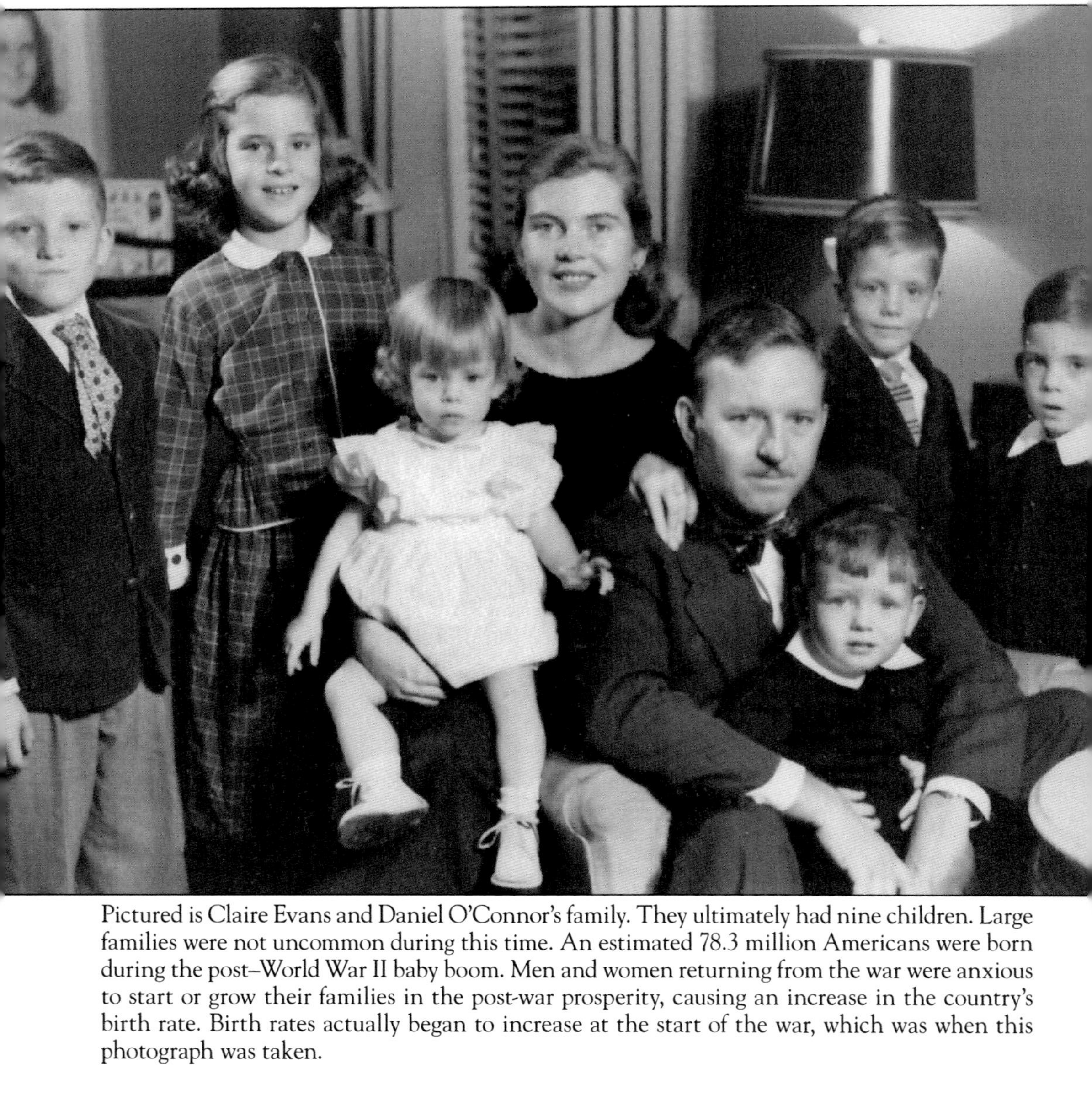

Pictured is Claire Evans and Daniel O'Connor's family. They ultimately had nine children. Large families were not uncommon during this time. An estimated 78.3 million Americans were born during the post–World War II baby boom. Men and women returning from the war were anxious to start or grow their families in the post-war prosperity, causing an increase in the country's birth rate. Birth rates actually began to increase at the start of the war, which was when this photograph was taken.

Three

LIFE IN LAKE MARY

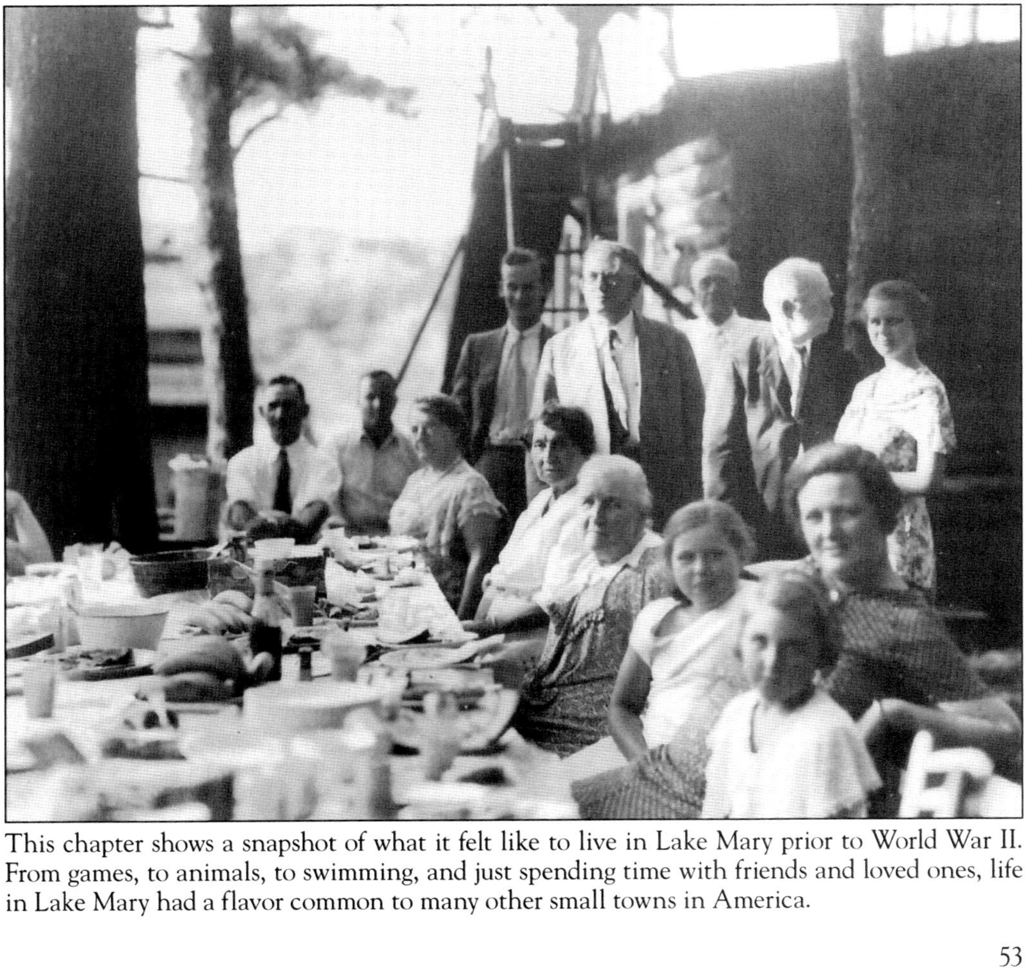

This chapter shows a snapshot of what it felt like to live in Lake Mary prior to World War II. From games, to animals, to swimming, and just spending time with friends and loved ones, life in Lake Mary had a flavor common to many other small towns in America.

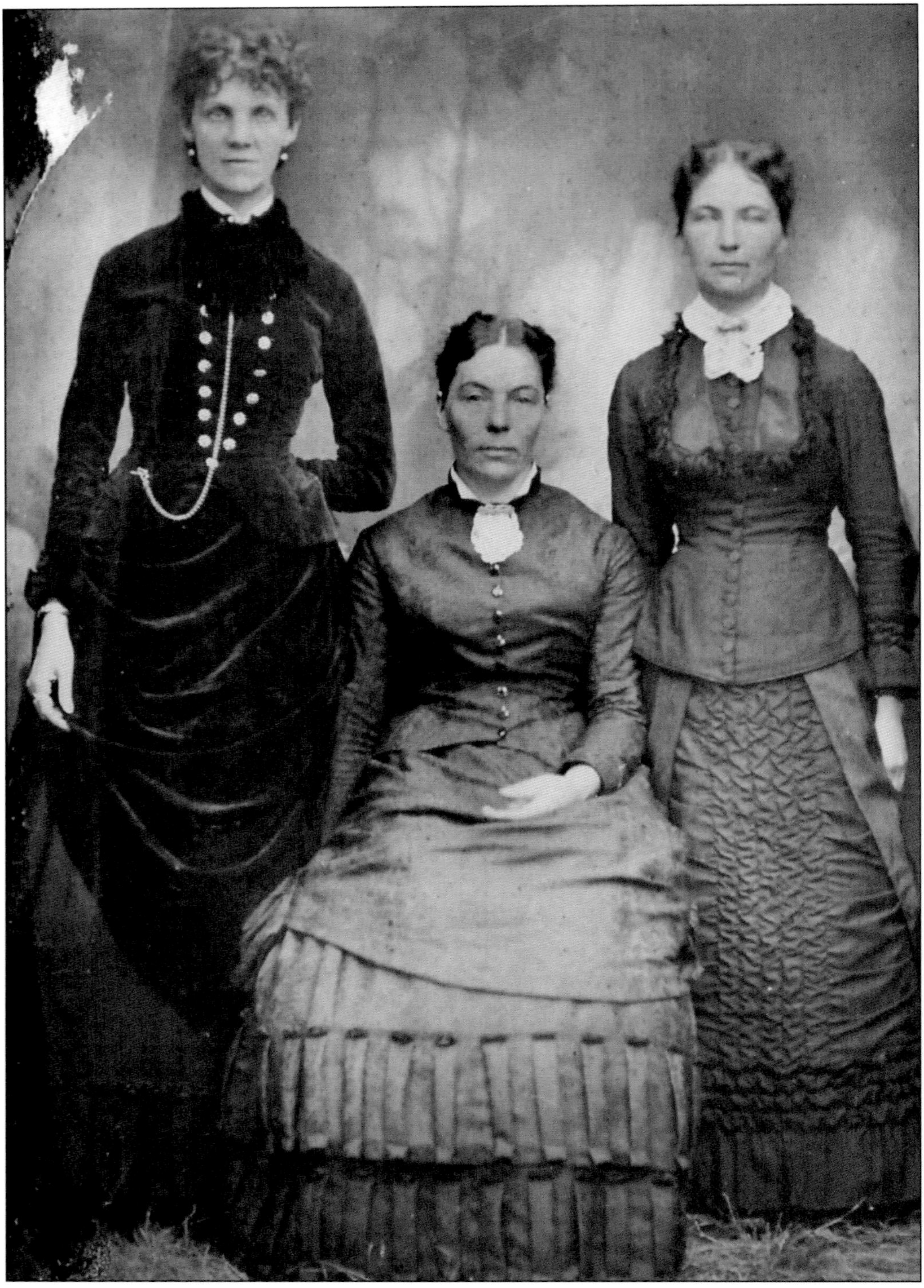

Three women pose in full-length dresses in the late 1800s. Nearly all the early residents came from colder climates. These two-piece wool and silk fineries kept ladies warm. In the days before air conditioning, wearing these undoubtedly required much personal fortitude in Florida's warm, humid weather.

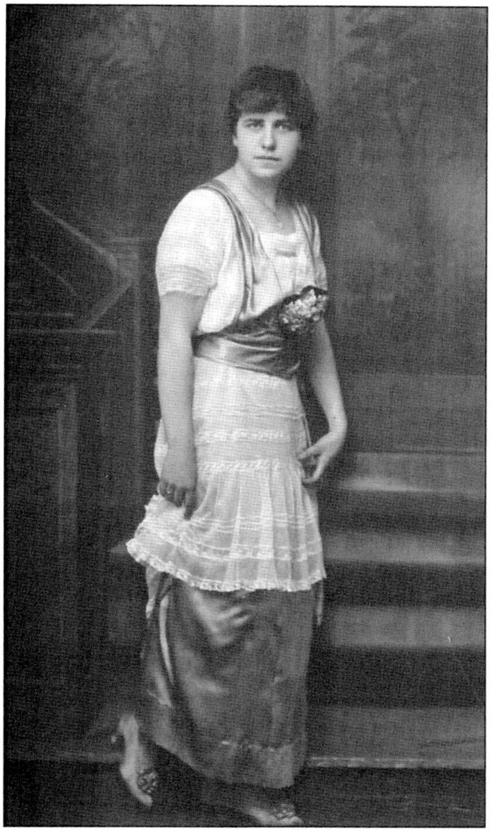

In these two photographs, one woman stands posed in a fancy satin and lace dress, and another sits with fur and a feather-covered hat. The early 1900s saw a rise in high fashion. Many French-made designs in this period were very extravagant and hard to make. Fashion in America took a more practical approach, though some extravagance made its way into American culture.

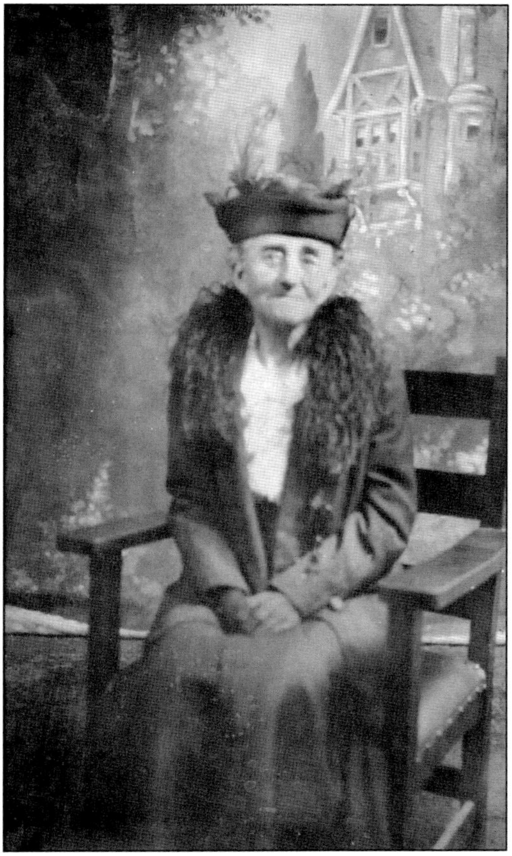

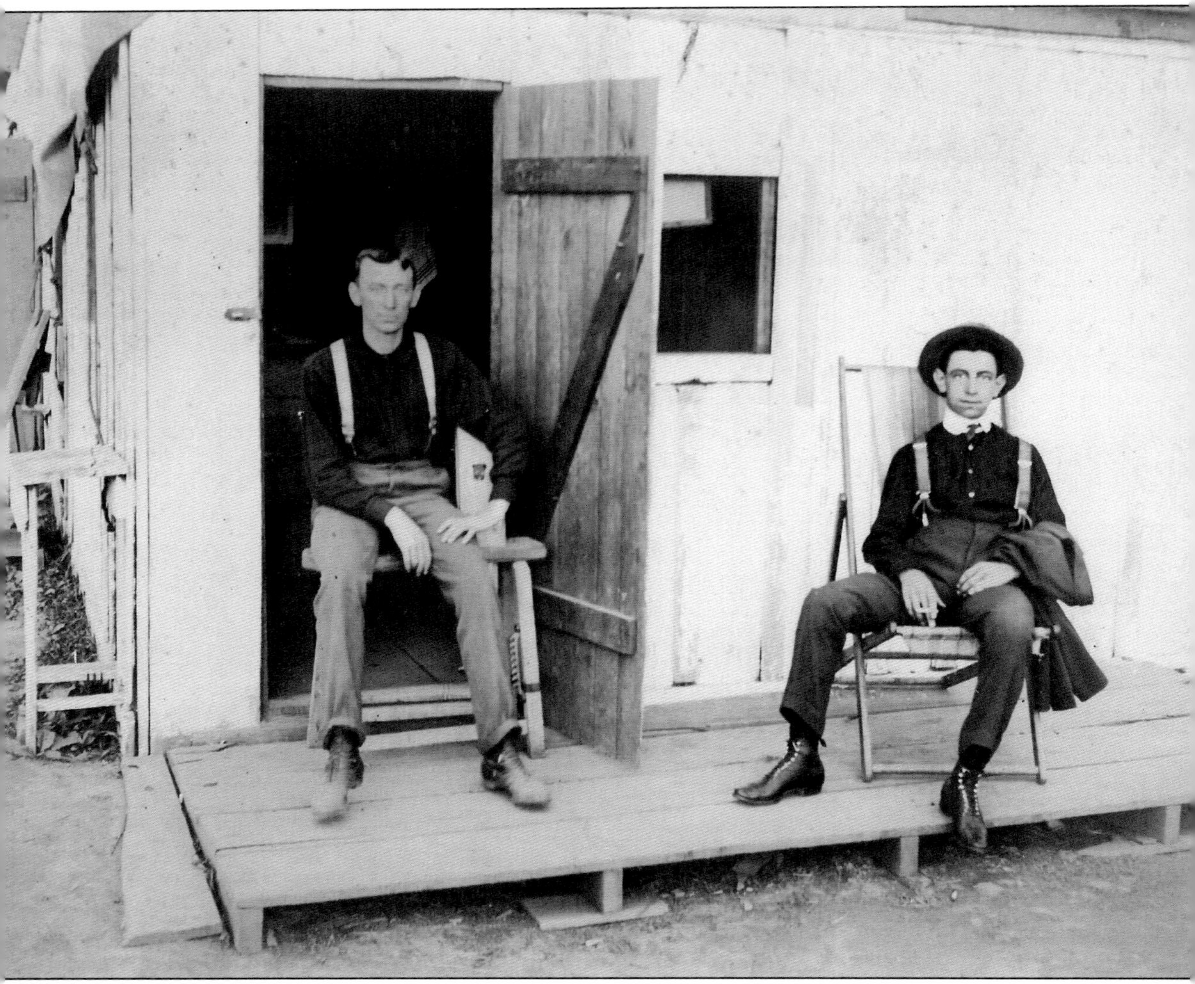

Captured here is a smoke break for a pair of businessmen in the 1920s. During this time, important Lake Mary business meetings were often held in seemingly causal settings such as this. New York–style high rises and fancy marble and masonry office buildings were nonexistent here. Yet their business deals, price negotiations, and discussions were handled with the same somber professionalism.

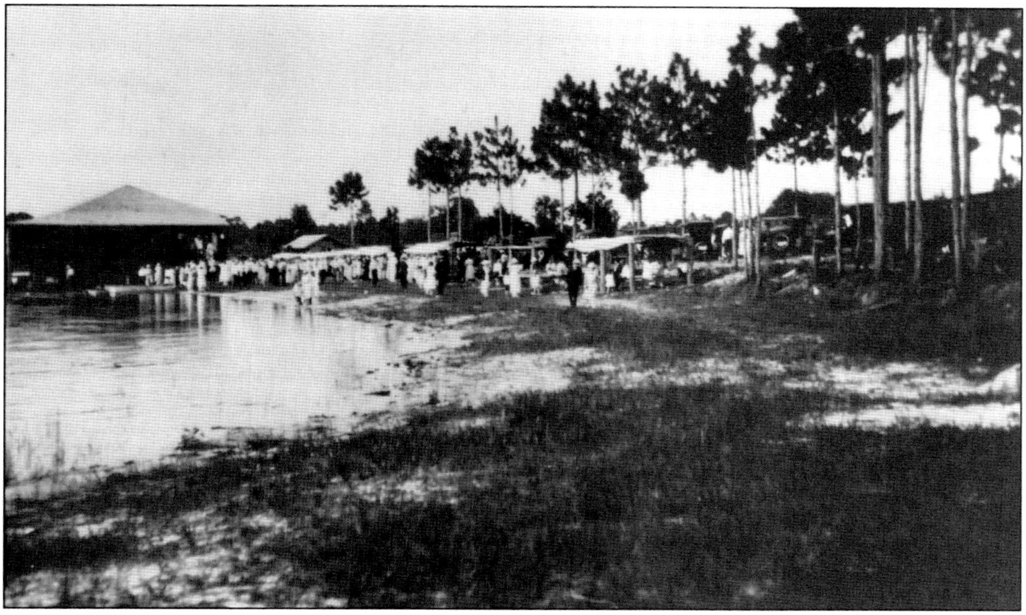

On the shores of Crystal Lake there once stood the Lake Mary casino and bathhouse. The top photograph is a rare shot of the casino in the 1930s. By this time, crime bosses Al Capone and Meyer Lansky had established Florida hangouts with casinos and speakeasies. The bottom photograph shows a number of shady characters, possibly drawn to the area by the casino's activities.

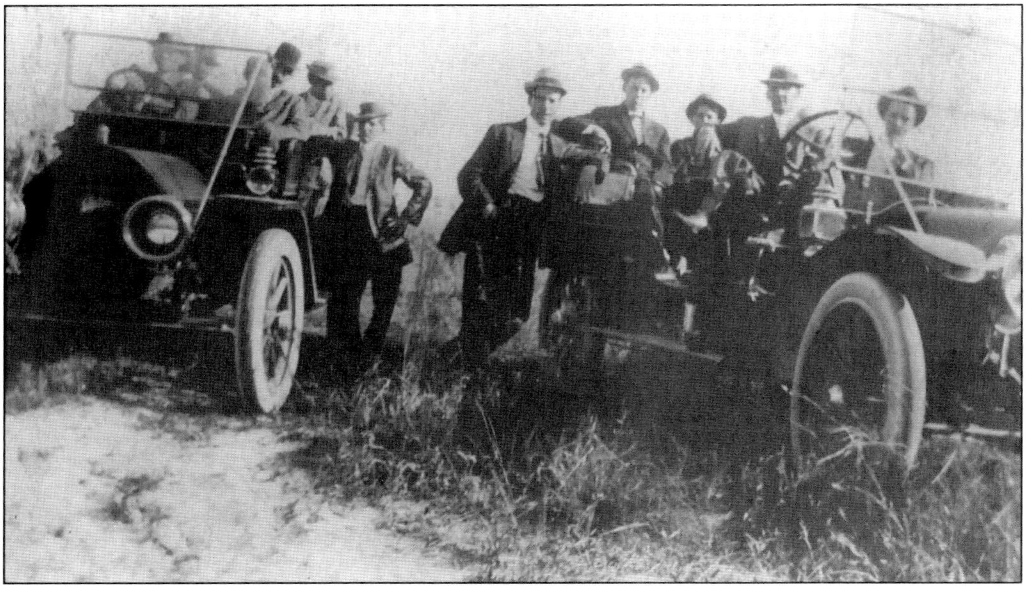

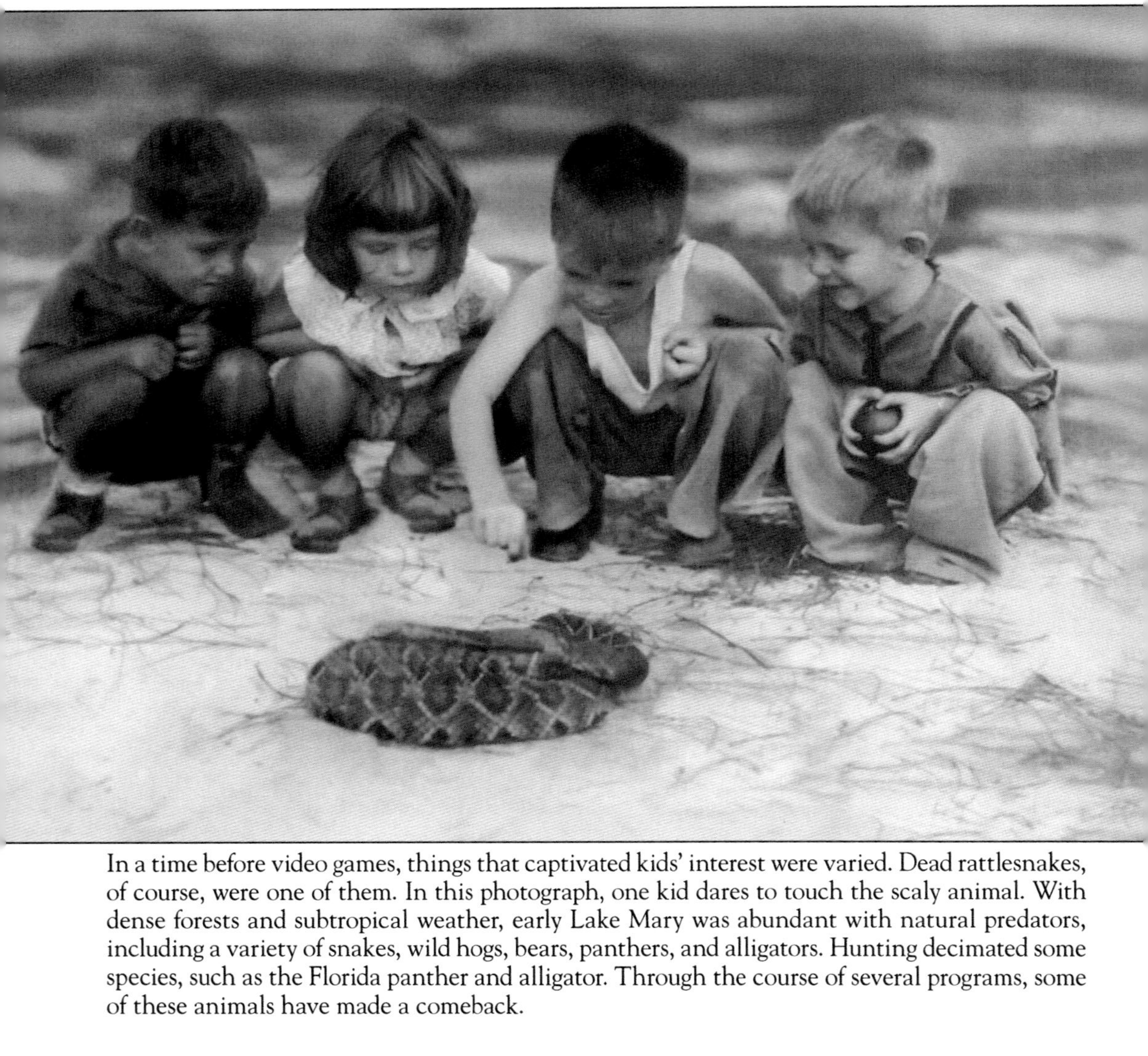

In a time before video games, things that captivated kids' interest were varied. Dead rattlesnakes, of course, were one of them. In this photograph, one kid dares to touch the scaly animal. With dense forests and subtropical weather, early Lake Mary was abundant with natural predators, including a variety of snakes, wild hogs, bears, panthers, and alligators. Hunting decimated some species, such as the Florida panther and alligator. Through the course of several programs, some of these animals have made a comeback.

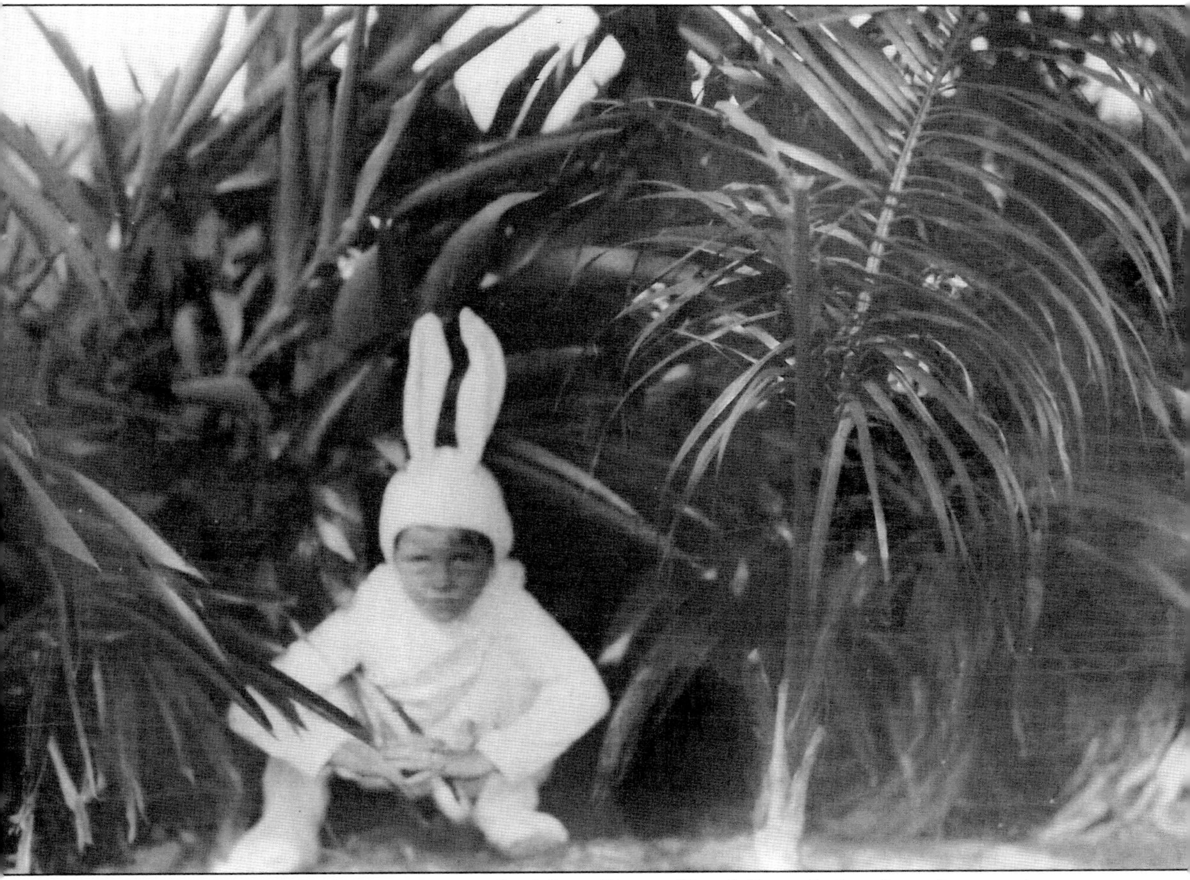

It appears whoever took this picture caught Claire Evans, Frank Evans's daughter, by surprise as she hid among the palm fronds. Costumes were all hand-made at this Halloween get together. One can only guess by the look on Claire's face whether or not she was happy being a bunny.

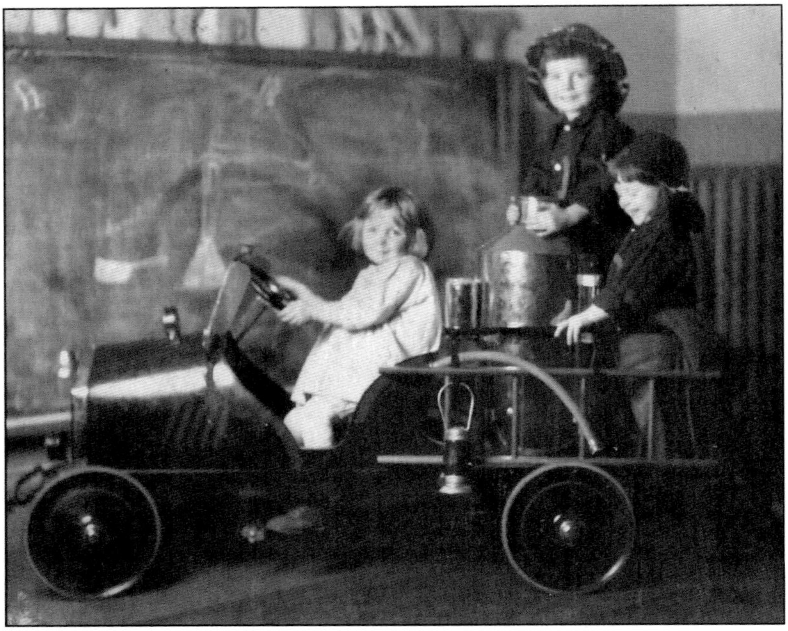

Some things never change. Like the children shown here pretending to be firefighters, every generation enjoys spending time in a fantasyland. In this case, the makers of this toy fire engine went to great lengths to make it appear authentic, with a ladder, hose, and water tank.

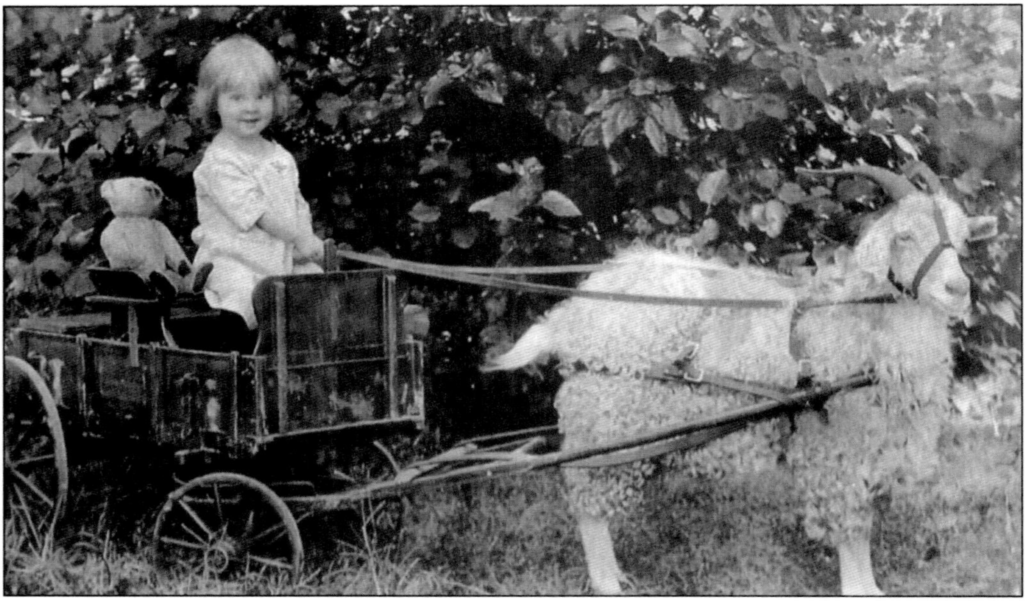

Posing with her trusty teddy bear at her side, this little girl is ready to be pulled off into the sunset, or perhaps just toward a grassy field, by the family goat. With the advancements in photography made by companies like Kodak in the late 1800s, the early 1900s saw a boost in photography as a commercial service. Photographs like this were often taken by traveling photographers who came to town with pricey equipment and sold prints—similar to professional photographers today.

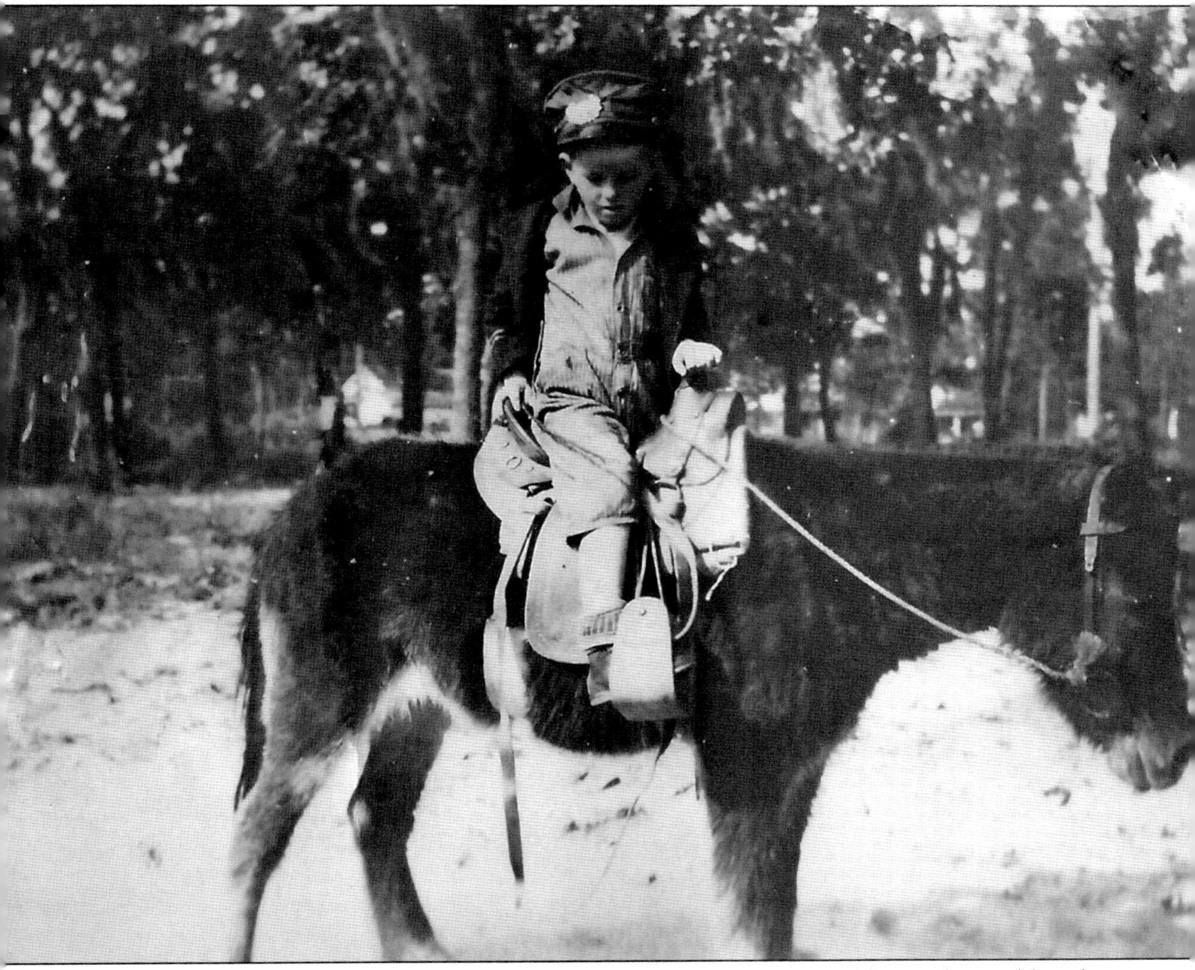

A boy sits on a family pony. With his sheriff's hat, he may have imagined being the cool hand of the law sent in to clean up the town. Although it was not uncommon to see people on horseback, the primary form of travel for kids in the 1920s was either by foot or in the backseat of a car. So for kids, riding a horse either meant helping with farm work or, like with this one, just playing around.

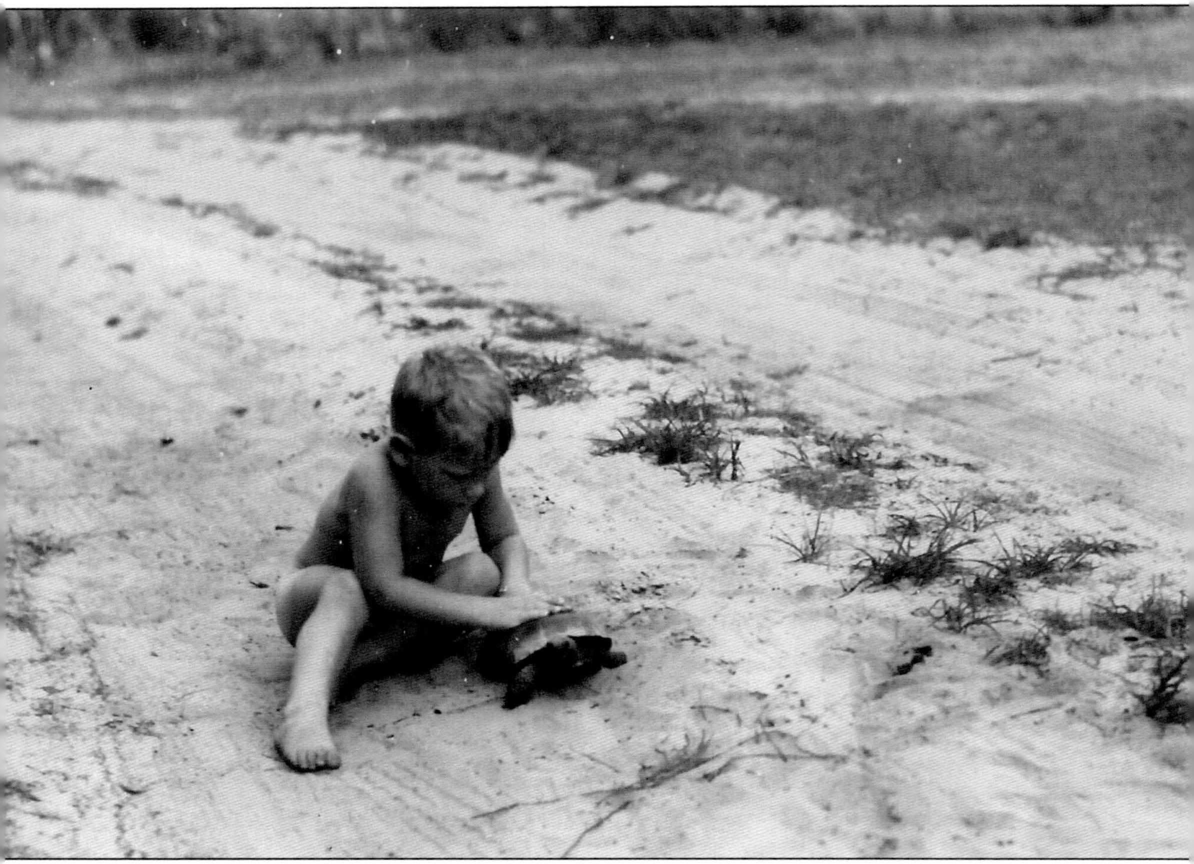

It looks like the gopher tortoise pictured here was not the only one out of his shell. Recognized as the state tortoise of Florida, at one time the gopher tortoise was commonly found throughout the southeastern United States. The US Fish and Wildlife Service has classified them as threatened due to predators and the destruction of their habitat.

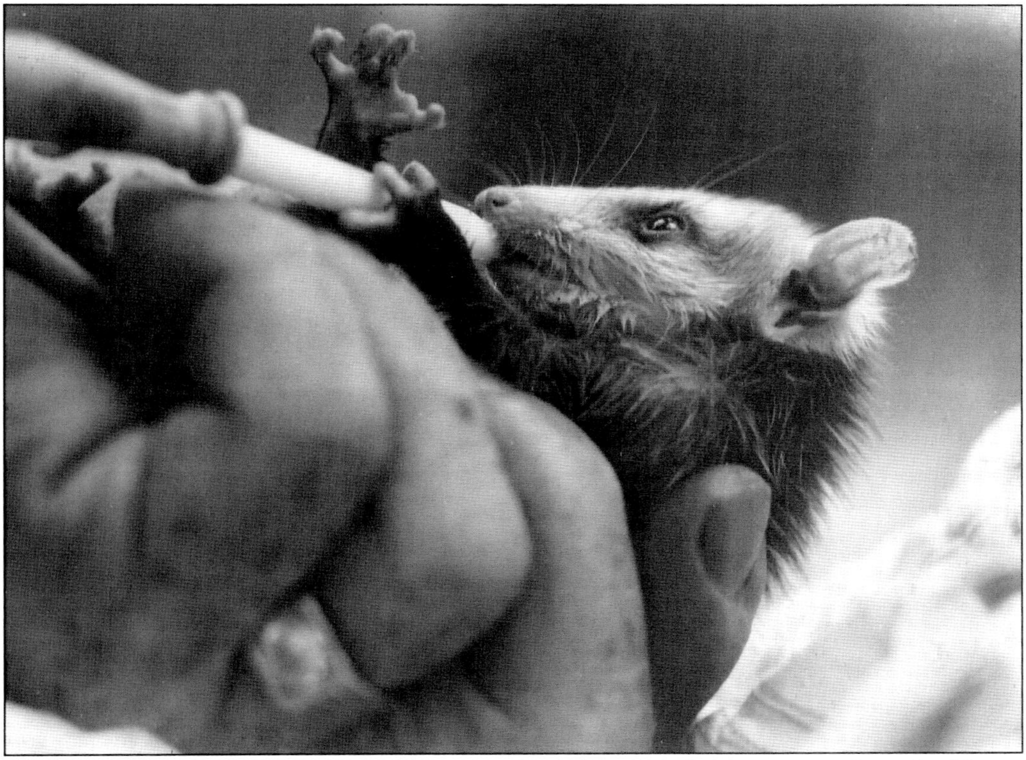

Pictured is someone hand feeding a baby opossum. This animal gets its name from the Native American Proto-Algonquian word meaning "white dog." They are classified as marsupials, similar to the kangaroos and koalas of Australia. The one pictured was found on a Lake Mary property.

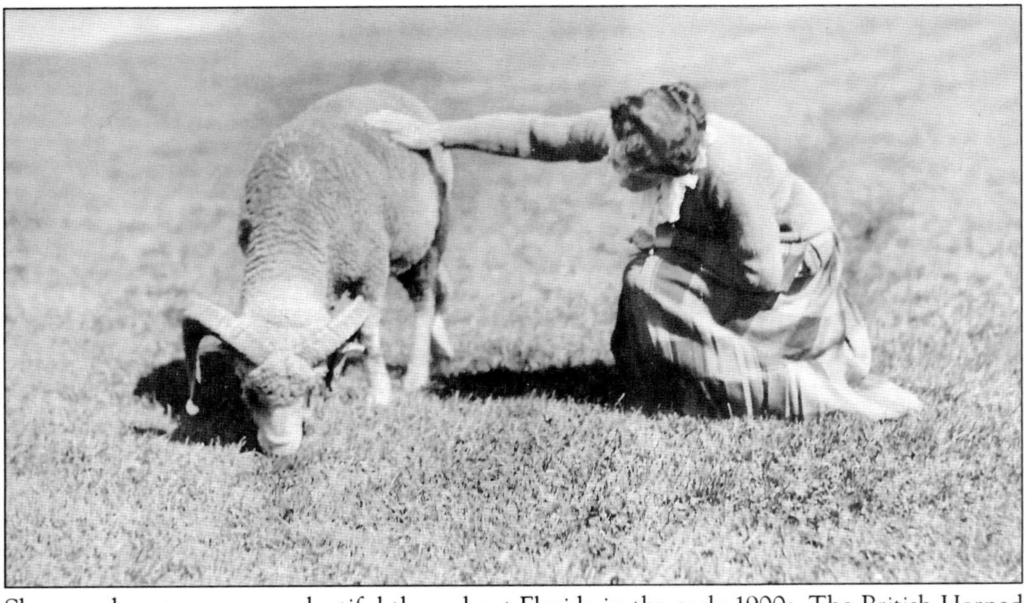

Sheep and goat were once plentiful throughout Florida in the early 1900s. The British Horned Dorset, as shown in this photograph, were brought to America and were once the most popular breed in the country. This breed was great for mothering and milking, and their lambs grew very fast, making them desirable among family farmers.

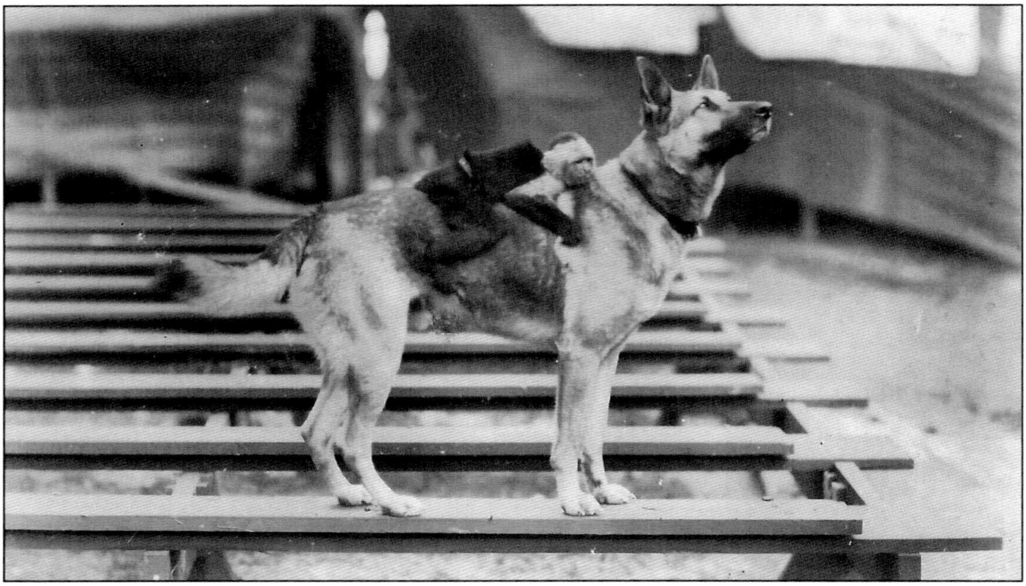

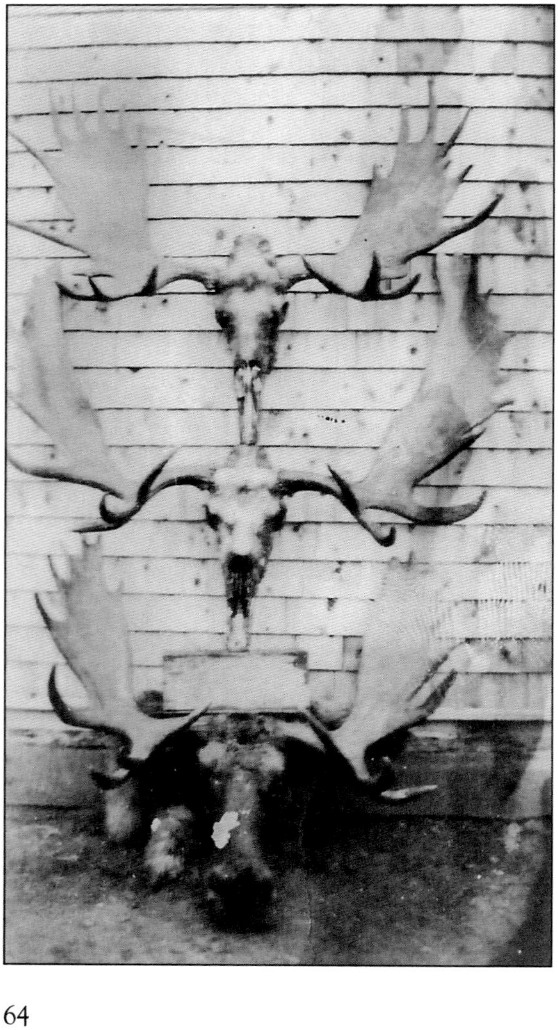

This German Sheppard literately has a monkey on his back. It is unclear where the monkey came from. With its quiet, isolated lakes, Lake Mary often attracted tourists from all over to spend some time to relax—even monkeys.

Did you expect to see moose in Florida? Neither did the people who swung by this Lake Mary residence. The owners acquired these heads from either northern states or Canada. Hunting was a popular pastime for residents, and they occasionally traveled elsewhere for a little change in scenery.

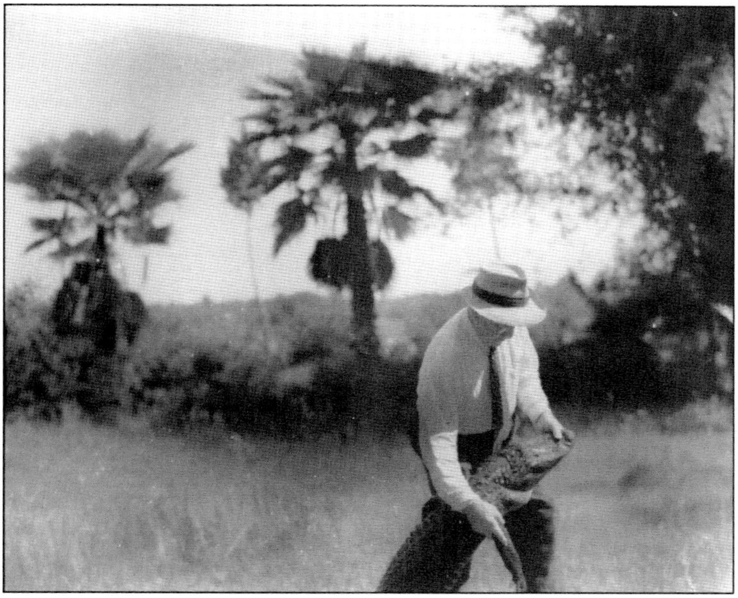

A photograph like this might have been titled: "Frank Evans Wrestles Man-Eating Gator to Make Lake Mary Safe for Tourists." In reality, the alligator was dead, but Frank often took advantage of publicity stunts like this to promote Lake Mary. He realized the power of making headline news to bring in money for the growing town.

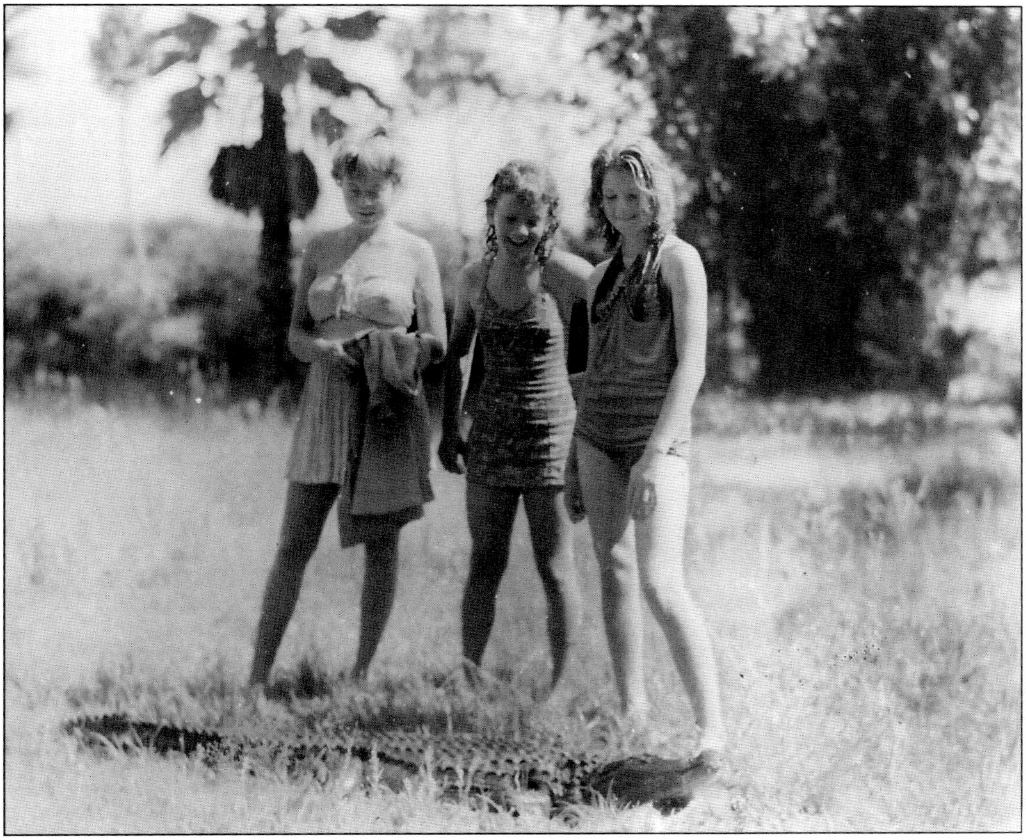

Hopefully this alligator was dead. Pictured are Claire Evans and her cousins, the Pellet girls from Jacksonville, staring at a five-foot alligator. Swimming in Lake Mary and Crystal Lake was not without its dangers. Alligator sightings may not have been as common as on notorious Lake Jessup southeast of town, but swimmers still needed to be cautious.

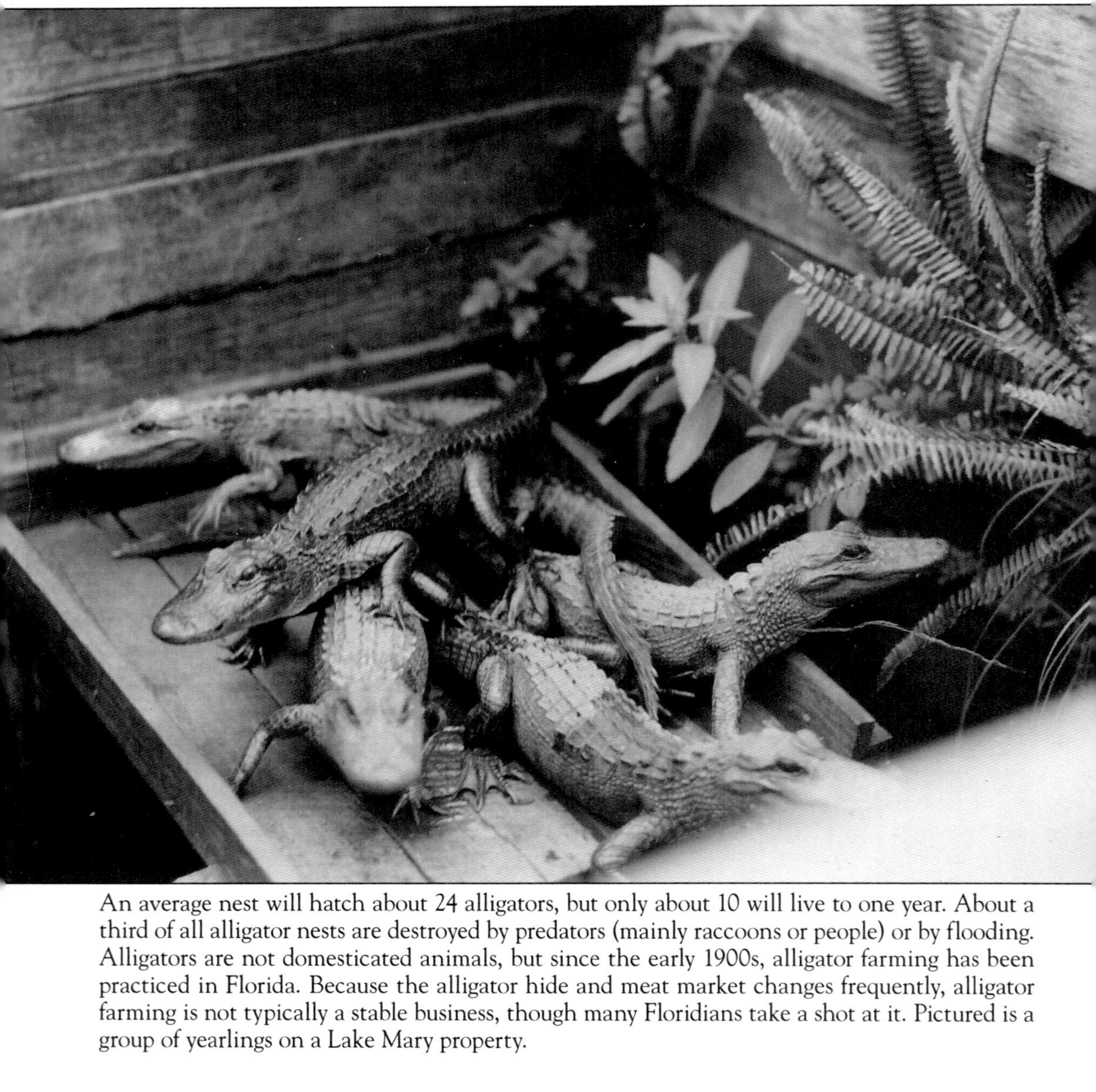

An average nest will hatch about 24 alligators, but only about 10 will live to one year. About a third of all alligator nests are destroyed by predators (mainly raccoons or people) or by flooding. Alligators are not domesticated animals, but since the early 1900s, alligator farming has been practiced in Florida. Because the alligator hide and meat market changes frequently, alligator farming is not typically a stable business, though many Floridians take a shot at it. Pictured is a group of yearlings on a Lake Mary property.

A deadly eastern diamondback rattlesnake prepares to strike. Although it primarily feeds on rats, mice, rabbits, and other prey considered pests, kids learned early on to stay away from animals such as this or risk injury or death. Living in early Lake Mary had its risks.

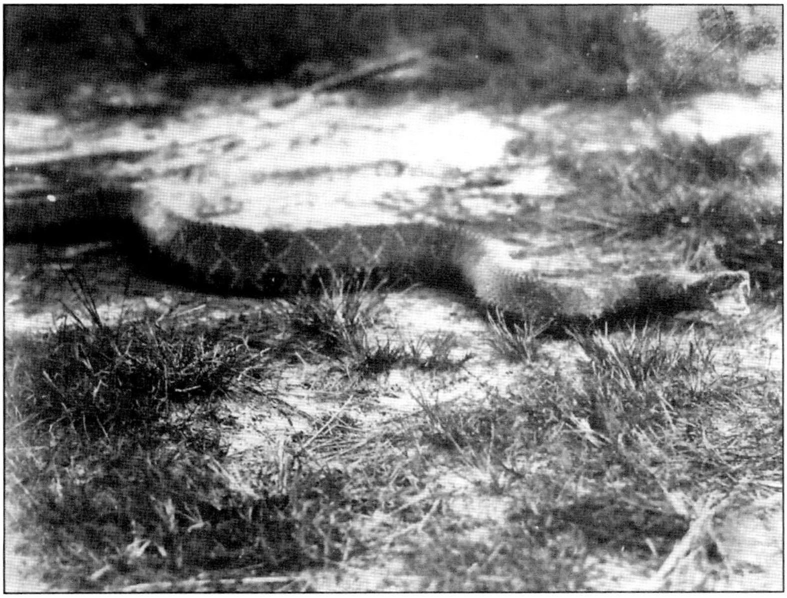

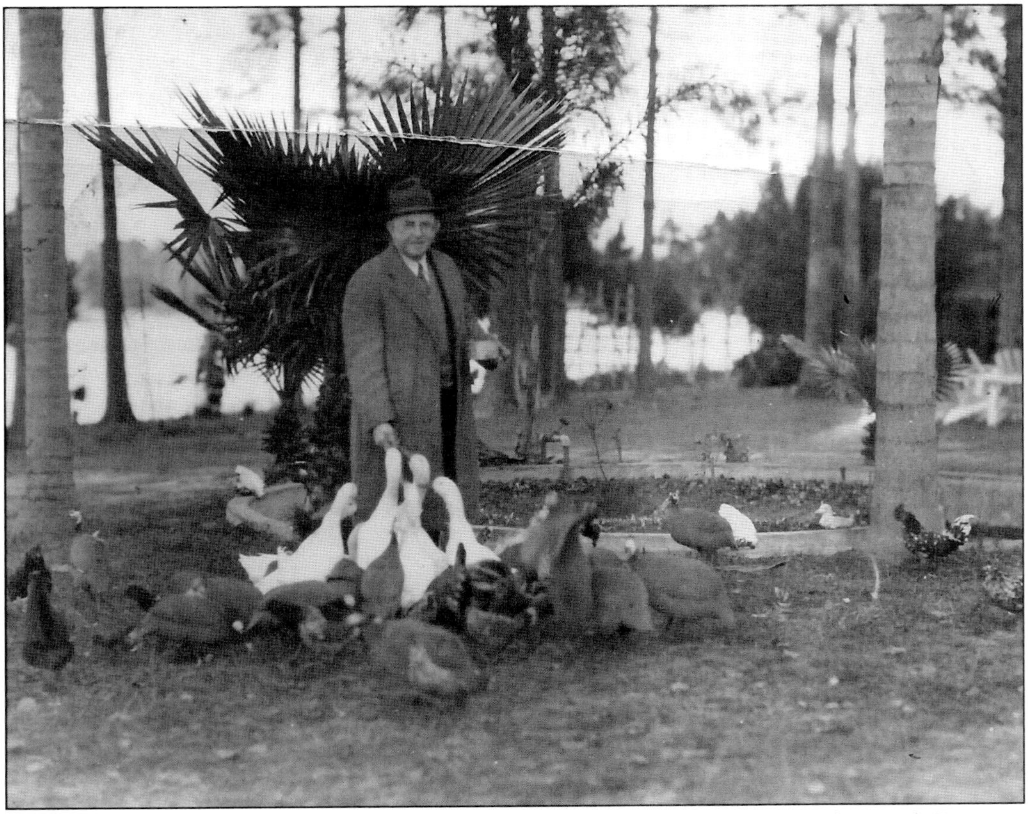

Feeding a group of ducks draws a crowd of various birds. In this photograph, Frank Evans is surrounded by ducks, chickens, and turkeys. All three birds were commonly raised and kept for food. The turkey, the only of the three once exclusively found in America, was a very aggressive bird until certain breeds were domesticated.

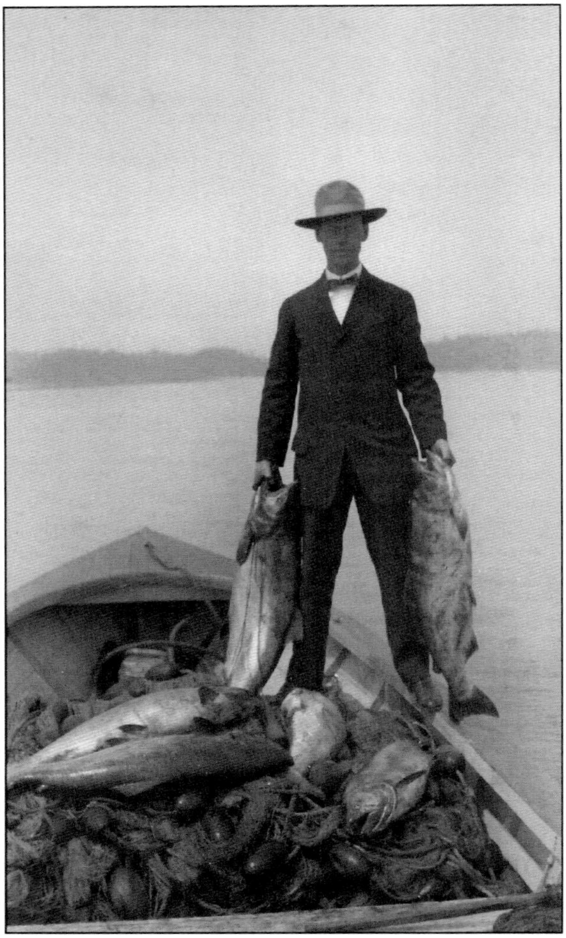

Naturally, fishing was quite popular in both Lake Mary and Crystal Lake. Neither lake was large enough to support any kind of industry, but that did not stop locals spending hours on their boats, patiently reeling in a healthy number of fish to bring home and eat.

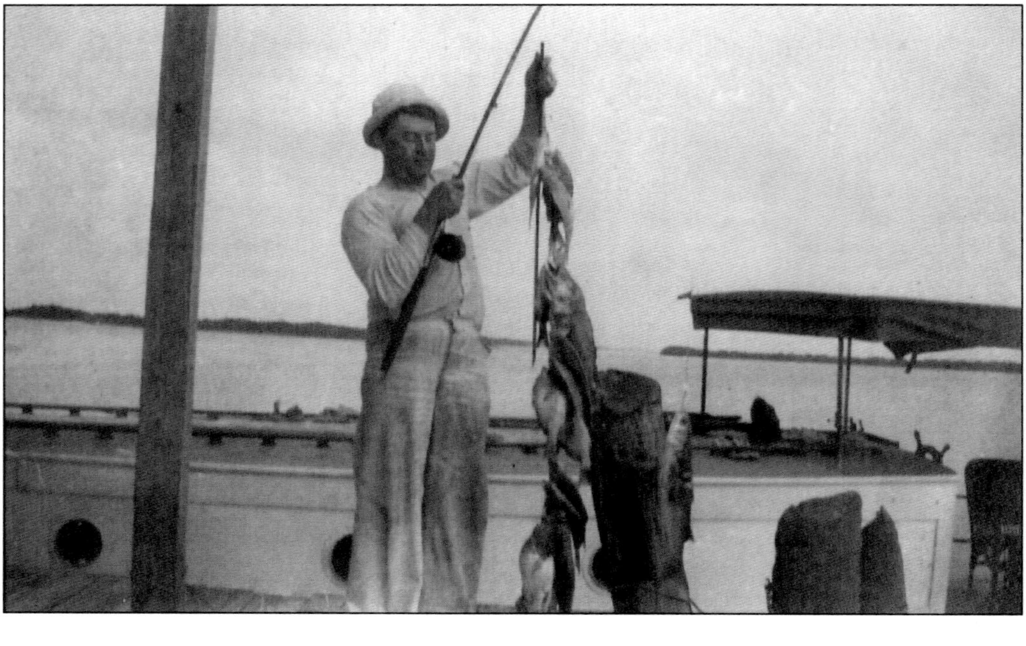

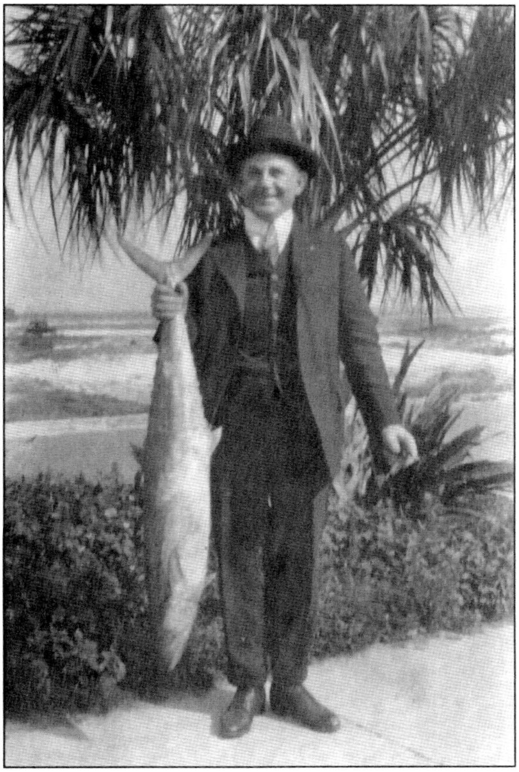

These two photographs show Lake Mary residents who traveled elsewhere for fish. The man on the right shows off a tarpon near St. Petersburg, and the woman below shows off a gray reef shark on a Florida east coast dock. Though Lake Mary's fishing was a popular pastime, it never could yield what the Atlantic Ocean or the Gulf of Mexico could offer.

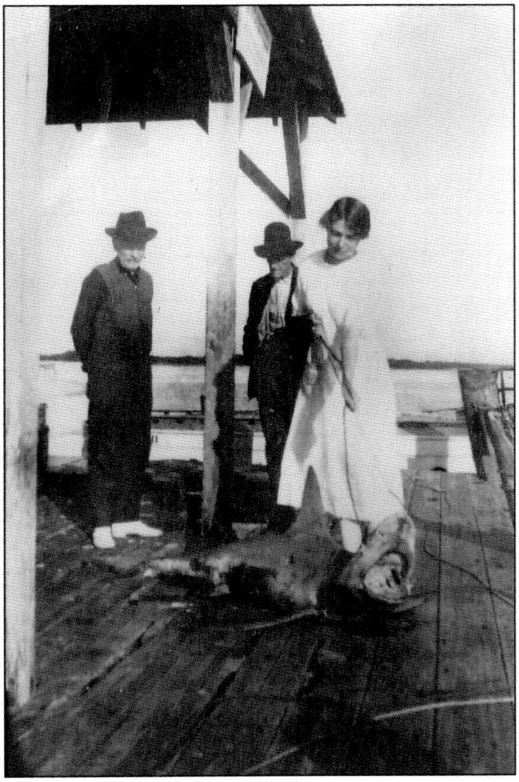

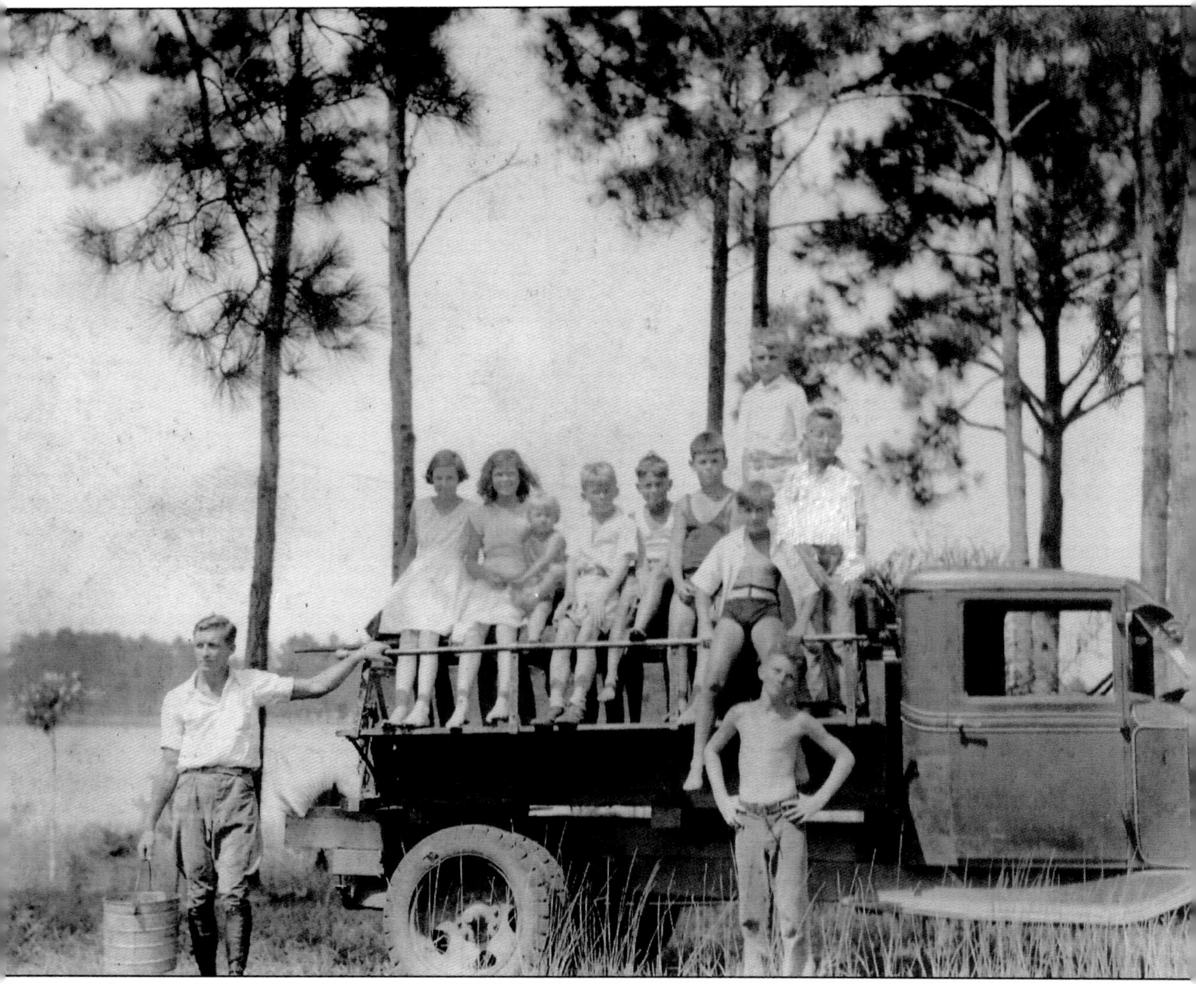

In this photograph from around 1932, kids pile onto a truck to watch a Florida Fish and Wildlife worker, standing on the left with a bucket. The worker visited the town to stock Lake Mary with fish. Starting in the early 1900s, the Florida Fish and Wildlife Commission raised non-native fish such as salmon and bass in hatcheries throughout the state and released them into selected lakes. Lake Mary is no longer stocked with fish, but the commission continues to stock lakes and rivers throughout Florida with a careful selection of fish species to avoid a negative impact on native species.

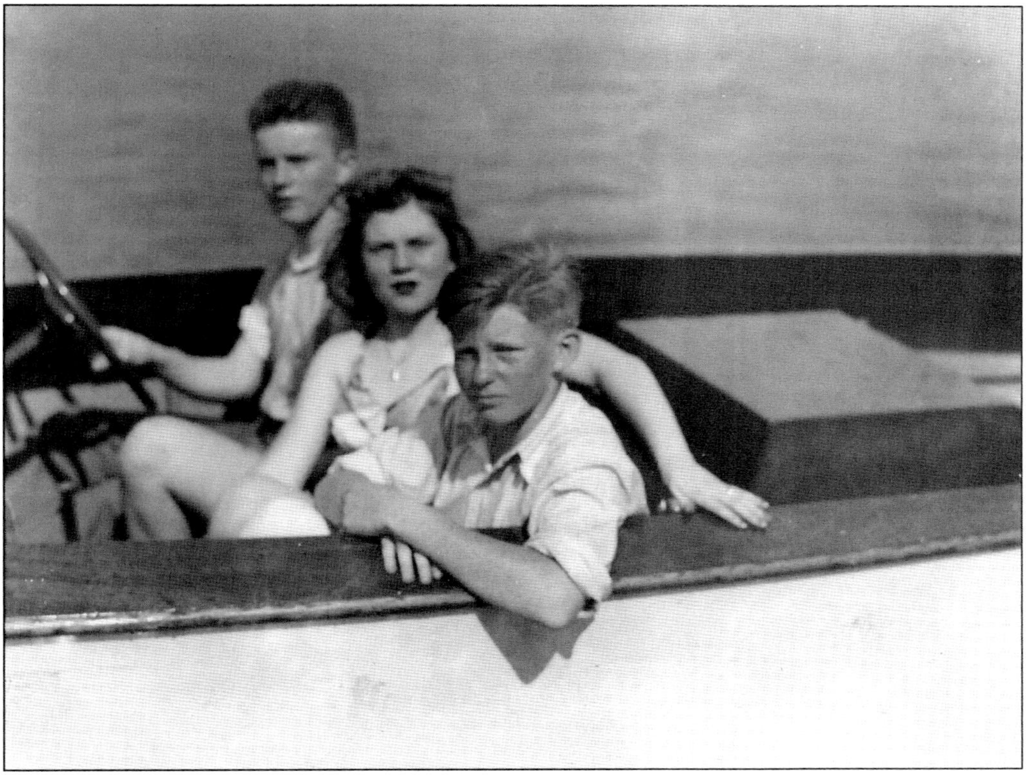

Pictured here are youths enjoying time out on the lake. Lake Mary was often seen as the perfect size for many—not big enough to concern parents with many dangers and not too small to bore those enjoying it.

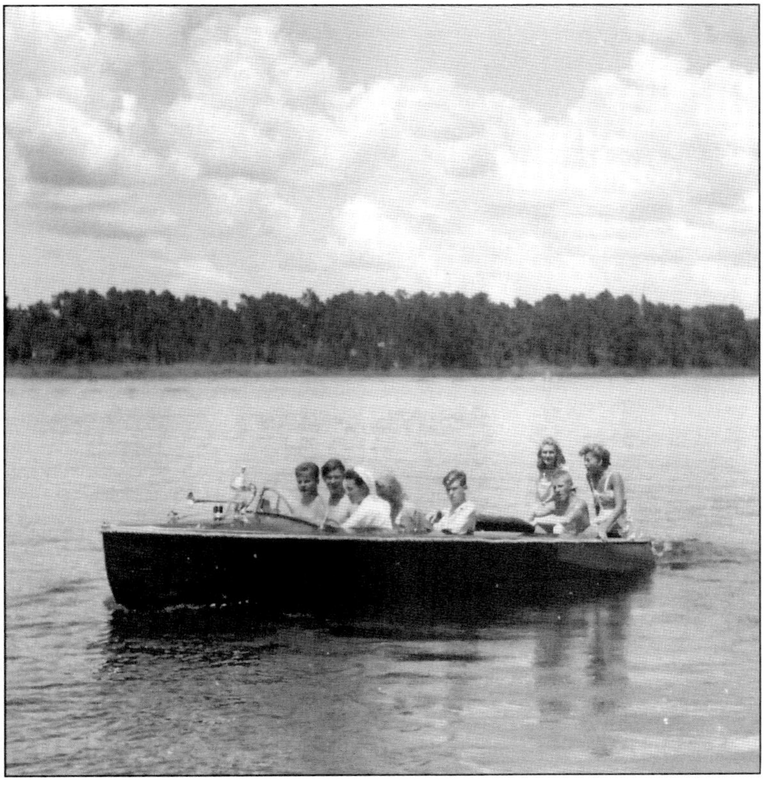

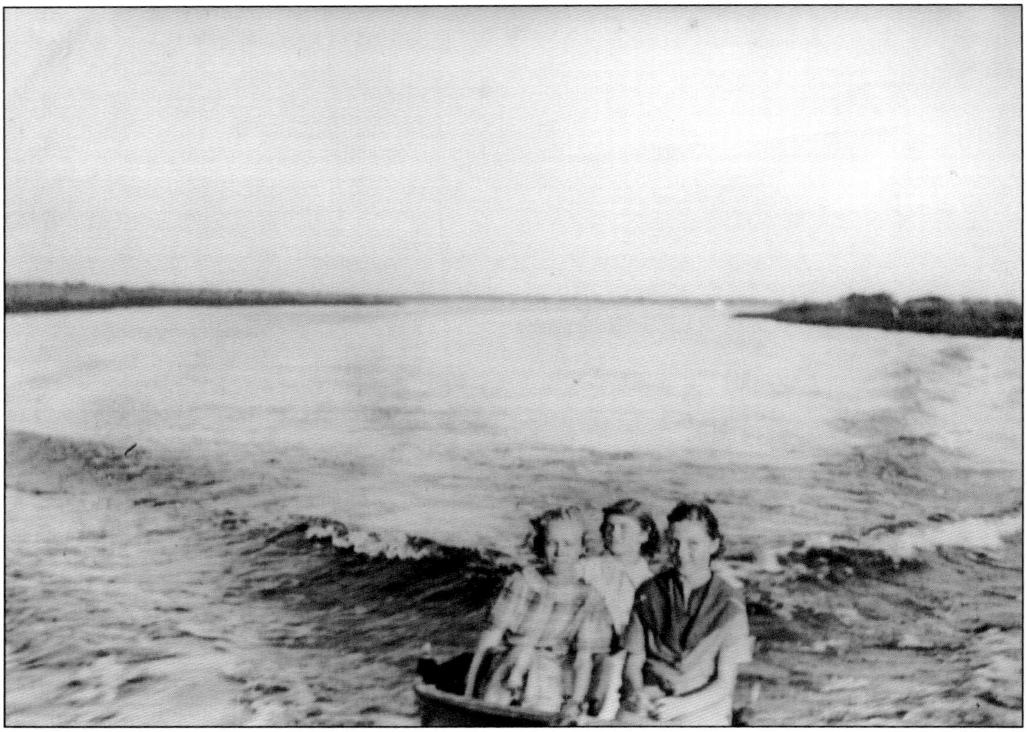

A group of girls enjoy a pleasant ride around Lake Mary in a large wooden bucket in the 1930s. Tubes and other flotation devices designed to be towed behind boats did not exist at this time. Fortunately, ingenuity often paid off for the sake of fun.

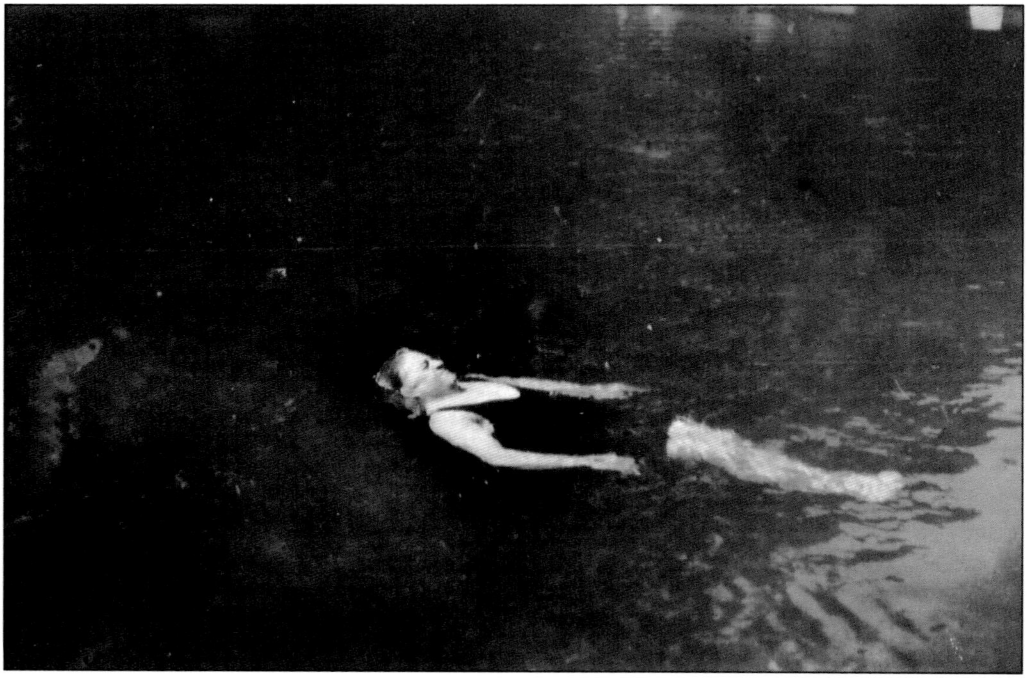

What is a lake without swimming? Unlike the ocean where bathers are troubled by waves and pesky animals like sharks, Lake Mary swimmers enjoyed serene moments like the one depicted here.

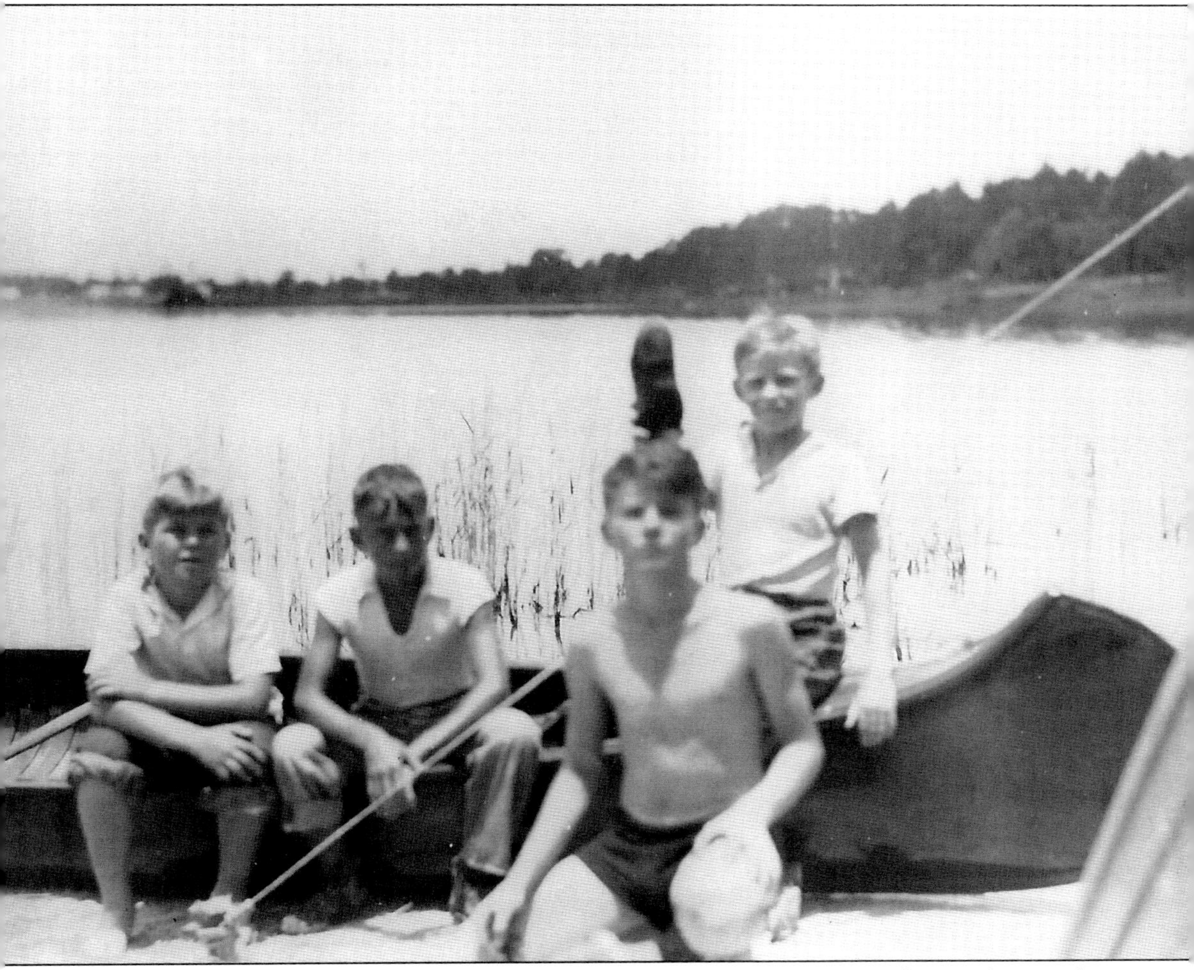

From left to right, Howard Botler, Jack Howell, Bill Evans, and Jackie Evans pull up to shore and rest after a summer canoeing trip on Lake Mary in the mid-1930s. Jackie holds up a waterlogged shoe as if it were a point of pride. The family of these kids was unsure if the shoe was his or if he fetched it from the lake.

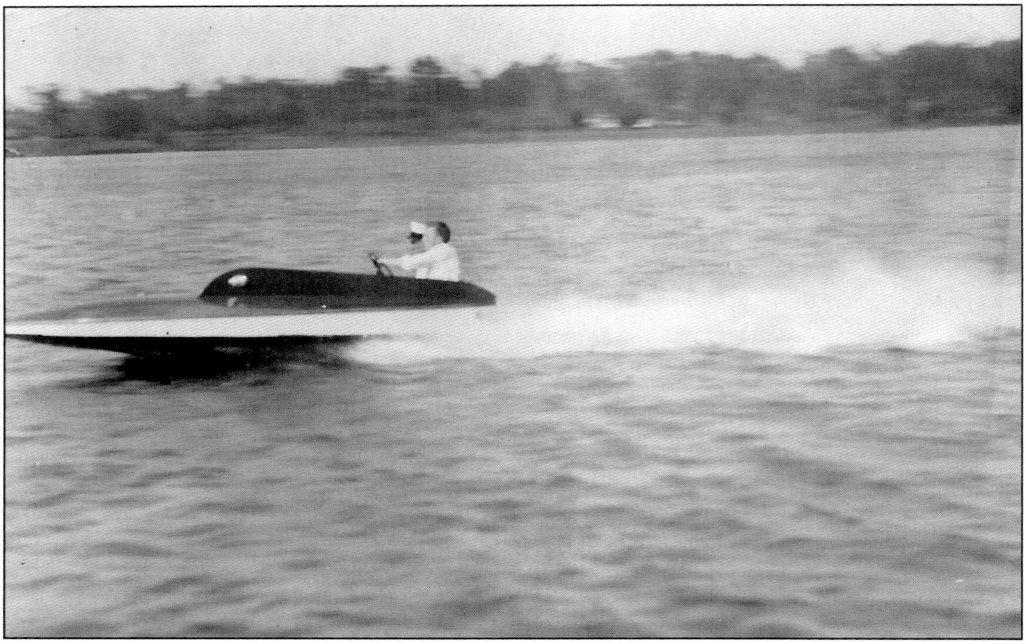

Two men enjoy a quick jaunt around the lake in a stylish, pre–World War II speedboat, barely big enough for two. Such boats were cutting edge at the time, and were only available to the few who could afford them.

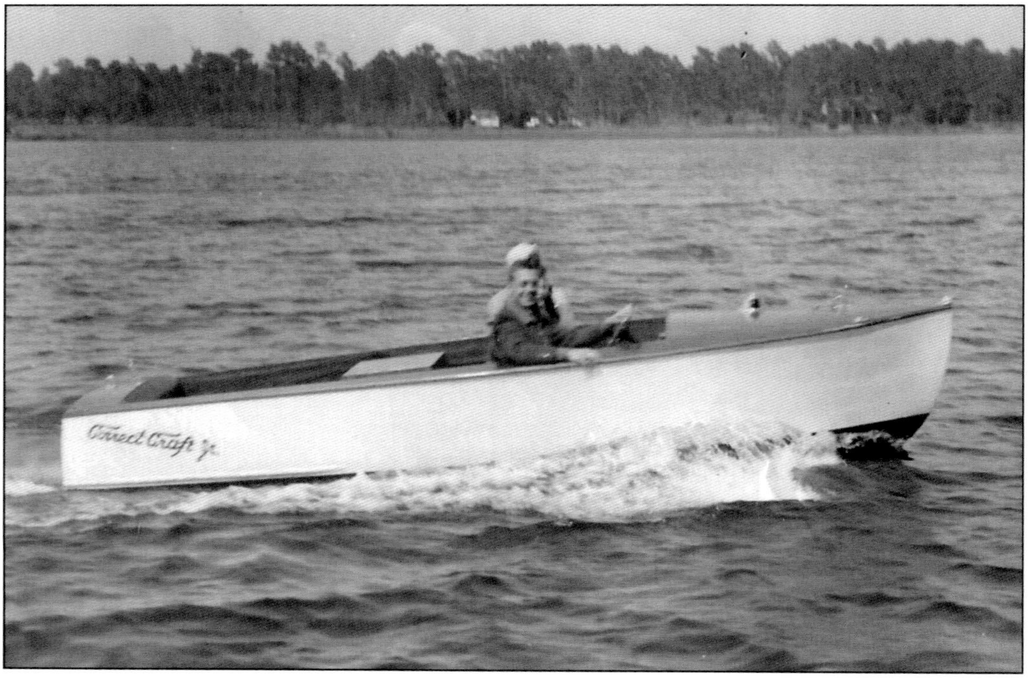

A young family cruises around the lake in a fairly common runabout motorboat. Runabouts were first built in the 1920s and were small, wooden, held four to eight people, and were very maneuverable. They were manufactured by a number of companies throughout the country and were portable enough to allow people from up north to trailer their boats to Florida and enjoy boating trips like this one.

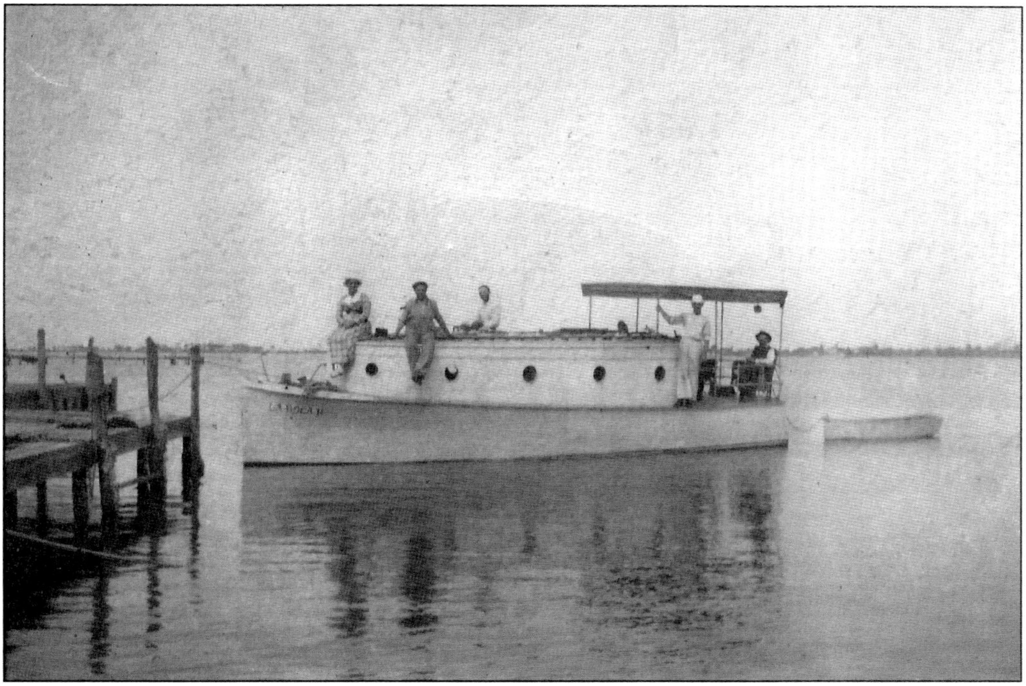

Both of these photographs show sizable boats with interior cabins. In the photograph above, the owners are towing a small dinghy, possibly to row into shallow waters for fishing or swimming.

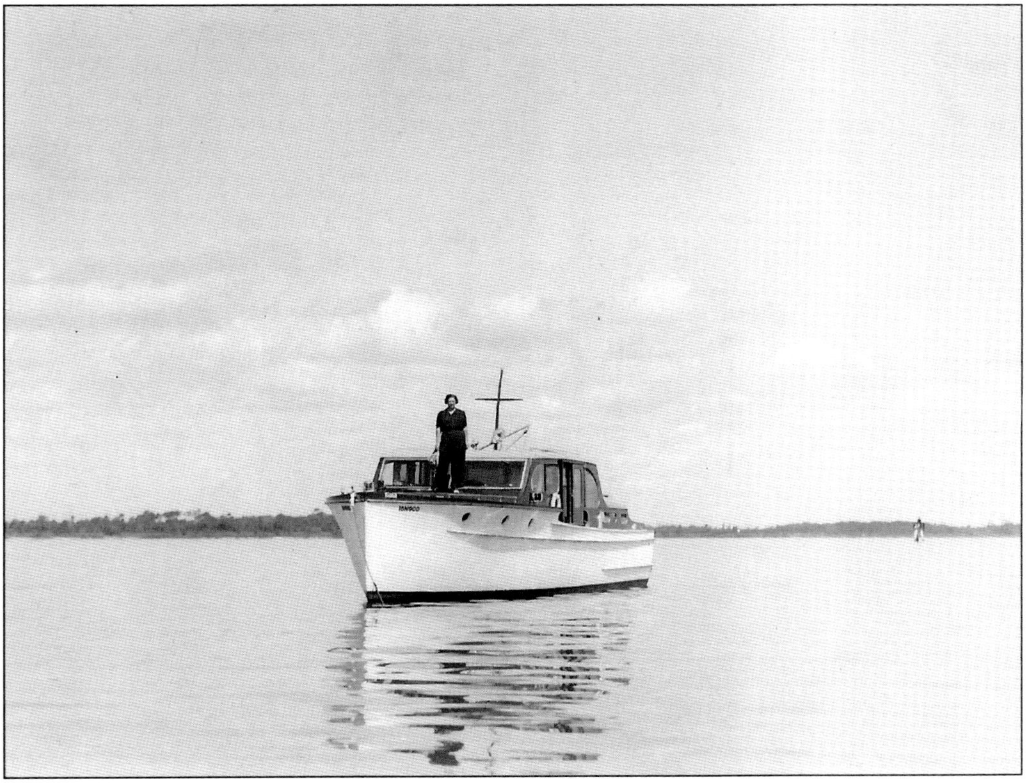

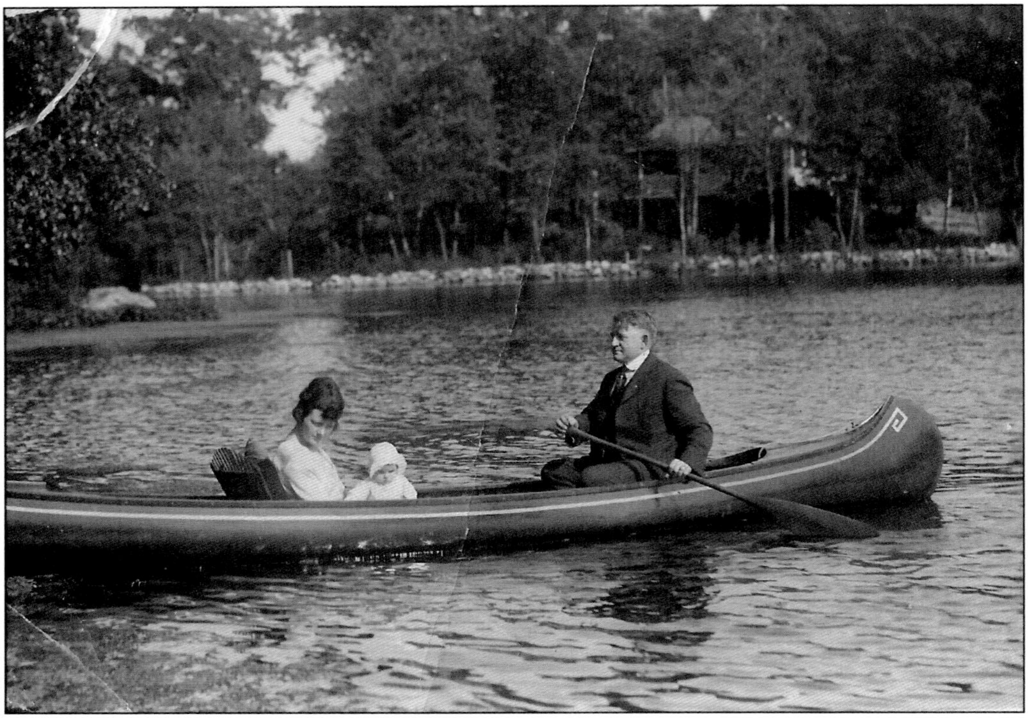

Frank Evans takes his wife and daughter on a boat ride in the family canoe, strangely while wearing a suit and tie. Often thinking about benefiting the town, Evans probably had this photograph taken as a publicity shot to help promote the lake.

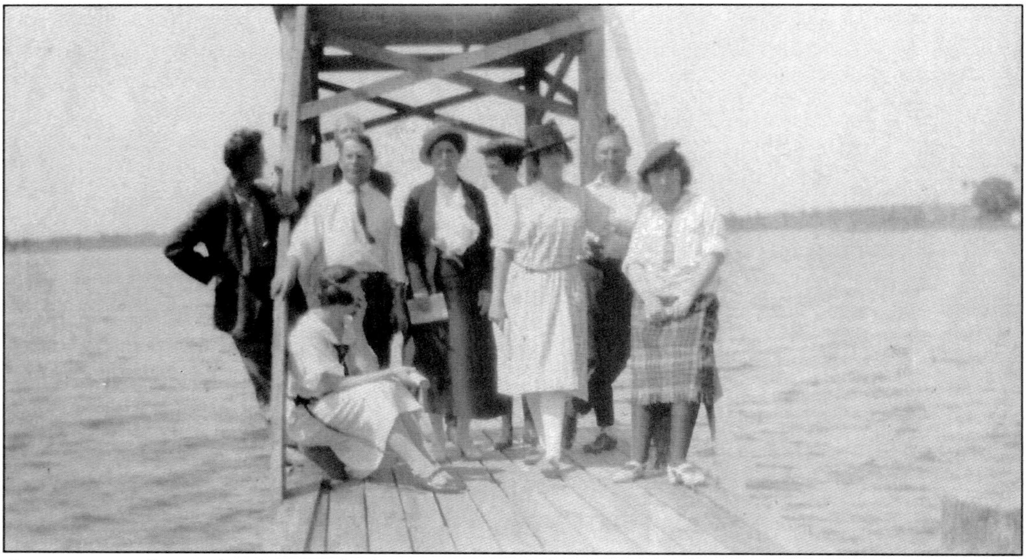

A group stands on the diving platform at Evansdale Park near the current intersection of Olde Park Way and South Country Club Road. Although this group does not appear ready to get wet, platforms like this were built due to diving's popularity. Diving as a sport originated in Sweden and Germany in the 1700s. By the late 1800s, it spread to England and America, and by 1904, diving events were a part of the Olympic games.

Schwinn bicycles were not just for kids. The Schwinn Bicycle Company came to America in the early 1890s during a sudden bicycle craze. At the turn of the 20th century, bicycle sales dropped with the popularity of automobiles and motorcycles. The stock market crash of the late 1920s hurt the automobile industry and virtually stopped all motorcycle production. This inadvertently gave companies like Schwinn a second wind.

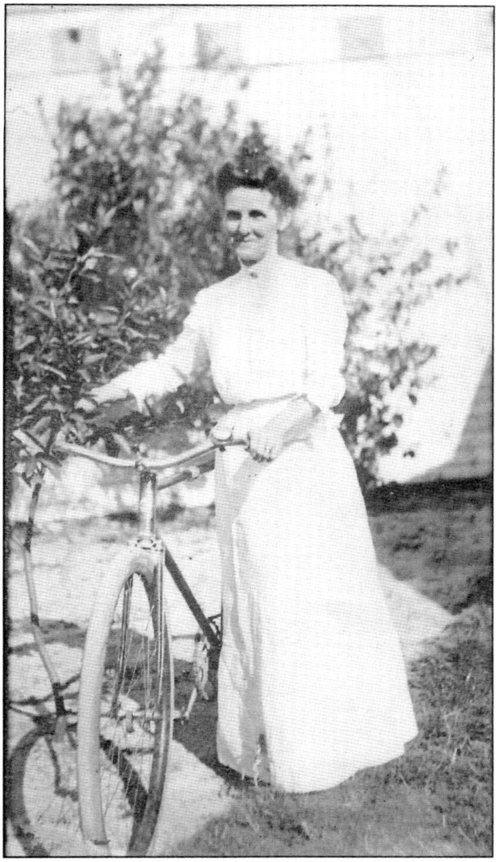

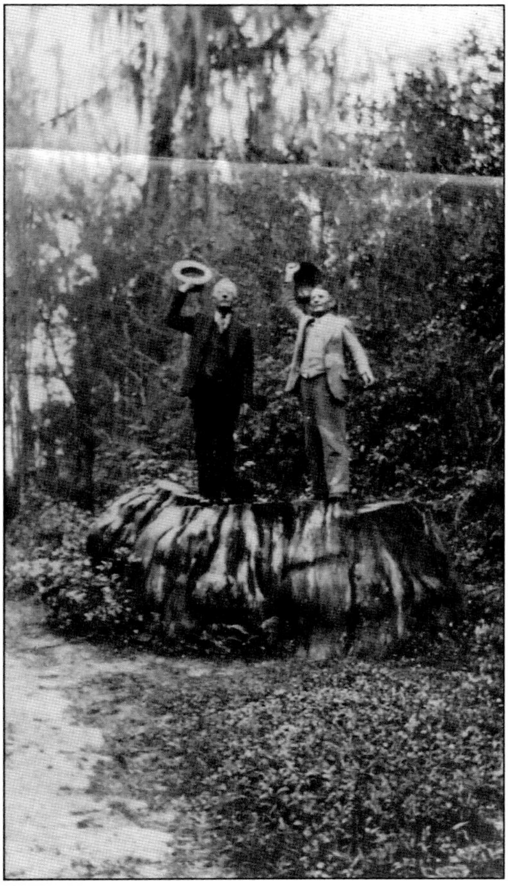

Using machines to accomplish traditionally manual jobs was still new to the country in the early 1900s. As such, tasks like cutting down large trees still required a large amount of sweat and muscle. Accomplishing this feat, even for the business owners shown here, was worth a raised hat.

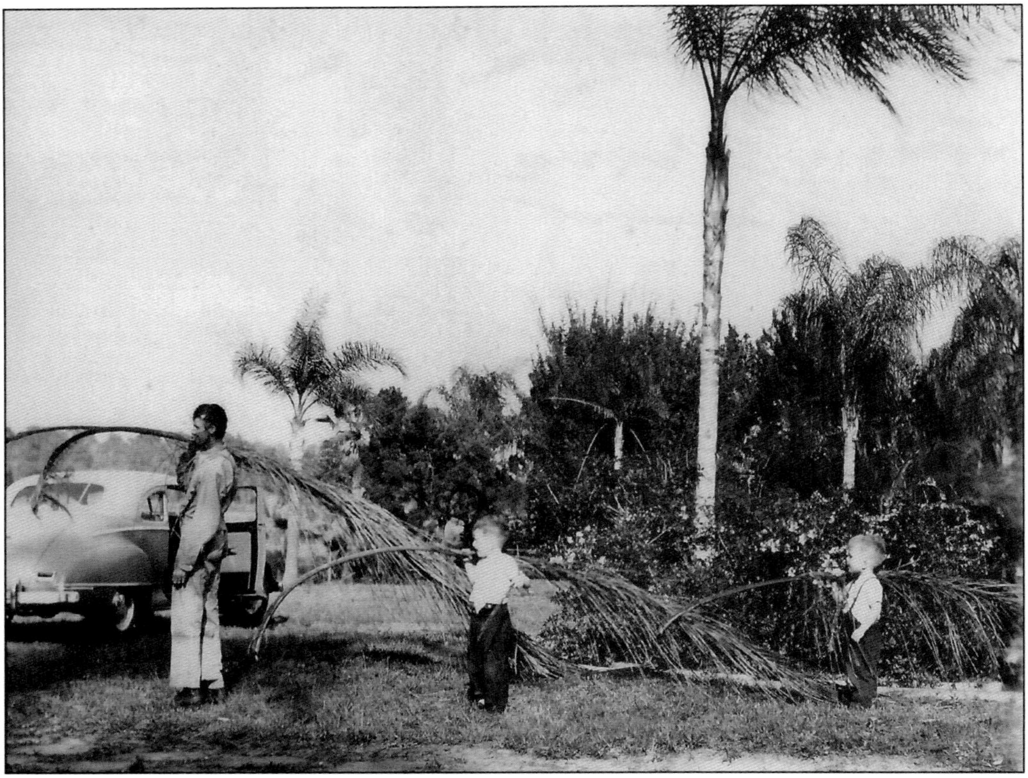

Yard cleanup was everyone's duty in Lake Mary. With plenty of sunshine and rain, especially during the summer months, maintaining lawns took quite a lot of work. In this photograph, two boys help their Uncle Jonnie with some fallen palm fronds.

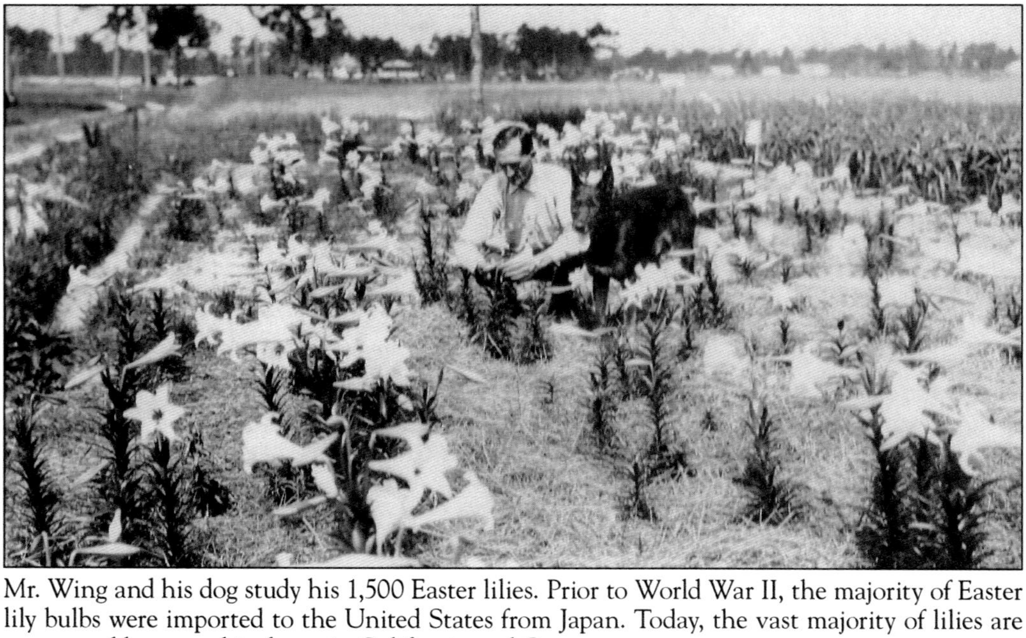

Mr. Wing and his dog study his 1,500 Easter lilies. Prior to World War II, the majority of Easter lily bulbs were imported to the United States from Japan. Today, the vast majority of lilies are grown and harvested in farms in California and Oregon.

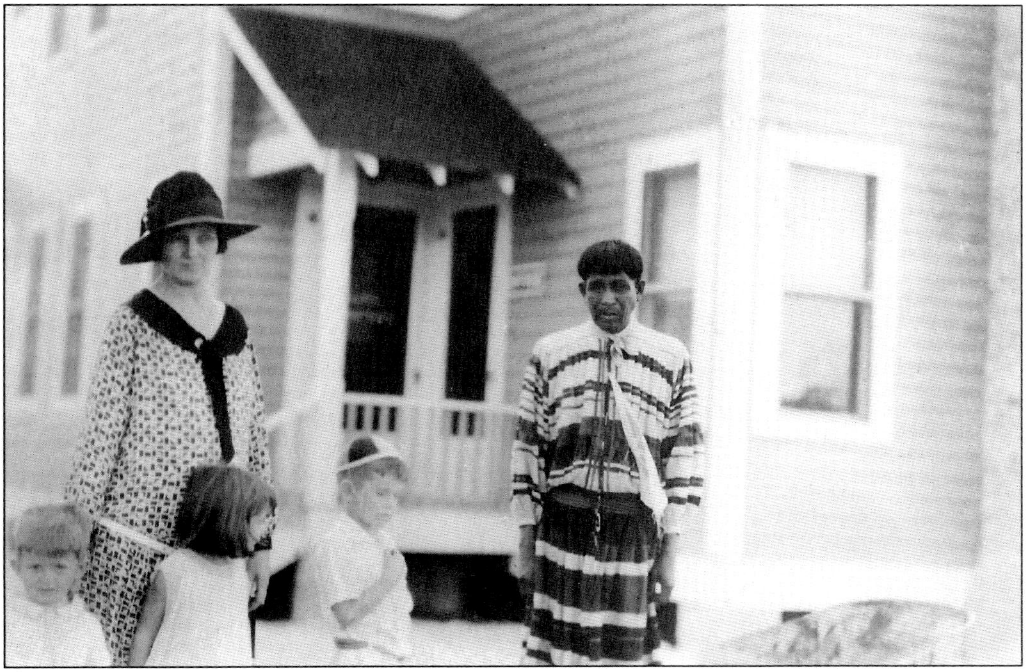

Though their ancestors were some of the original settlers in Florida, Seminole Indians were forced to live on the outskirts of American society. Their clothing, speech, and skin color often led white Americans to treat them as unusual novelties. Residents today recall interacting with them in a civil manner with no malice between each other. Their communities were segregated "and that's just the way it was," a Lake Mary resident recalled.

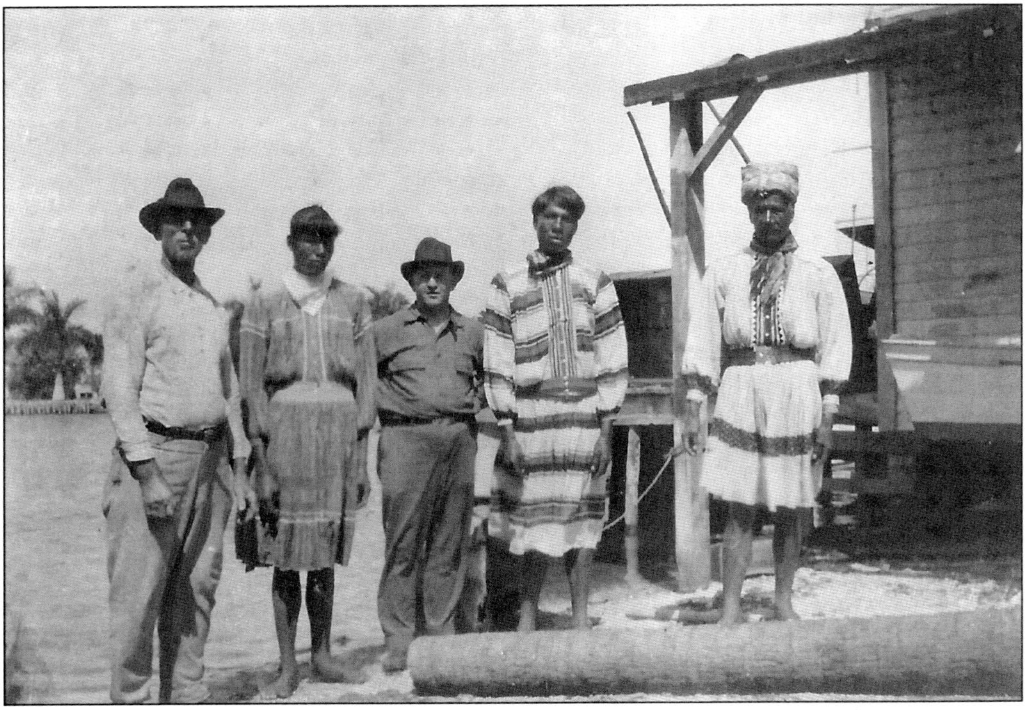

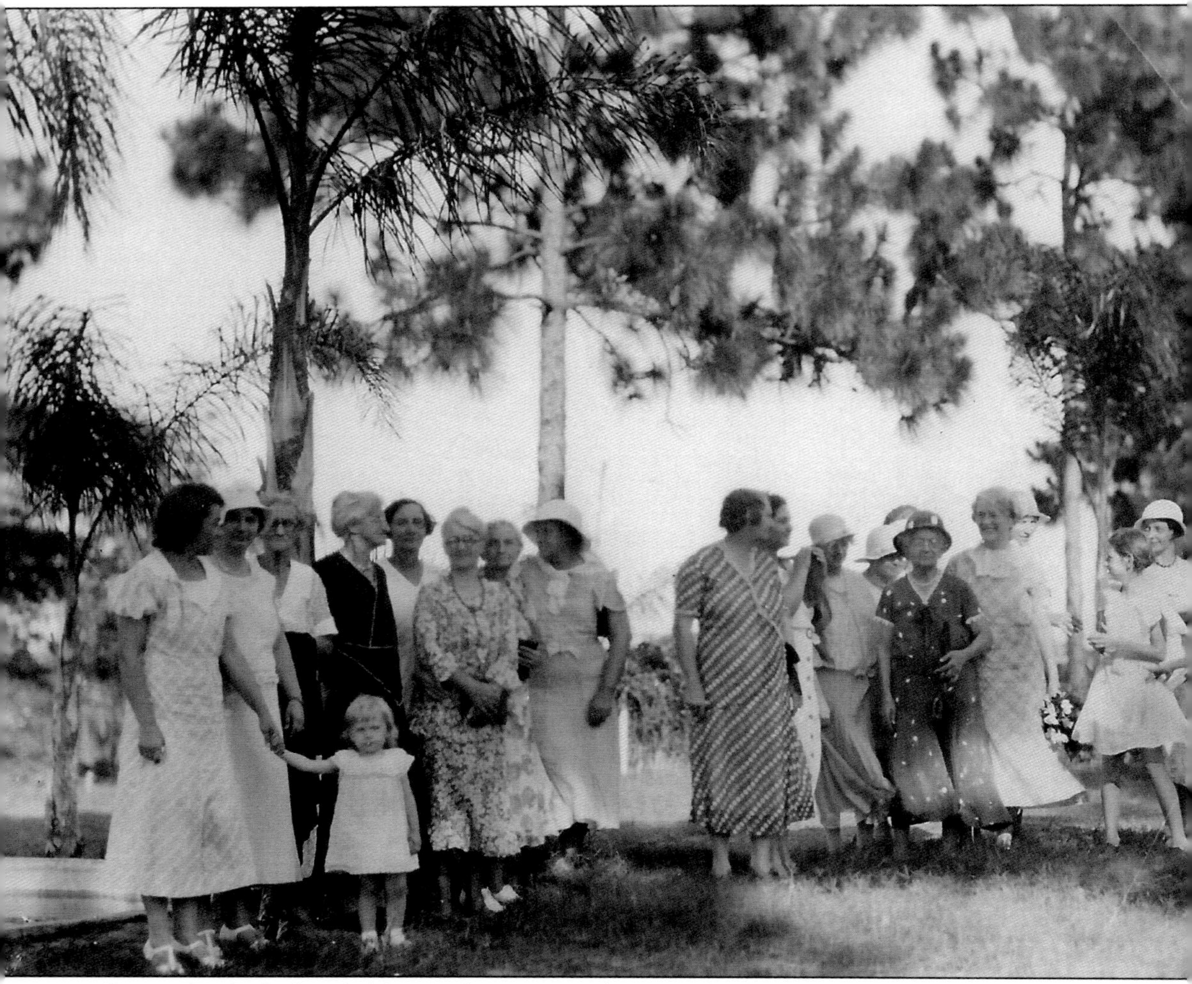

Pictured is the Ladies Aid Society hosting a garden party for the women and girls in town. Garden parties were formal picnics where the women took a break from their daily activities and causally mingled with friends. For the young girls, these were often learning events as their elders educated them on party etiquette.

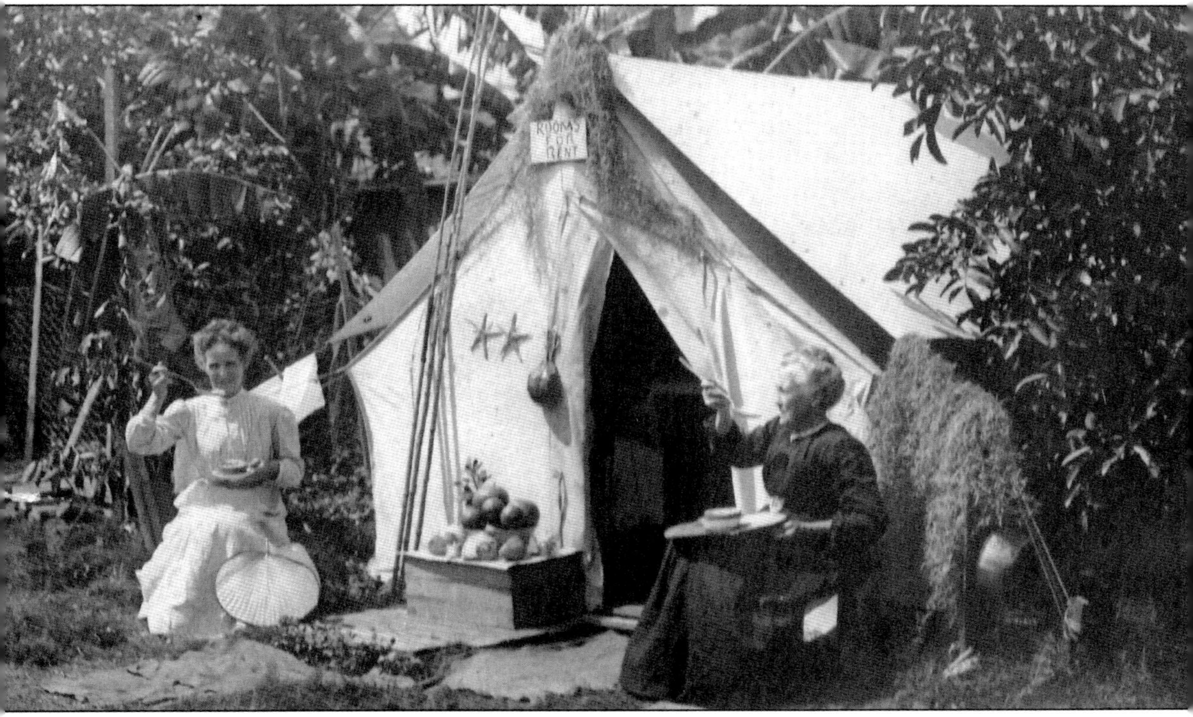

A couple of ladies pretend to offer rooms for rent while enjoying bowls of stew. This photograph was taken in the 1930s, over 50 years since families had lived in tents in Lake Mary. Early in the community's history, temporary dwellings similar to this were a necessity before families could build more permanent houses on their homesteads.

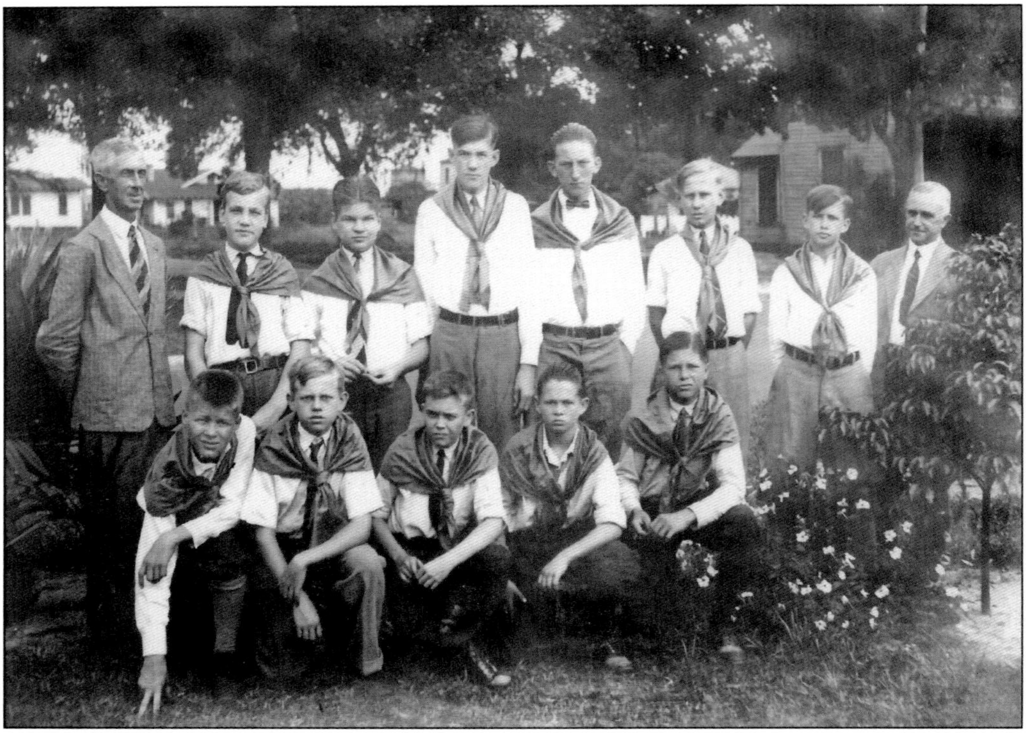

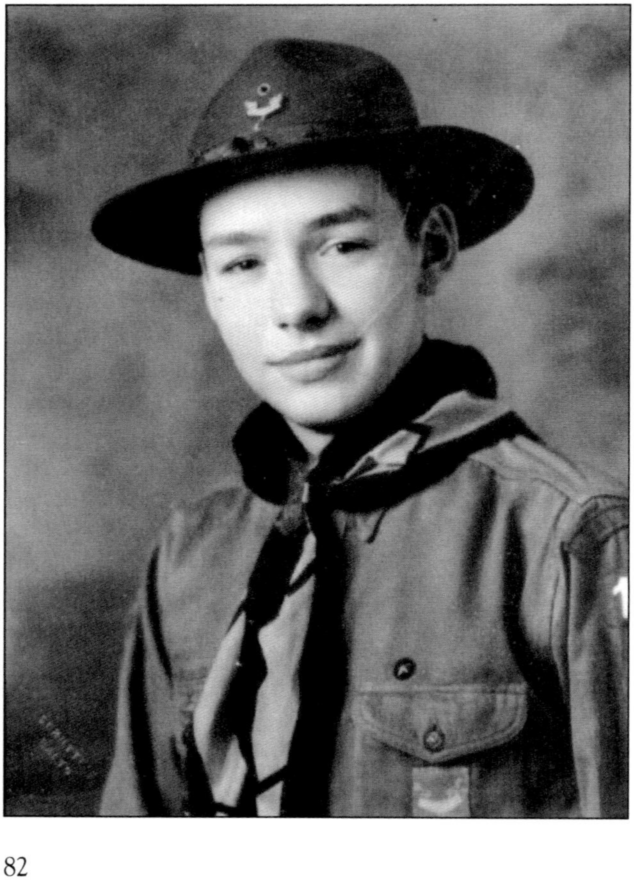

In 1922, the Central Florida Council of Boy Scouts of America was chartered, headquartered in Apopka just west of Lake Mary. A small community outside of Apopka called Plymouth hosted their summer camps, named Camp WeWa after an American Indian term meaning "many waters." Scouts returning home to Lake Mary likely used their outdoor skills in the still very rural town and surrounding area.

Pictured is Bob Lippincott in his youth as a Boy Scout. He later became a scoutmaster and owner of Lippincott's Ink Spot Inc., a local commercial printing company. Since its start, Lake Mary's scouting groups have built leaders out of boys.

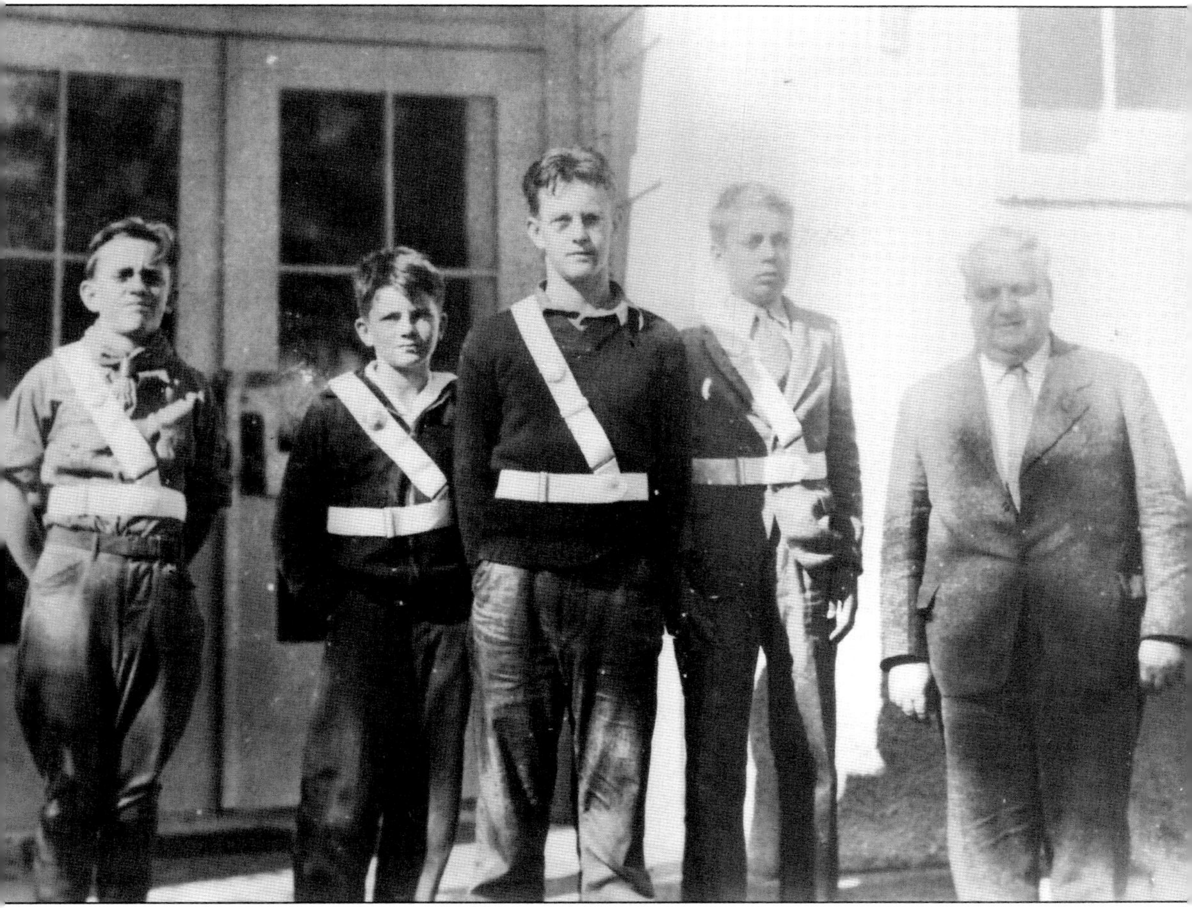

From left to rigth, "Patrol Boys" Roy Howell, Bill Evans, Thomas Wansley, and Joe Isbell stand at attention in 1933 with their official Sam Browne belts crossing their chests. Roy, the boy on the left who is apparently taking the job very seriously, also wears his Boy Scout uniform. The School Safety Patrol, started by the American Automobile Association in the 1920s, came to Lake Mary in cooperation with the Lake Mary School and in response to the increase in vehicle traffic.

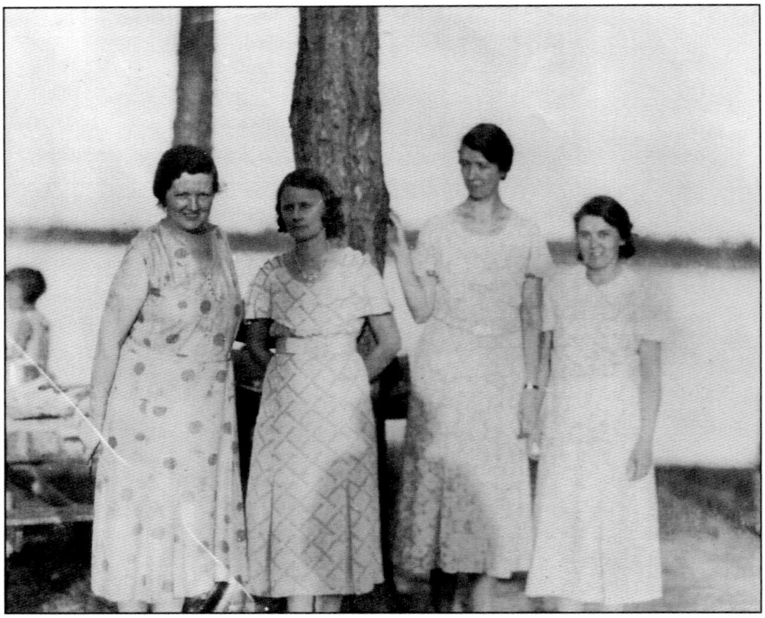

In early 1933, Stella Evans, Mabel Cole, and Isabelle Booth Thompson—the three ladies pictured from left to right—formed a committee to establish the first registered Girl Scout troop and Brownie Pack of Lake Mary. Booth served as the troop committee chairman.

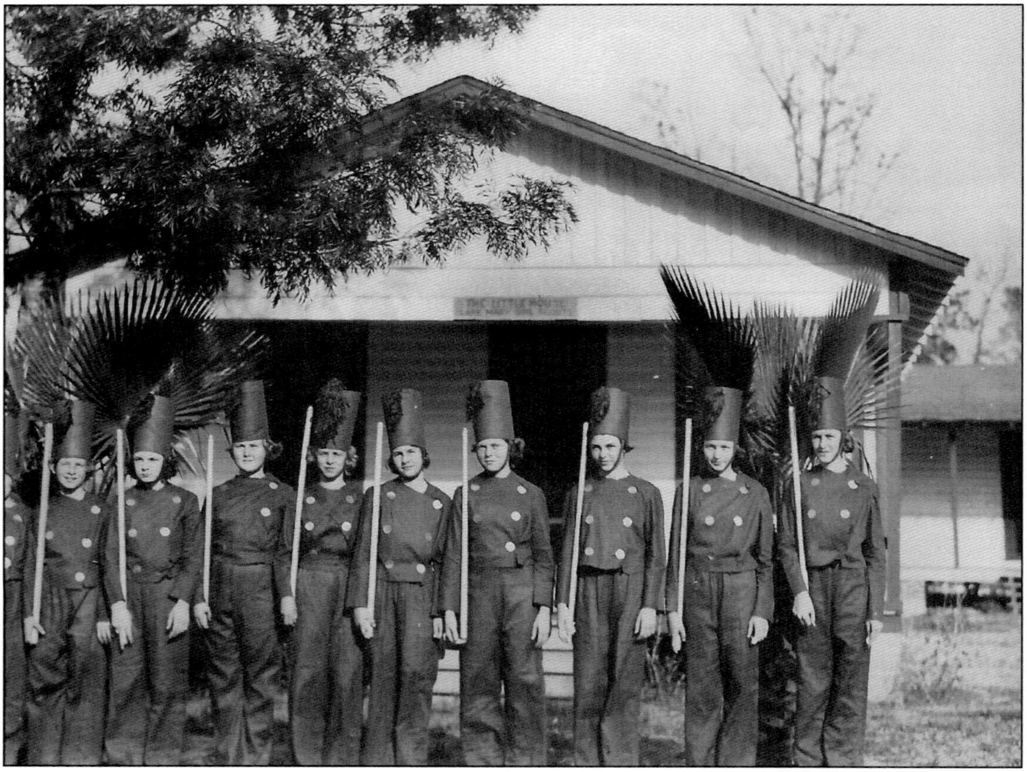

In this photograph, the Girl Scouts wear whimsical toy soldier costumes. Although the scouts followed the guidelines and standards established by the Girl Scouts Association, occasionally they deviated from the norm.

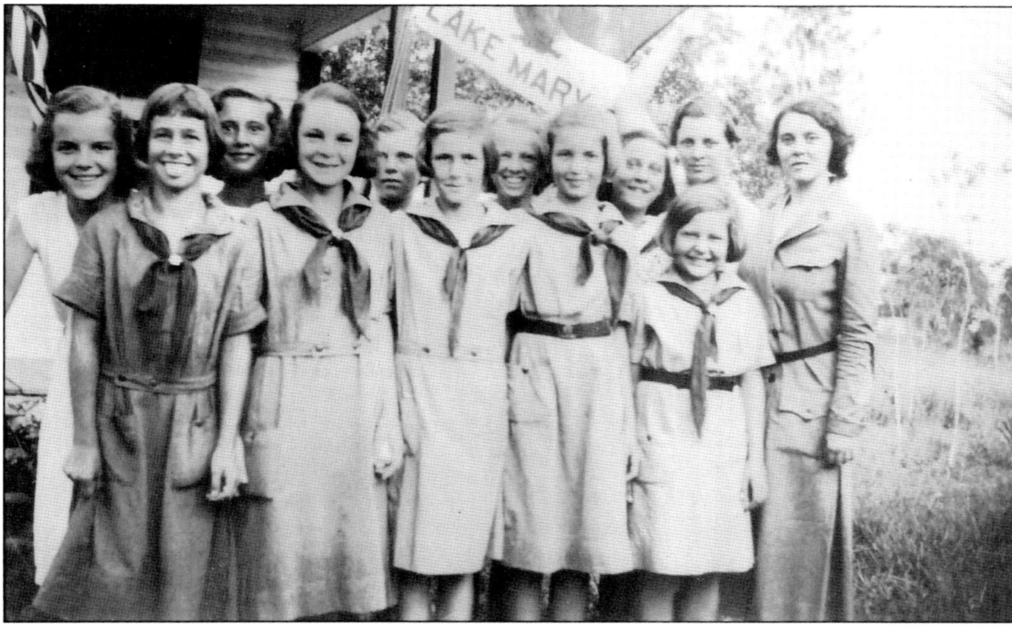

Girl Scout and Brownie uniforms were expensive, so Isabelle Thompson, Stella Evans, and others spent many hours sewing to ensure the girls were properly outfitted. Pictured are the results of some of their hard work. The Girl Scouts pose in front of "The Little House," a building on Country Club Road across the street from the Community Center built specifically for the scouts. In the house, the scouts met and worked on projects and merit badges. Today, a sign from The Little House is kept in the Lake Mary Museum.

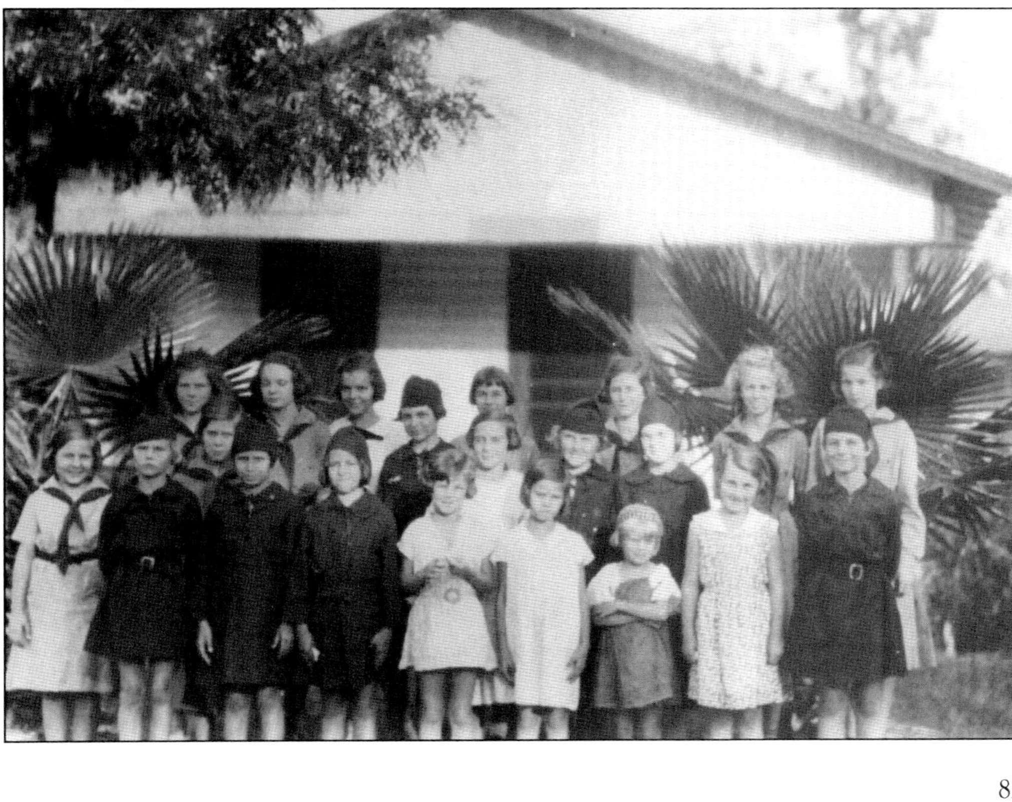

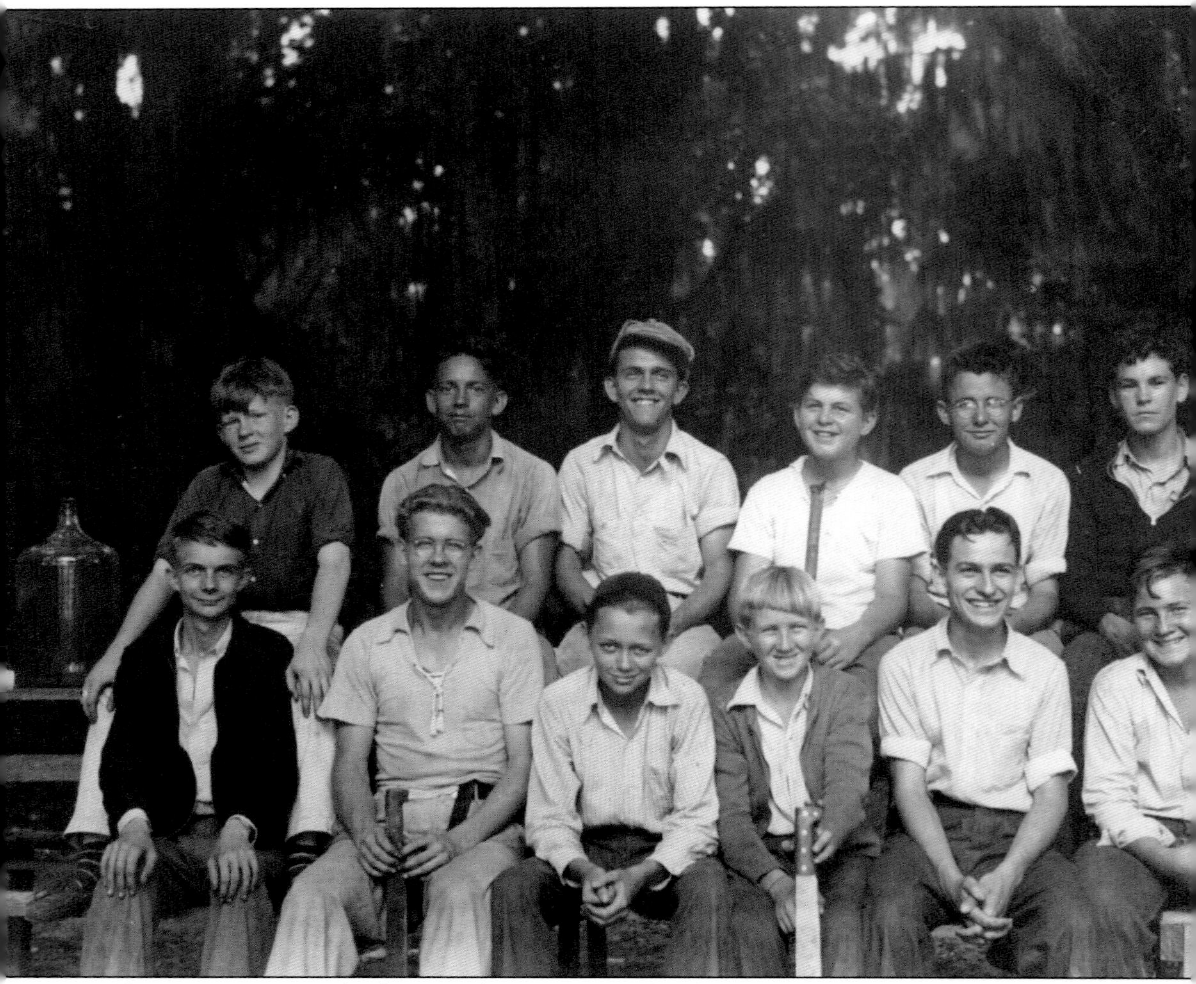

Shown are a group of Lake Mary boys in 1938. The photograph includes Jackie Evans, Jackie Howell, Roy Howell, Howard Boteler, Cracker Donaldson, Donald Hendrix, John Fennell, Ray Ball Jr., Wallace Smith, Jimmy Reaves, and Glenn Coachran. With two kids holding machetes, it is likely this group might have been clearing some foliage when the photograph was taken.

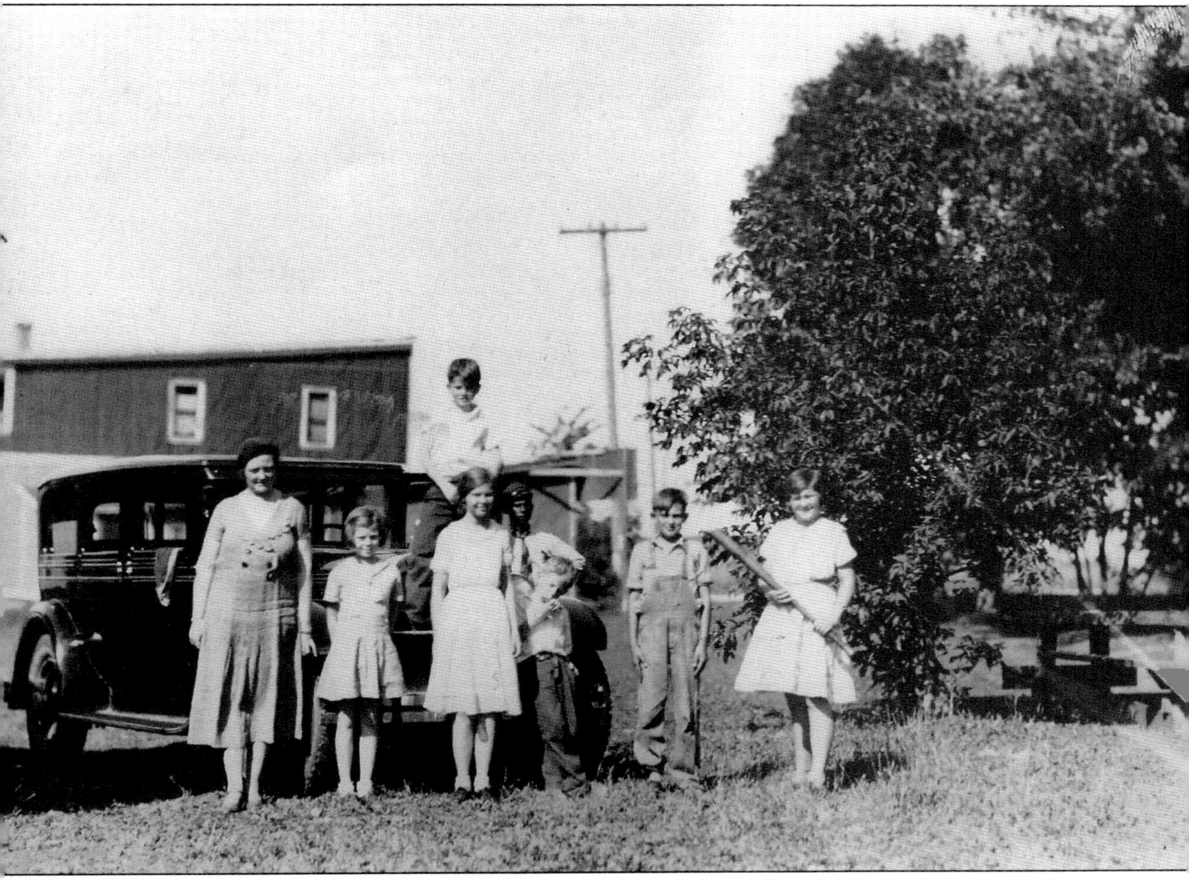

Kids assemble in this photograph, one with a baseball bat in hand. But the game they planned to play did not require a ball or a cleared field. A common pastime for kids was snake bashing. The rules were simple. They tromped through the woods, one or two with a bat or stick, and once a snake was spotted, they would corner it and kill it.

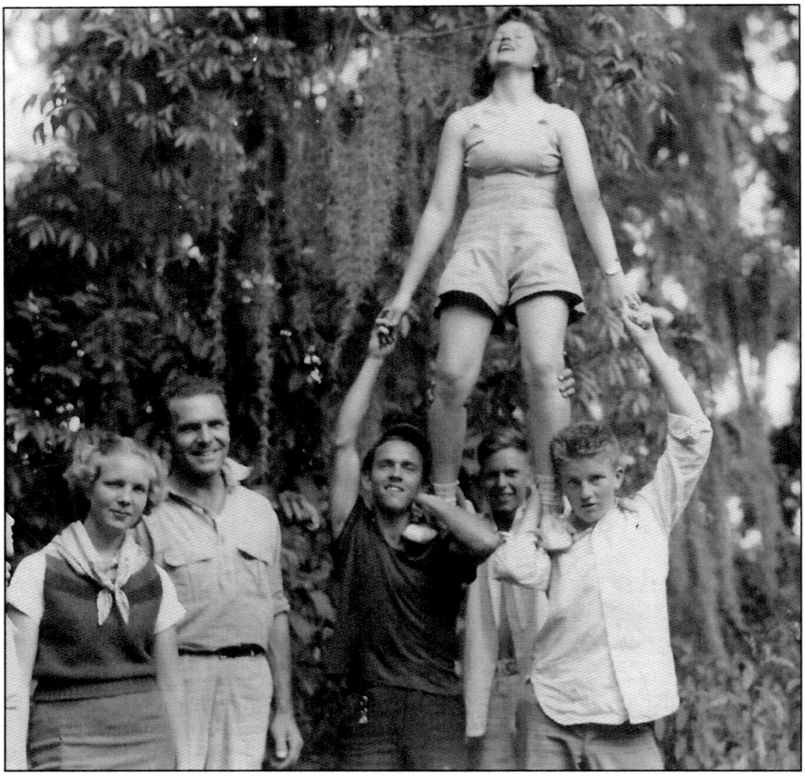

Pictured is a common sight in any generation—teens goofing around. In this case, the boys prove their strength and gymnastic prowess by balancing a girl on their shoulders while the girl tests her nerves and balance.

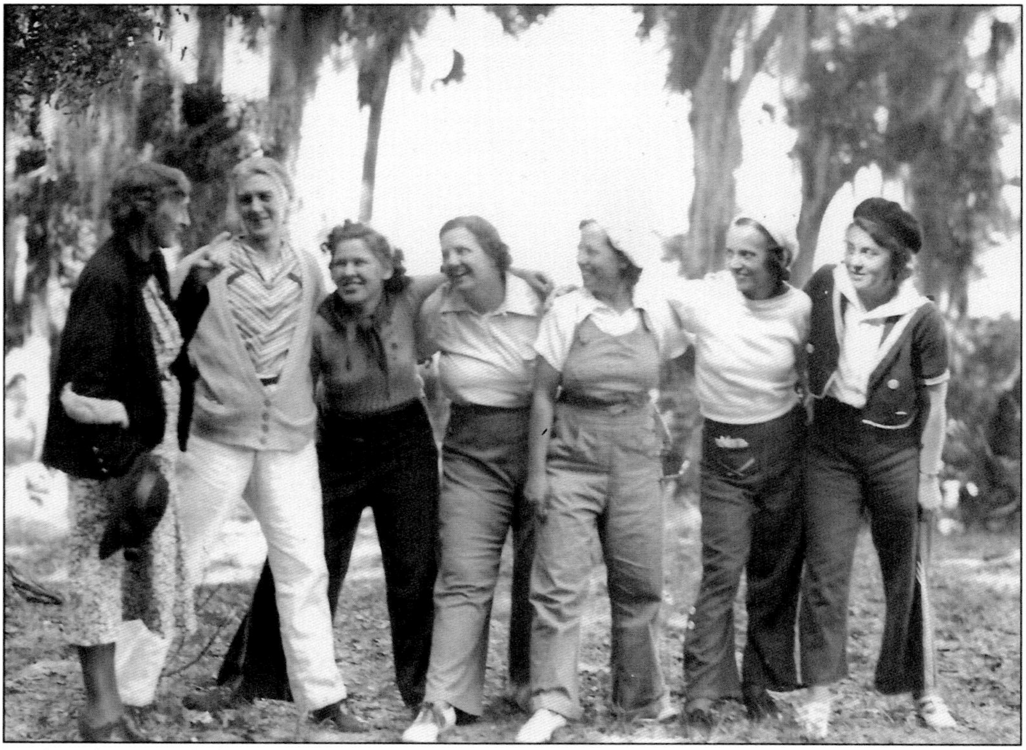

In this photograph, local women get together for a women's club project.

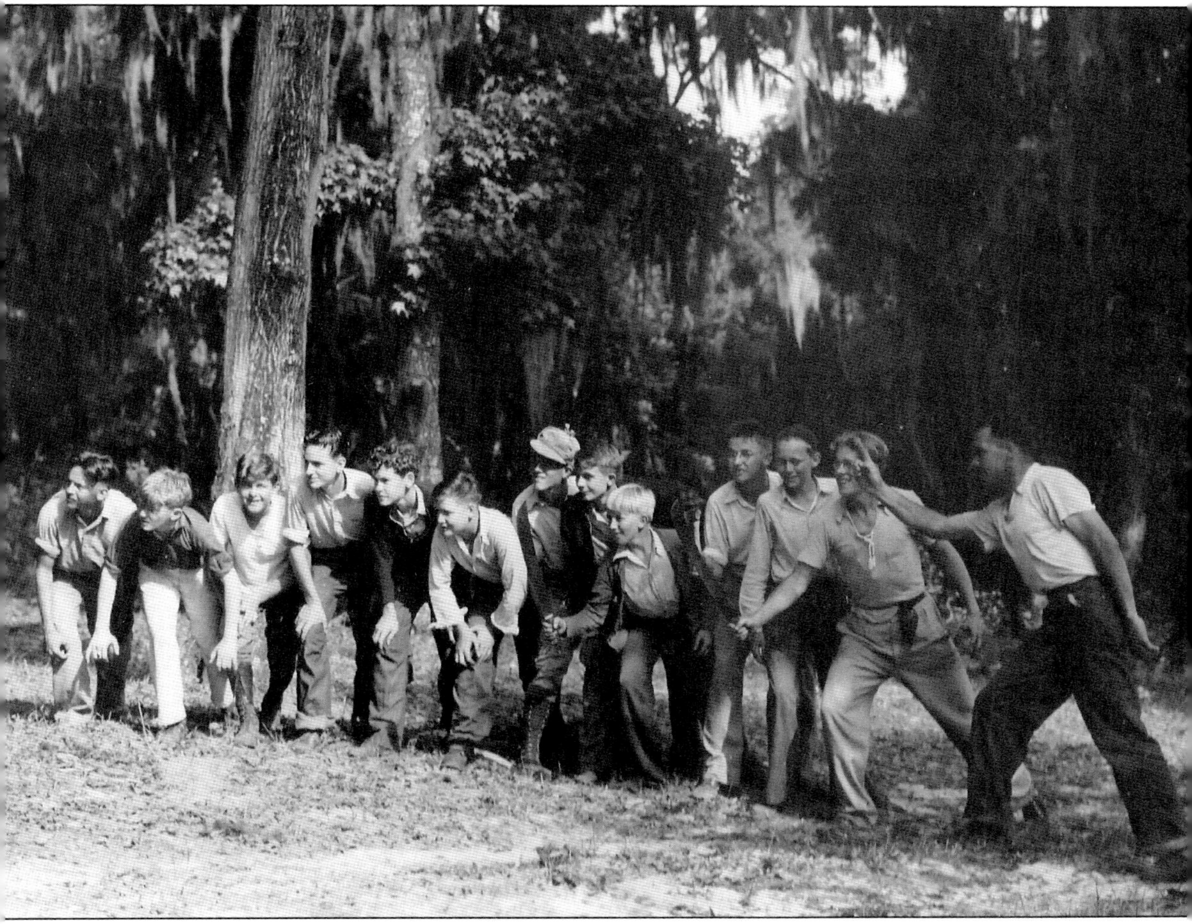

Pictured are a group of boys lined up and ready to race in Evansdale Park. Today, Lake Mary has multiple facilities for its residents, including the popular Cross Seminole Trail. In the late 1930s, options were more limited. But judging by the looks on these boys' faces, they do not seem to mind.

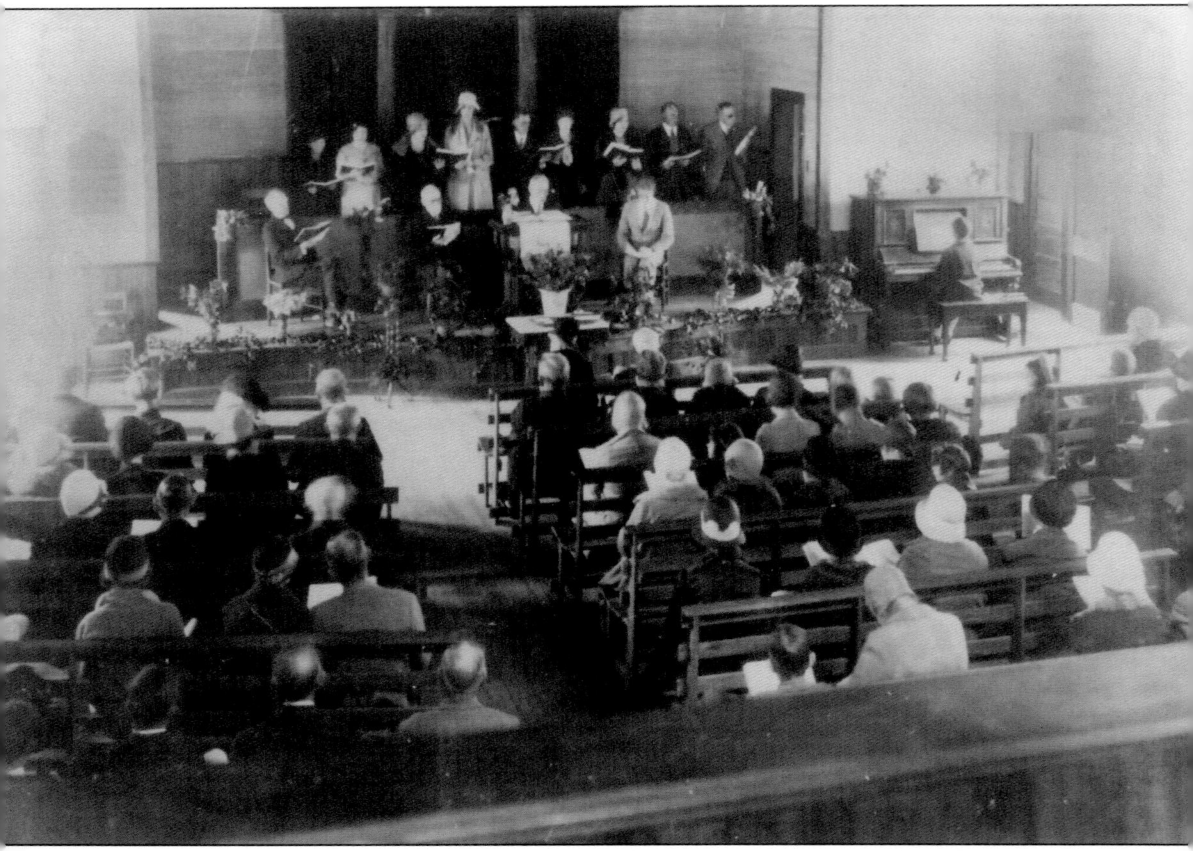

This was a typical church service at the newly built Community Church. Rev. James Moore Thompson sits at the pulpit while the choir sings behind him and Reverend Thompson's wife Isabel plays hymns on the church organ. The congregation, dressed in their Sunday best, sits in rows of wooden pews while breathing in the fragrant flowers and plants lining the stage.

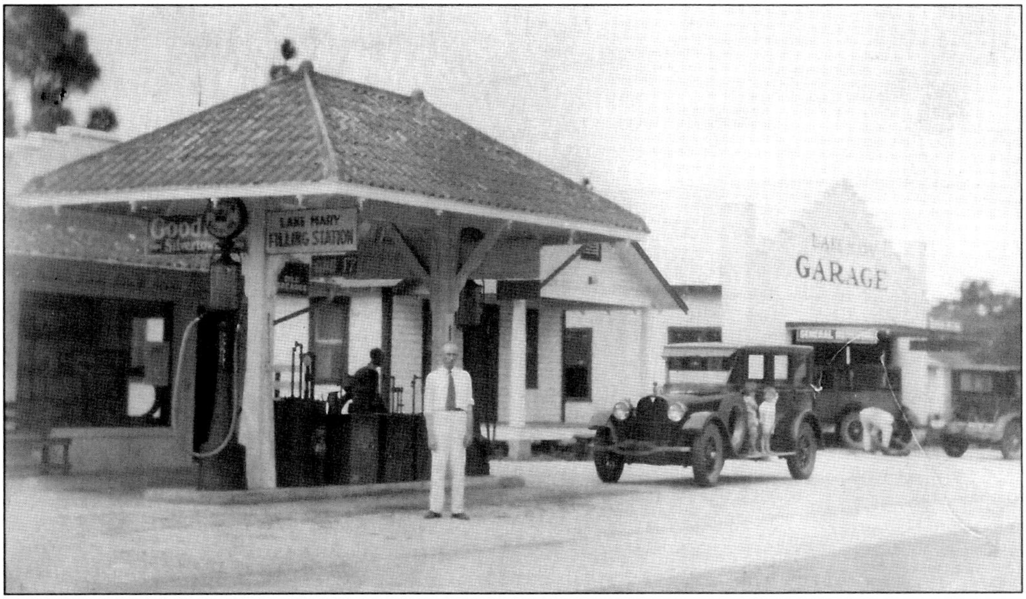

Commonly known as the filling station, this area of Lake Mary was a regular spot for residents to meet and talk. Often, people passing through Lake Mary on their way north to Jacksonville or southwest to Tampa stopped off at this midway point for a refill and/or service. Standing in front of the filling station is Rev. James Moore Thompson.

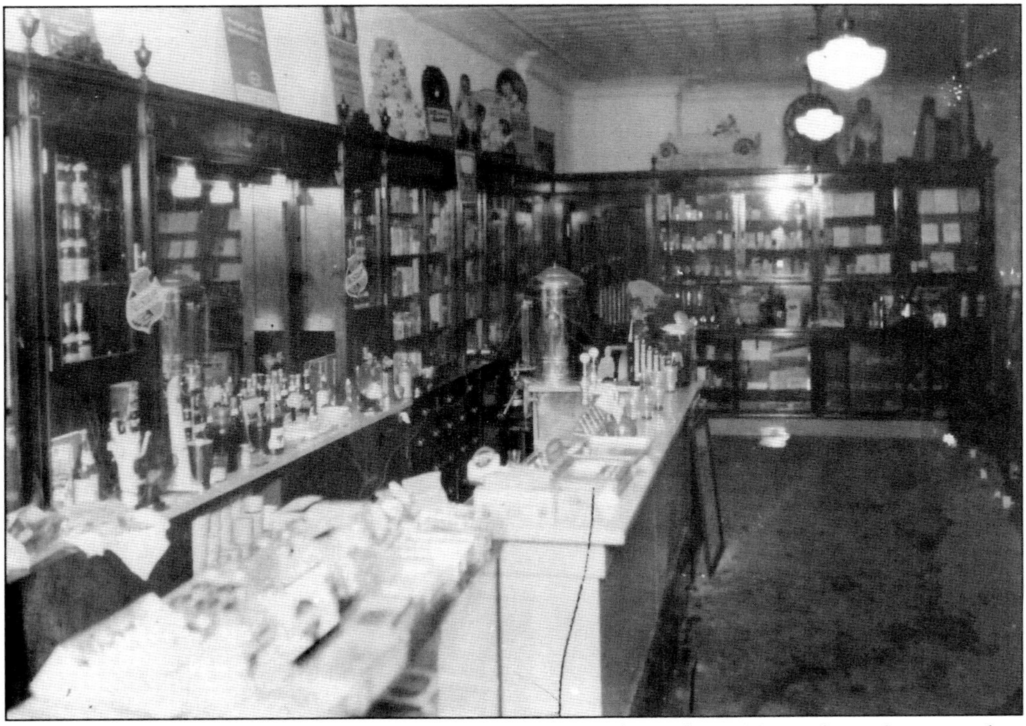

Pictured is the inside of Millers Drug Store on opening night in the 1920s, with its gleaming glass cases stocked full and ready for business. Miller's Drug Store was in the Evans building, which Frank Evans built and owned until he sold it to Ottis Sjoblom in 1960. For opening night, the entire town gathered outside, with the Lake Mary Orchestra playing and kids eating ice cream.

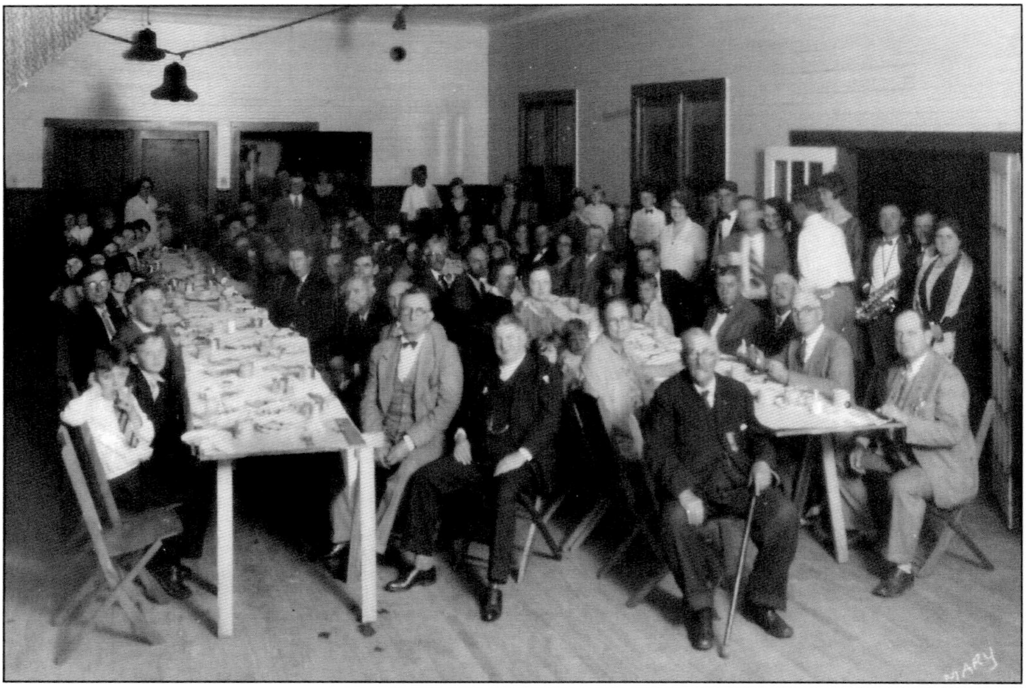

Here, a gathering enjoys a meal during Pioneer Night on January 10, 1929, an annual meeting of Spanish-American War veterans. At the side doors stand members from the Lake Mary Orchestra, possibly preparing to provide some entertainment for the evening.

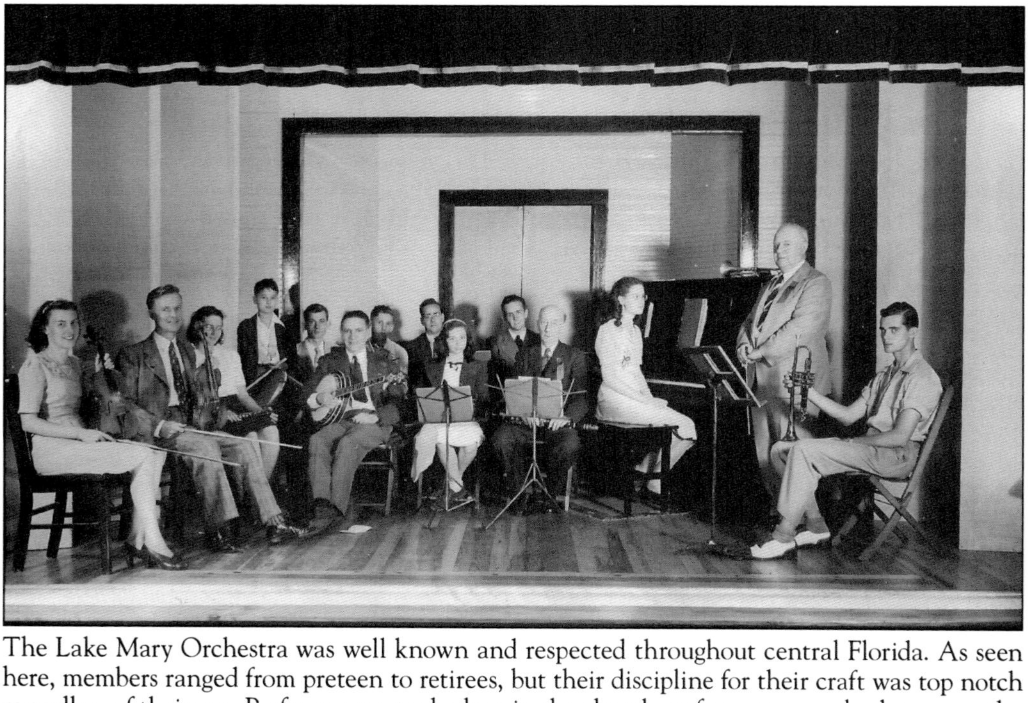

The Lake Mary Orchestra was well known and respected throughout central Florida. As seen here, members ranged from preteen to retirees, but their discipline for their craft was top notch regardless of their age. Performances took place in the chamber of commerce, also known as the Community Building, which houses the Lake Mary Museum today.

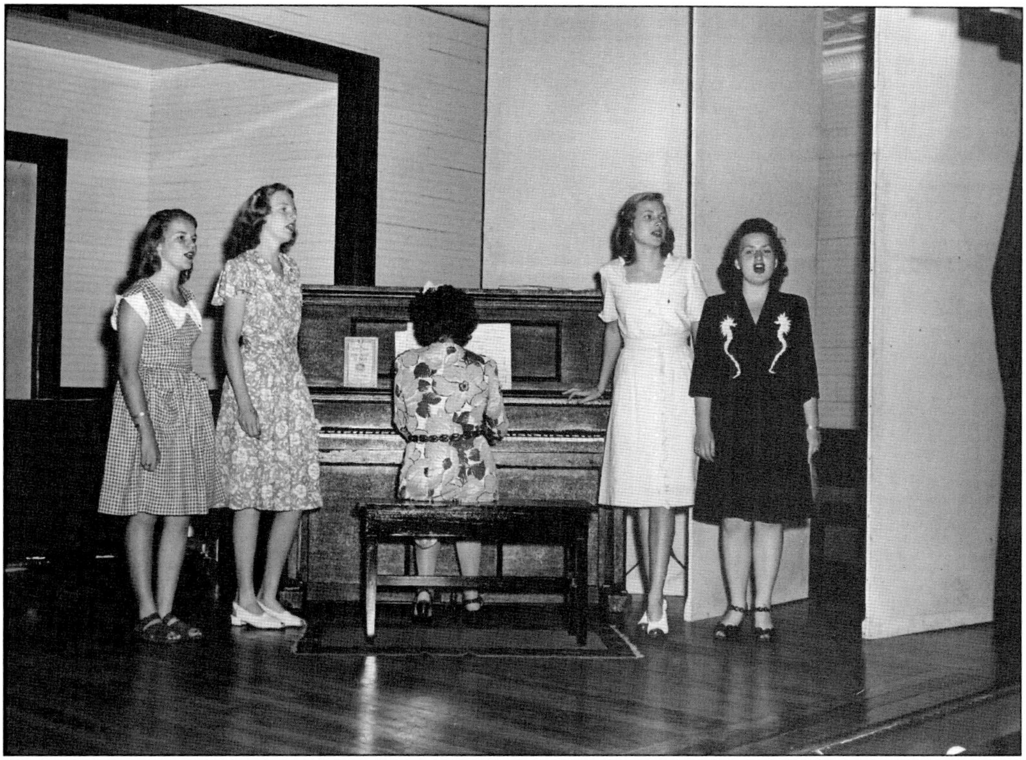

Pictured is a singing quartet at the Community Building on Pioneer Night. These nights featured talents that ranged from small groups to a full orchestra, including nationally recognized groups and bands. The Pioneer Nights were held for Lark Mary "Old Timers," residents aged 60 and older.

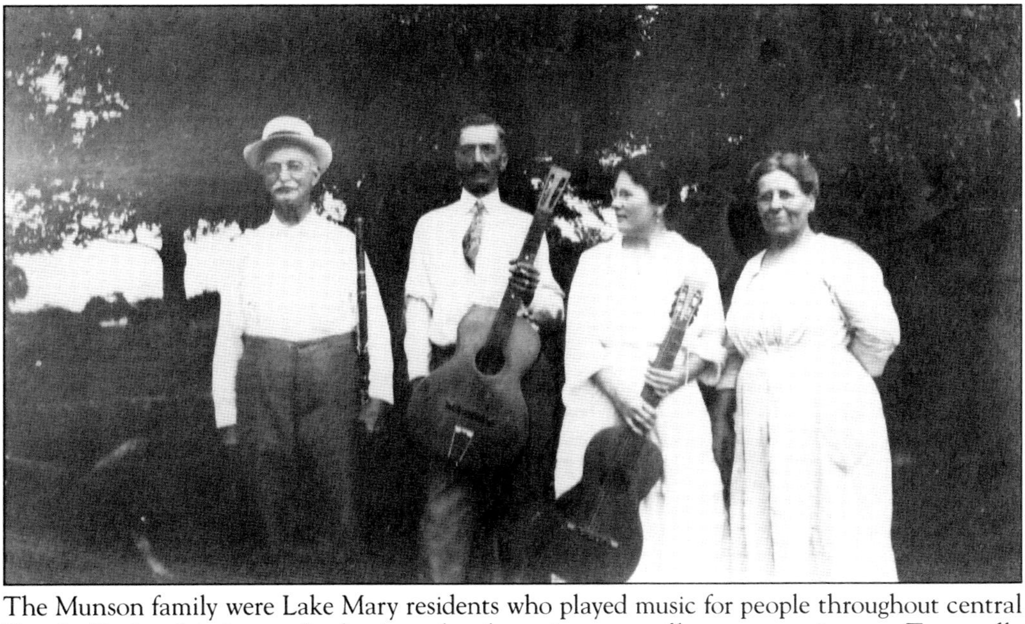

The Munson family were Lake Mary residents who played music for people throughout central Florida. During this time, radio dominated as the main source of home entertainment. To actually see performers, people were required to go to theaters and other venues. This high demand for in-person entertainment was often filled by mom-and-pop groups like this.

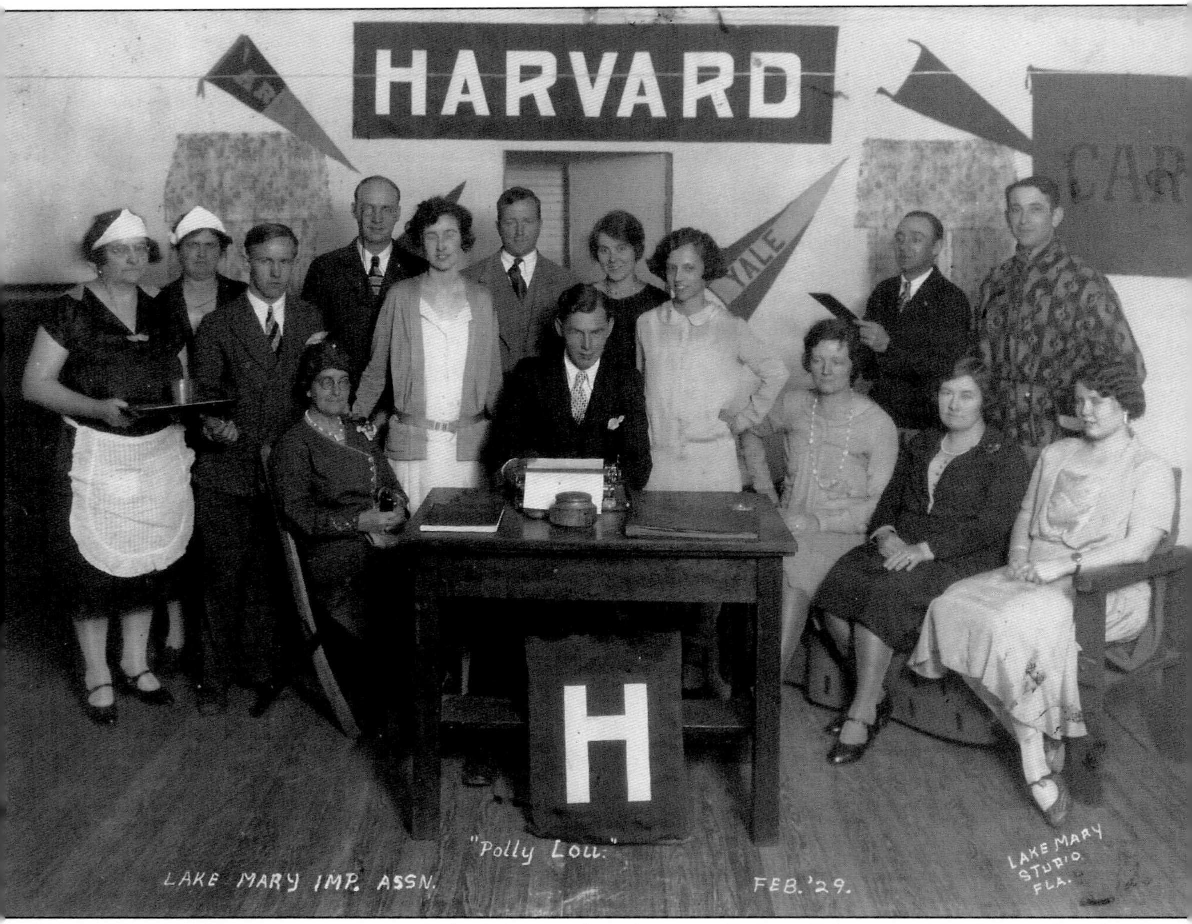

Harvard University comes to Lake Mary in this photograph from February 1929. Pictured is the cast of one of the many plays performed at the Community Building. This one, entitled *Polly Lou* by Gladys Ruth Bridgham, takes place in a Harvard fraternity. Plays were a great form of entertainment in Lake Mary during the long, quiet evenings when residents retreated inside to get away from mosquitoes and other insects. Some of the actors pictured include Homer Gleason, Robert True, Arolyn True, and Roy Howell.

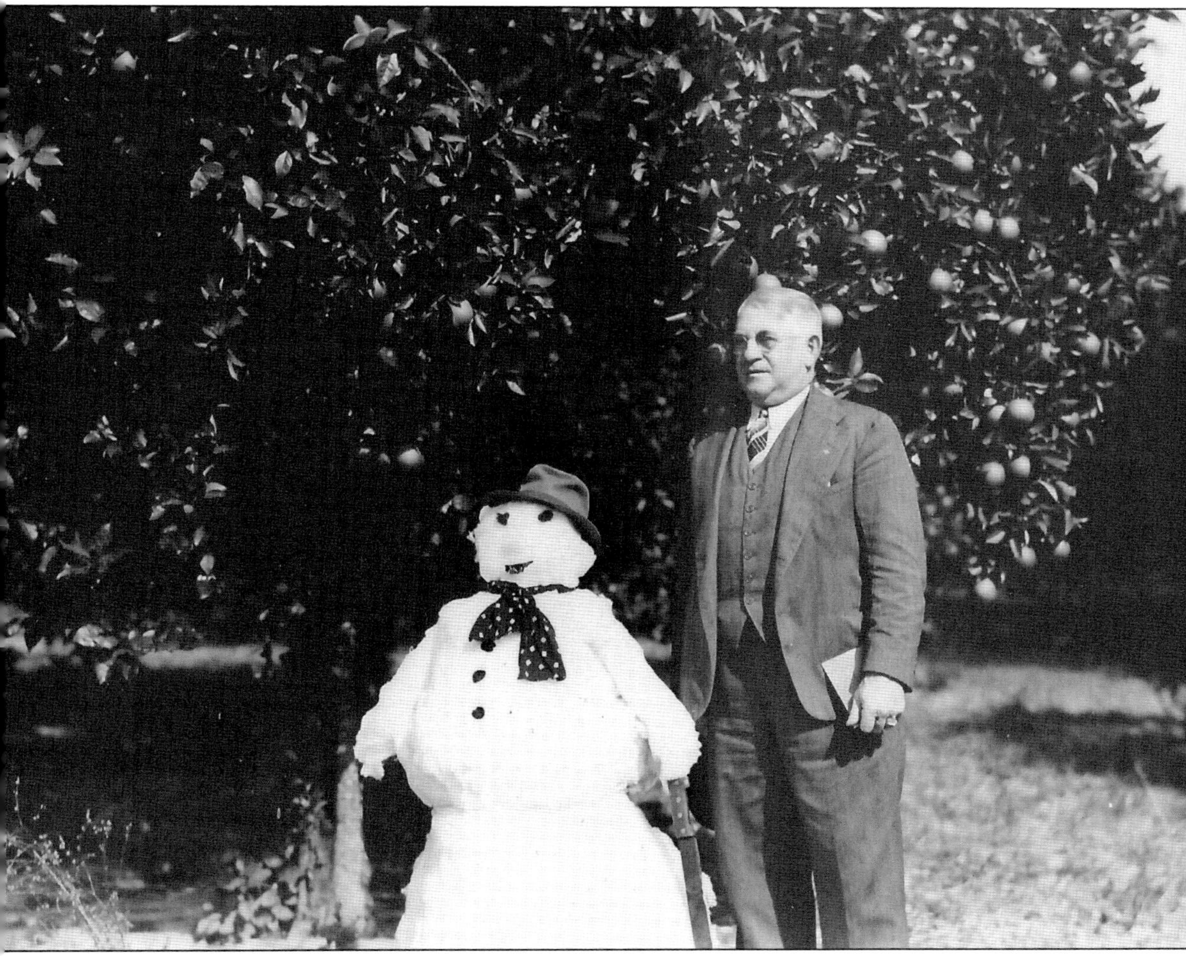

Frank Evans poses for an obvious publicity shot at Christmas in 1939. A photograph like this was likely targeting frigid residents up north, enticing them to head south for the winter and perhaps spend their Christmas surrounded by green orange groves like the one pictured. Note that the fake snowman welds a machete—a common implement for folks hiking through the wooded trails surrounding Lake Mary.

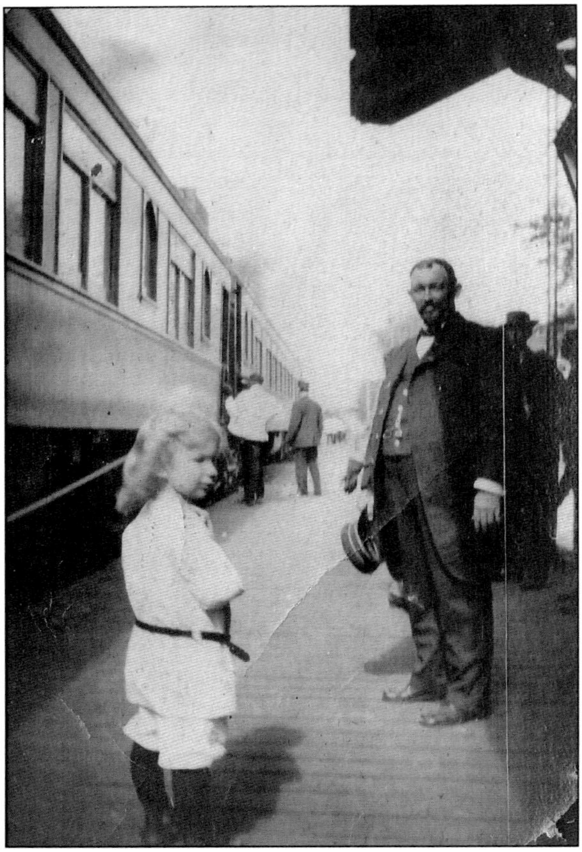

At left, a girl is hesitant to meet the train conductor at the Lake Mary station. Below, Mrs. Evans poses with the kids in 1936 on the Tampa Special. This Atlantic Coast Line train ran between Jacksonville and Tampa, with stops along the way including Lake Mary. Fueled by a land boom in the 1920s, this railroad, along with competitors Florida East Coast and Seaboard Airline, invested in excess of $100 million into expanding their routes and services. At their peak, the three had about 6,500 miles of track in Florida alone, compared to 2,800 miles in 2014.

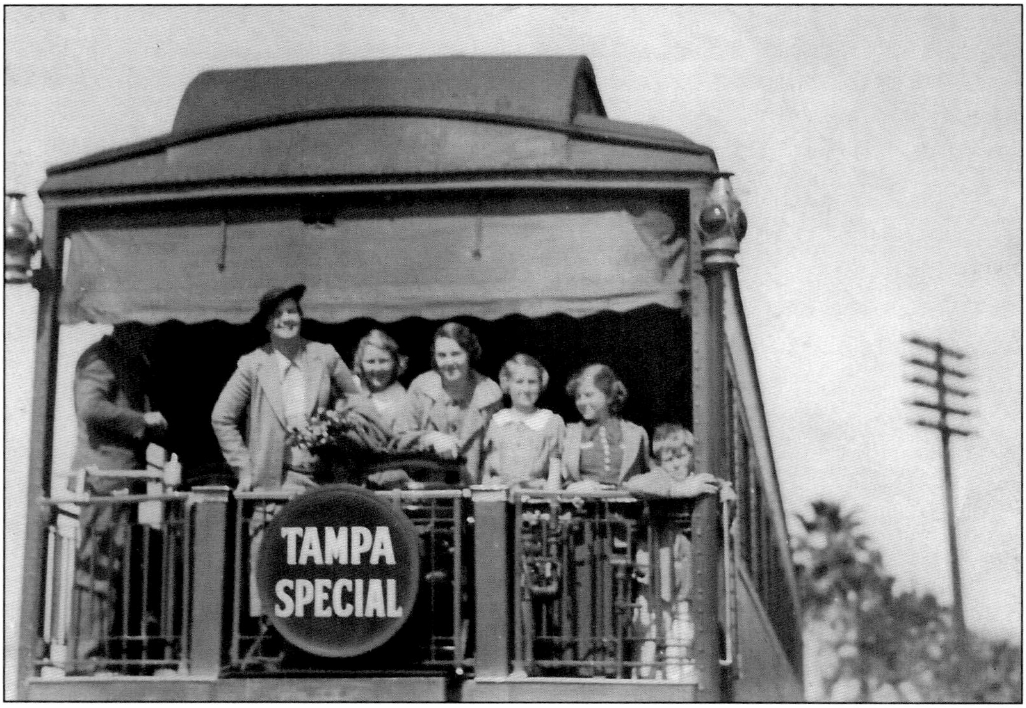

Four

From World War II to Hurricane Donna

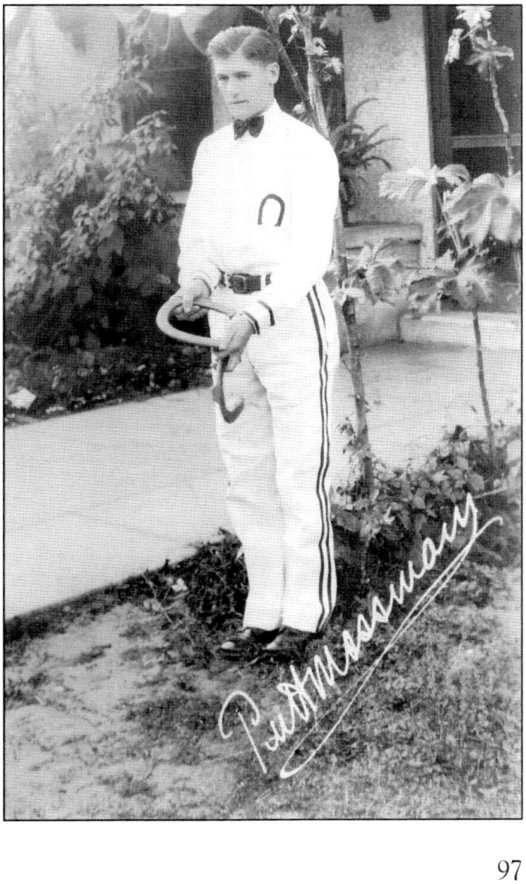

This chapter covers a period spanning two turbulent events in Lake Mary's history. World War II swept the town and the world into a fight for democracy, sacrificing personal freedoms and loved ones. Hurricane Donna, one of the costliest storms in the nation's history, destroyed many Lake Mary houses and took away a community leader in its wake.

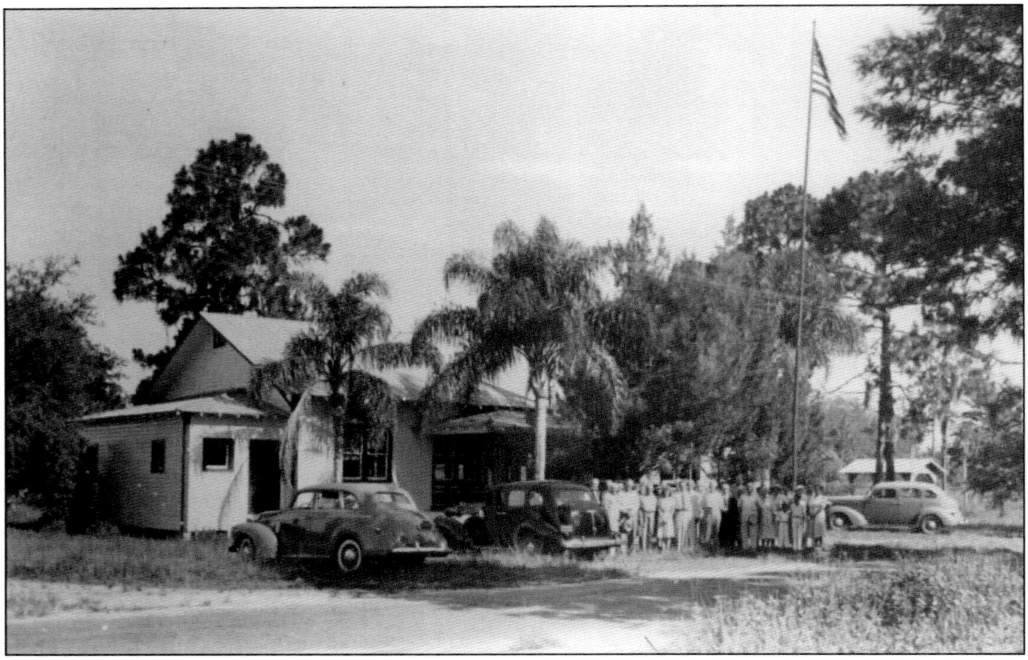

A group poses in front of the Community Center in the early 1940s. By the start of World War II, the assorted anti-Nazi propaganda resulted in a swell of patriotism, hence the impressively tall flag pole topped with the stars and stripes. Despite the war, the Community Center continued to be the center of town life, hosting events, shows, and town meetings.

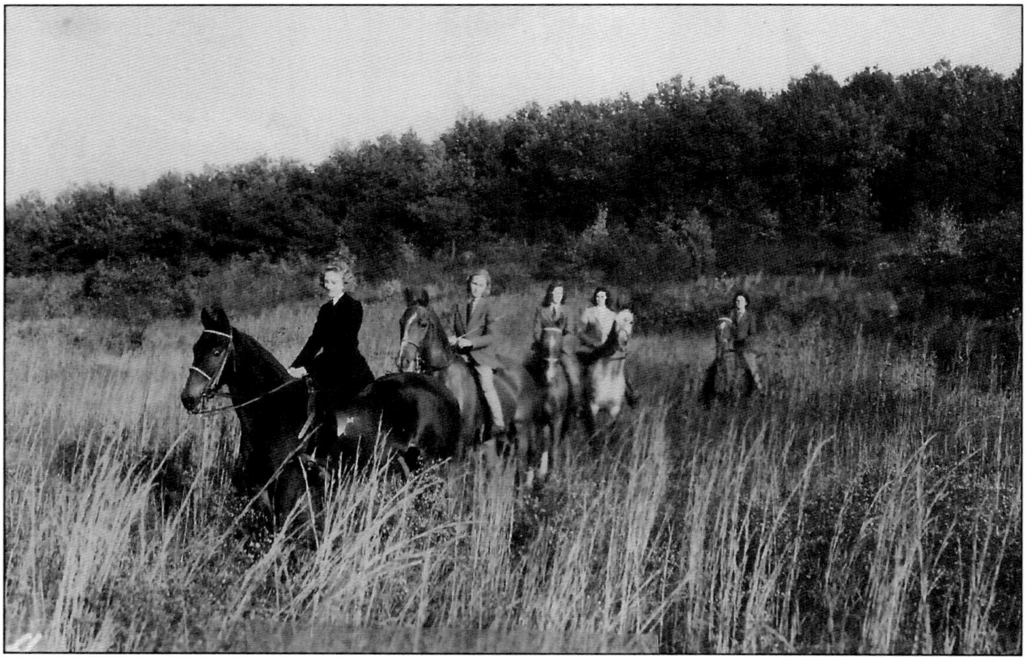

A group of equestrians enjoy a pleasant ride through the tall Florida grass fields. By the 1940s, automobiles ruled the streets. Still, there was nothing quite like riding horseback. Equipped with their formal suits and riding crops (a horse whip without a lash), this group may have been taking their horses on a trail ride to better acquaint themselves with their horse, and vise versa.

William Holden, one of the most popular movie stars of his era, signs autographs for Lake Mary youngsters. In this photograph, he is dressed in his US Army uniform. He served in the Army during World War II and later won the Academy Award for Best Actor in 1953 for his role in *Stalag 17*.

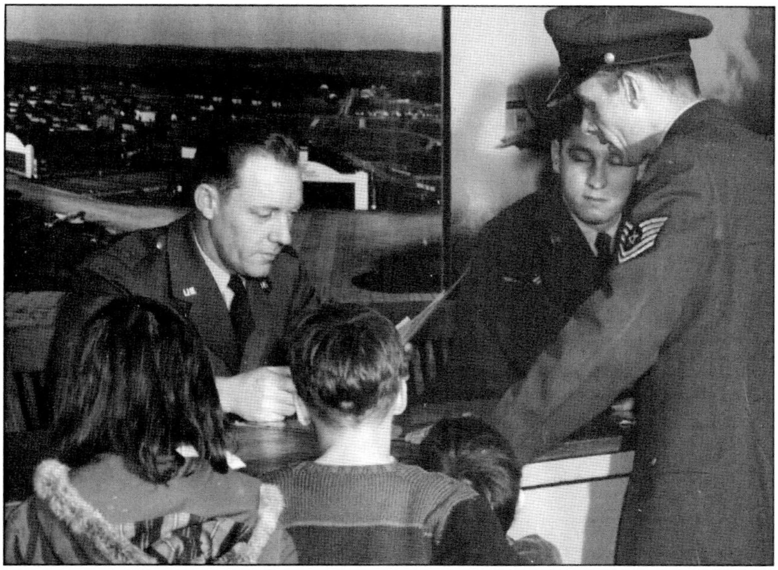

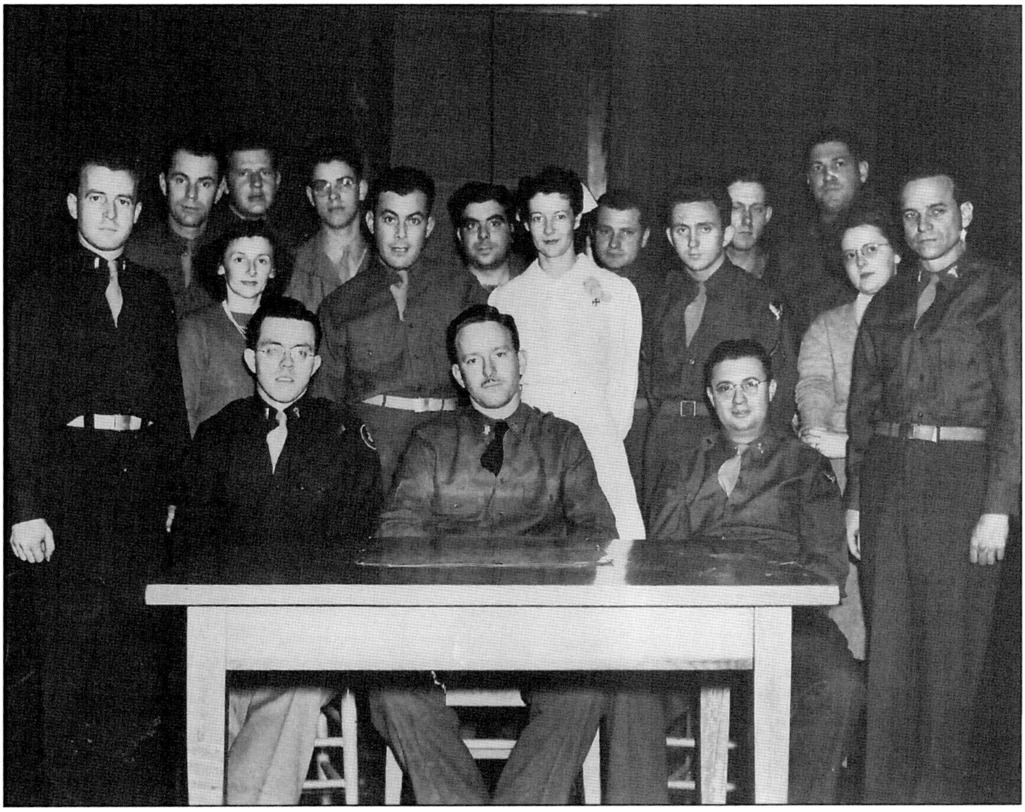

There are no actors in this photograph. Pictured are men and women from one of the various Military Entrance Processing Stations established during the war. Their job was to screen and process applicants into the US armed forces. Doctors and nurses checked that the young men and women met the physical and mental requirements.

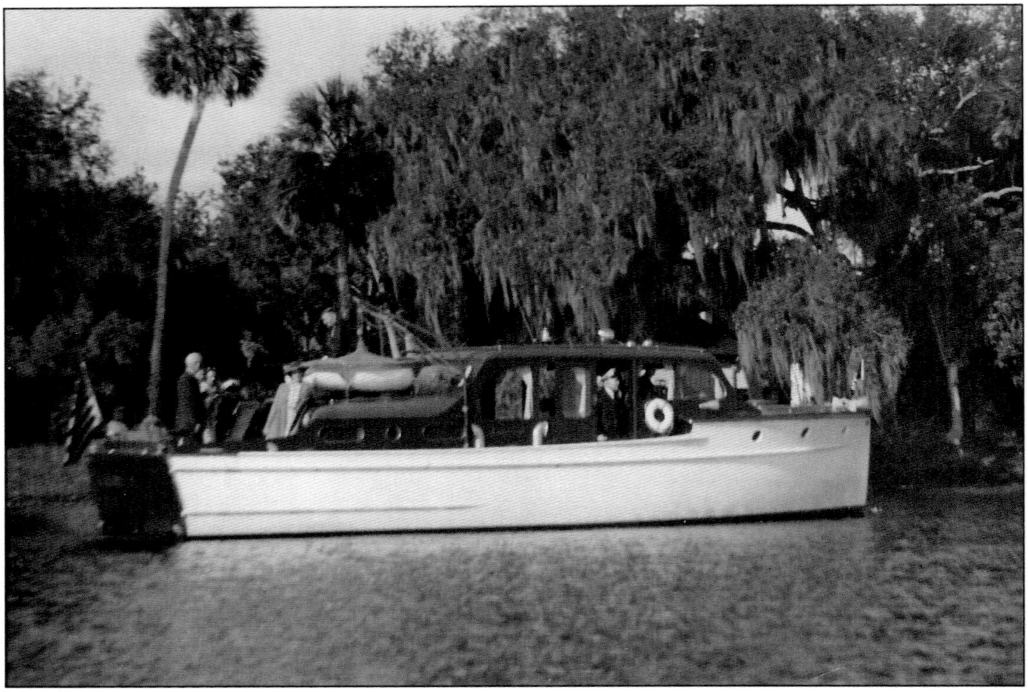

The boat seen here was owned by a Lake Mary family who donated it to the US military to be used for the war effort. At the start of World War II, the military had the enormous task to transition from peacetime to war. Commandeering privately owned vessels like this was critical to the Allies' initial success. In his book *Twelve Desperate Miles*, Tim Brady chronicles the story of a privately owned New Orleans banana boat called the *Contessa* used in the successful invasion of Casablanca. The war was filled with other stories that were essential to the country's success.

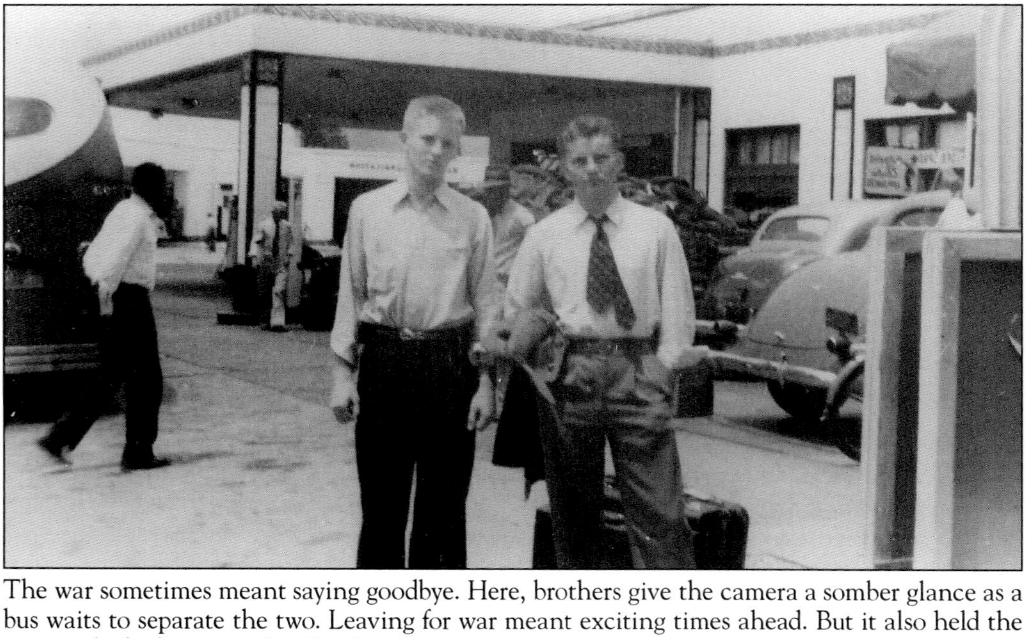

The war sometimes meant saying goodbye. Here, brothers give the camera a somber glance as a bus waits to separate the two. Leaving for war meant exciting times ahead. But it also held the potential of splitting up families forever.

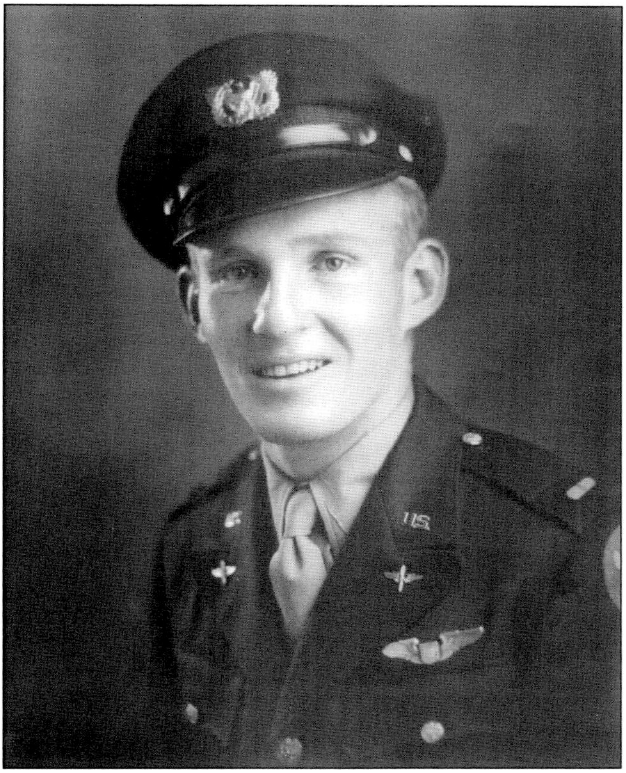

Pictured are two Lake Mary residents who helped the war effort by becoming Army pilots. The US Army Air Corps and later the US Army Air Force predated the separate military branch of the US Air Force. Created in World War I and formalized thereafter, their contribution proved to be an invaluable tool for all sides of the war. Jackie Evans, shown here and as a child in the previous chapter, sacrificed his life in the war.

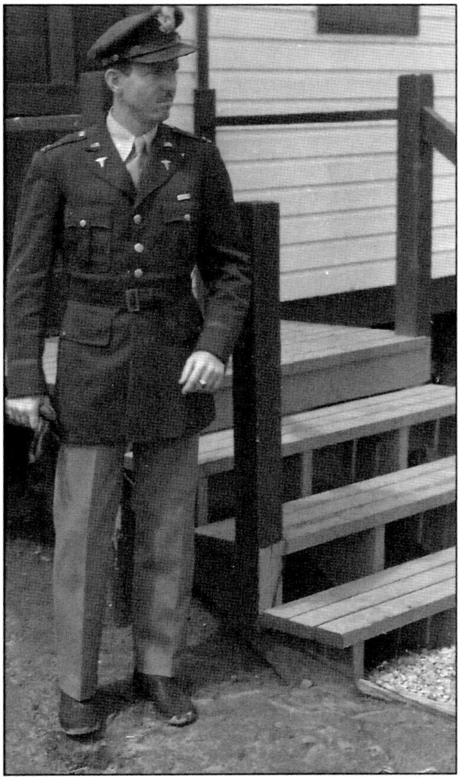

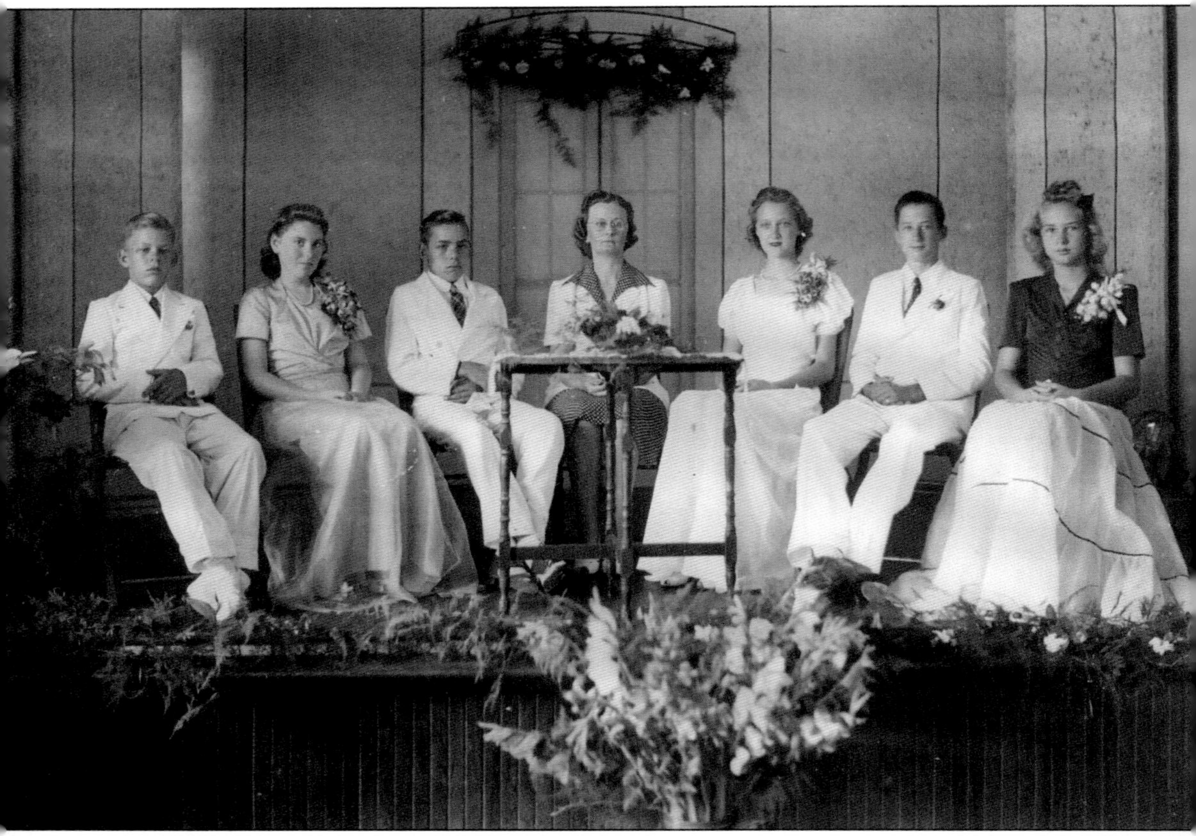

This photograph shows the entire Lake Mary High School graduating class of 1943 and their teacher, seated in the middle. Before the new campus opened in 1981, the high school was housed in a small building on Country Club Road and was staffed by a handful of teachers who taught every subject for 10th to 12th grade.

Don Reno and Red Smiley and the Tennessee Cut-Ups performed in Lake Mary's Community Building to bring some musical entertainment such as the band's most famous gospel song "I'm Using My Bible for a Roadmap." Nationally known groups like this toured the country to promote their records and occasionally drew crowds to the quiet town.

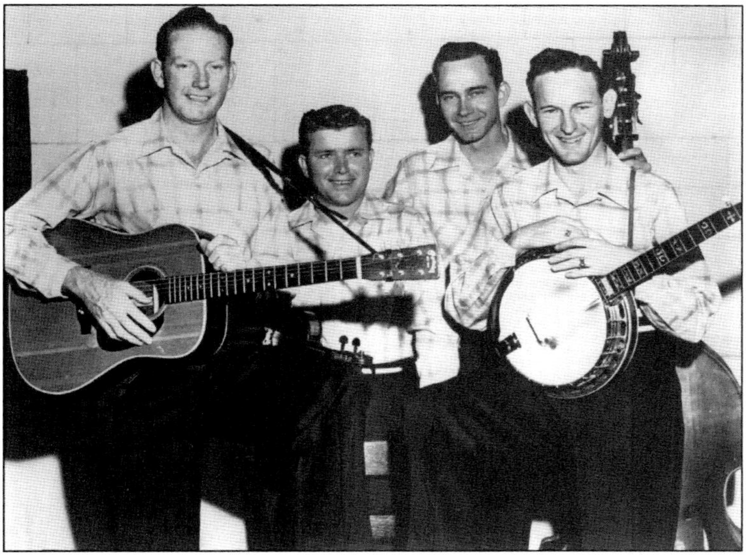

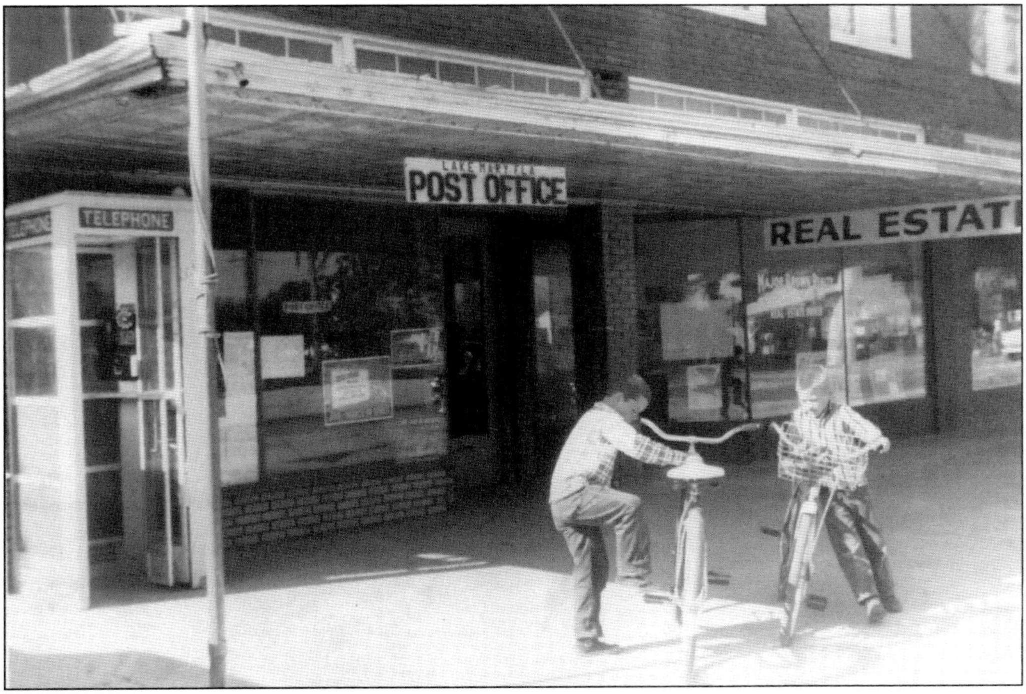

Bicycles were the typical mode of transportation for these boys in downtown Lake Mary in the late 1950s. In this case, they might have been dropping off or picking up mail from the post office. The post office relocated a number of times throughout Lake Mary's history. Starting in the home of William N. Webster in 1887, it moved to an old freight building, then to the home of Bertie C. Martin, then to the A.E. Sjoblom store on Crystal Lake Avenue at the railroad, then to A.E. Sjoblom's third store at the corner of Crystal Lake Avenue and First Street, and then to the Frank Evans building in 1932, as seen here.

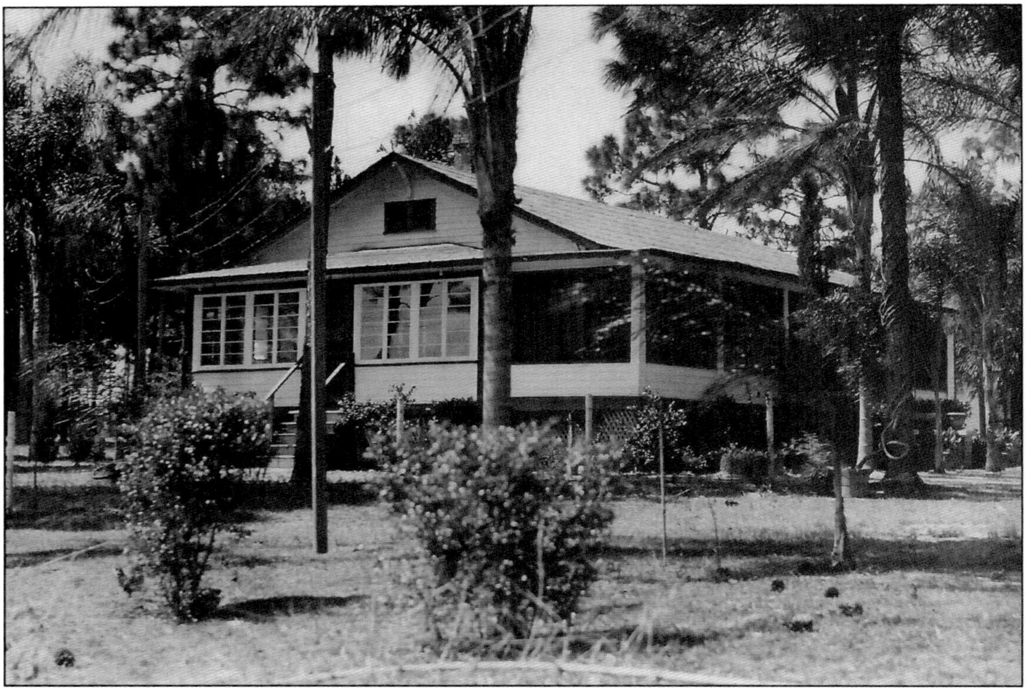

Pictured is a typical Lake Mary house in the 1940s. Homes varied in shape and size, but most were one story and had a porch or "Florida room" and a crawl space underneath the house. Aerial power lines provided the house with electricity. Buried power lines were not common in Florida at this time.

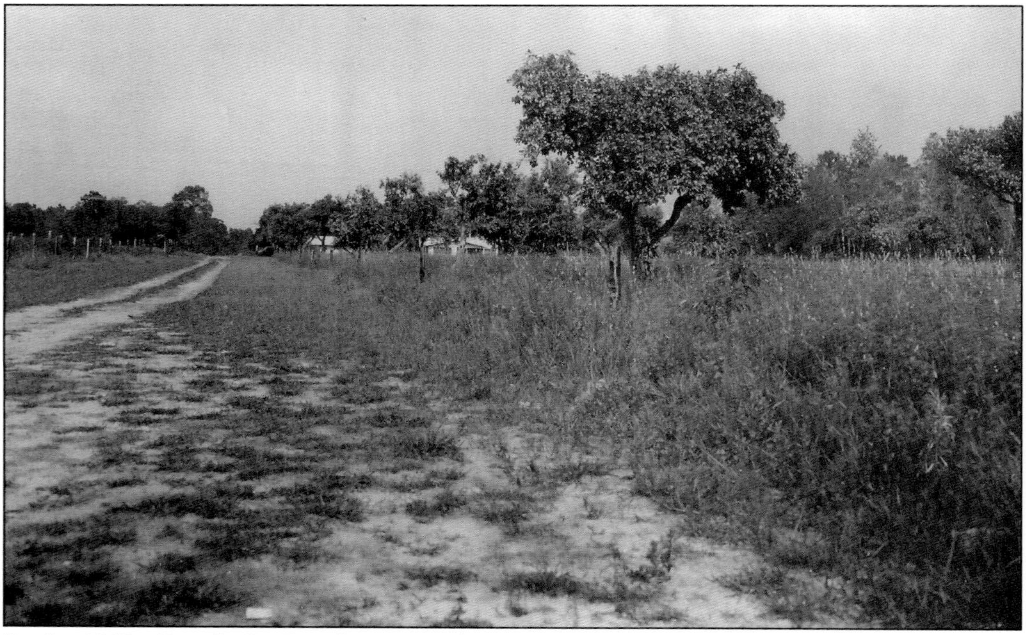

By the 1950s, Dwight D. Eisenhower saw his vision of duplicating Germany's autobahn come to light with the passing of the Federal Aid Highway Act. Limited-access interstate highways sprung up throughout the country in multiple construction projects. Meanwhile, most of Lake Mary remained unpaved.

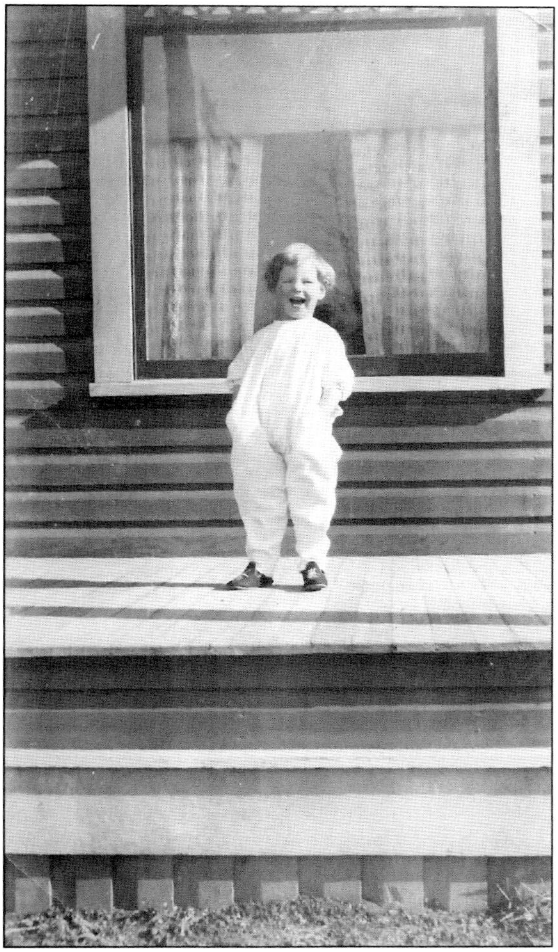

A child enjoys herself one evening on her open porch in a dated one-piece outfit. Meanwhile, two elderly women sit and rock in their lawns, reading and flipping through photo albums. Both of these were common scenes in Lake Mary in the 1950s. Life here was not often exciting or fast-paced. These gentle, low-key moments were why residents loved to call this place their home.

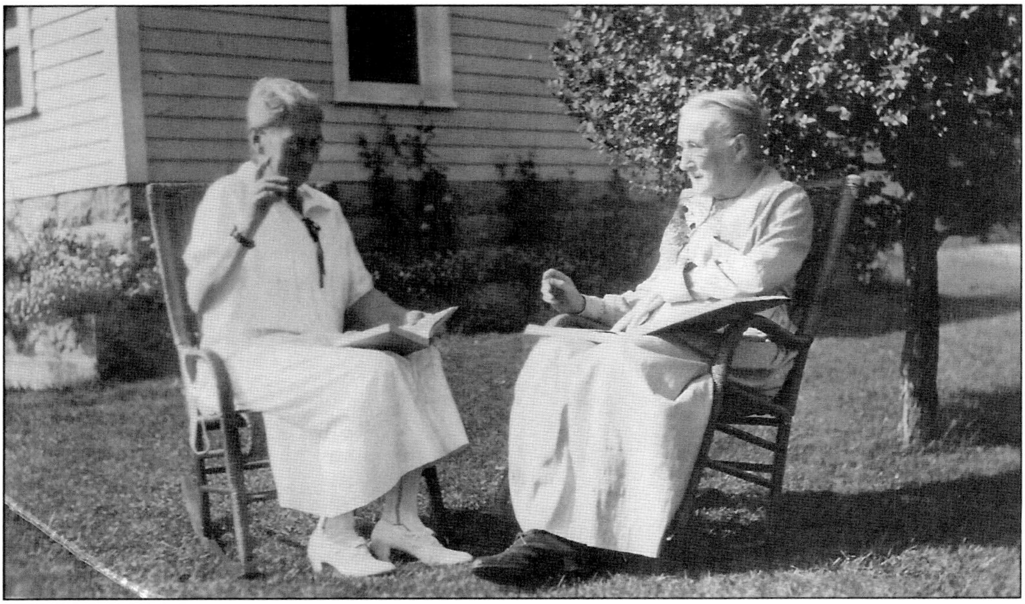

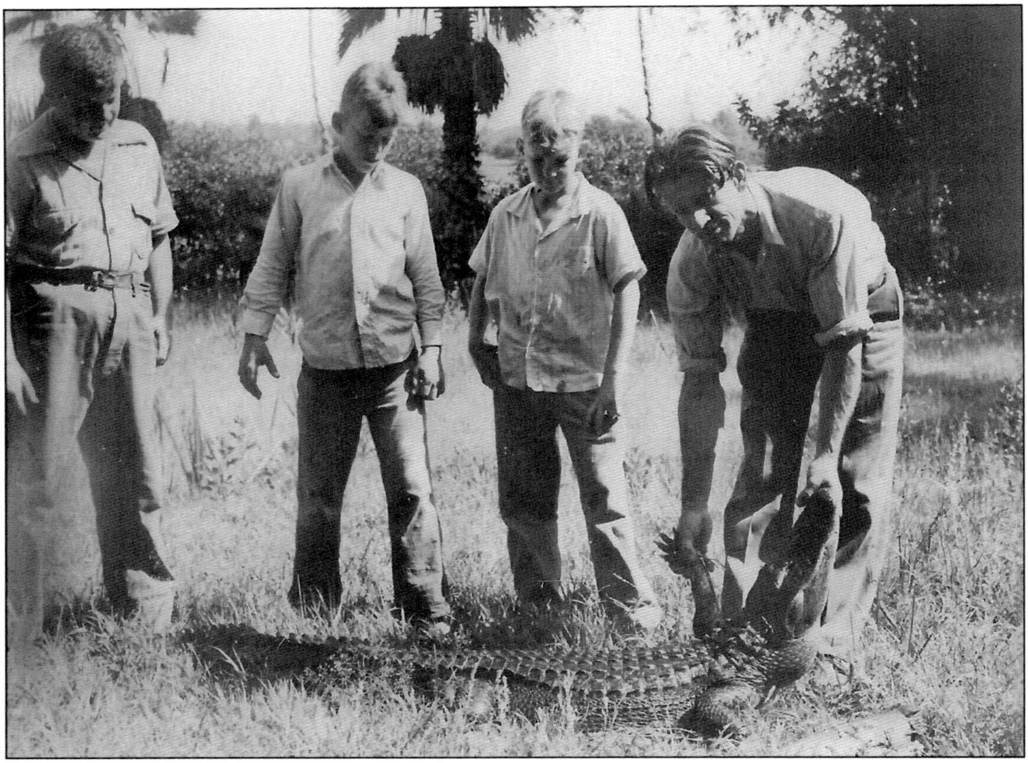

Pictured are residents wrestling alligators. Since the late 1940s, there have been close to 300 documented alligator attacks on people. Their reputation and mystique led to overhunting, and by the 1970s, the American alligator was considered an endangered species. Conservation efforts allowed them to be removed from the endangered list in 1987. Since then, the state has allowed hunters to kill a limited number of alligators during certain times of the year.

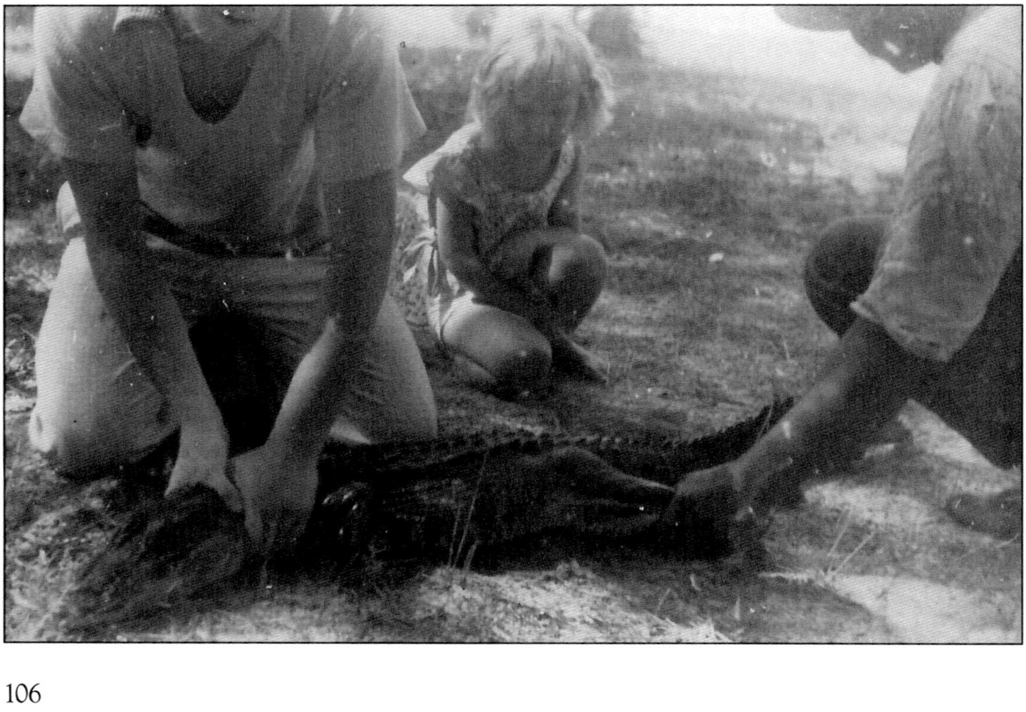

Kids jump off a dock at Evansdale Park on the west end of Lake Mary. Hot summer months provided good incentive to cool off in Lake Mary and Crystal Lake's waters. Elevated, two-story docks like this served as a high dive for kids and adults to work on perfecting their diving form. At the time, swimming pools and associated diving facilities were a rarity in central Florida.

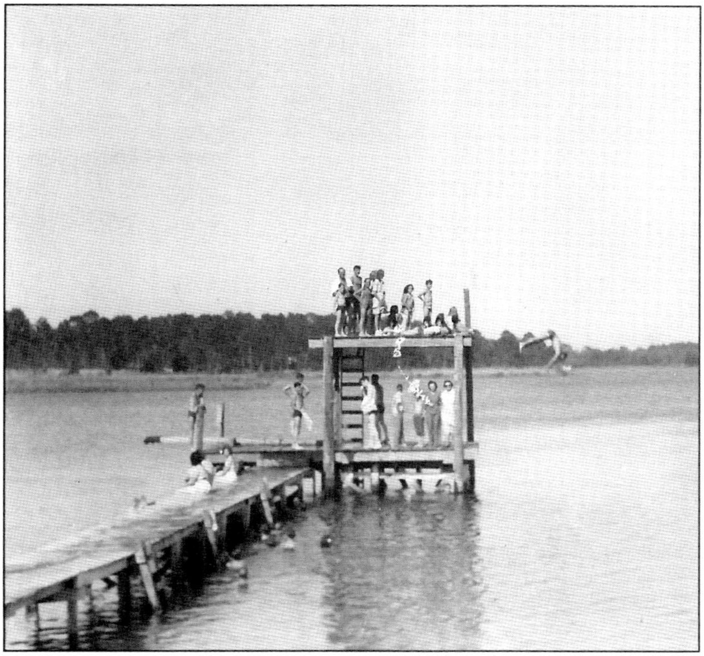

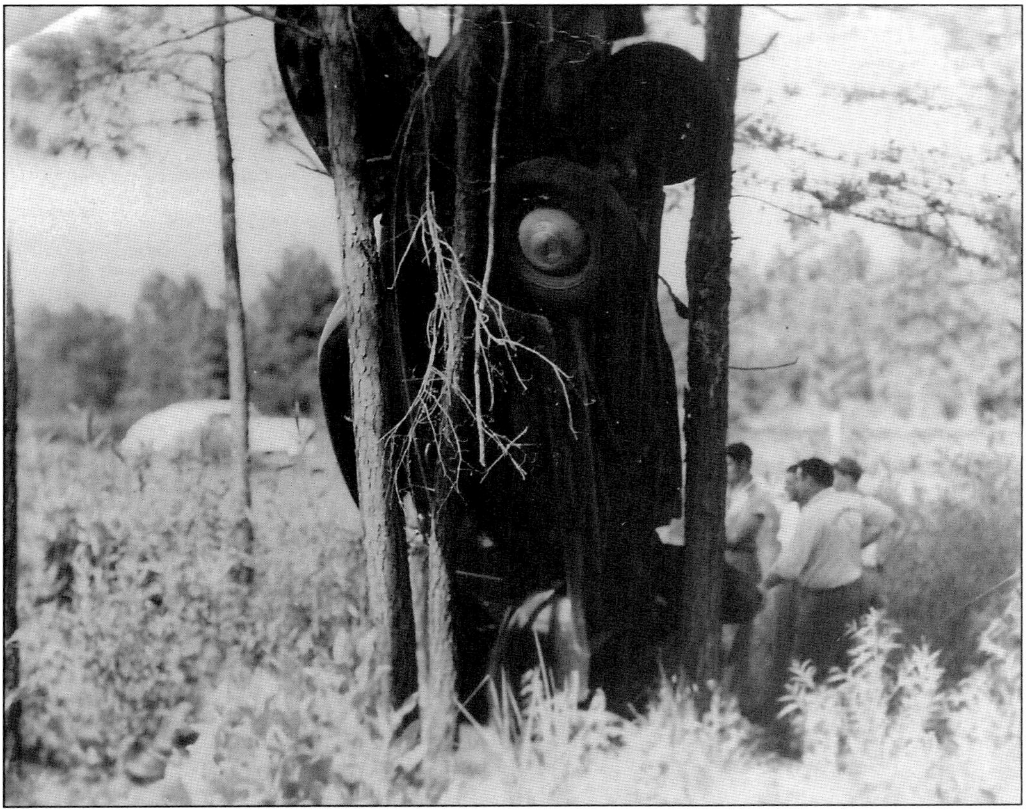

What happened in this photograph has been lost to history. One can only imagine what might have transpired to result in a car standing upright like this. Even in small towns, the strangest events could happen.

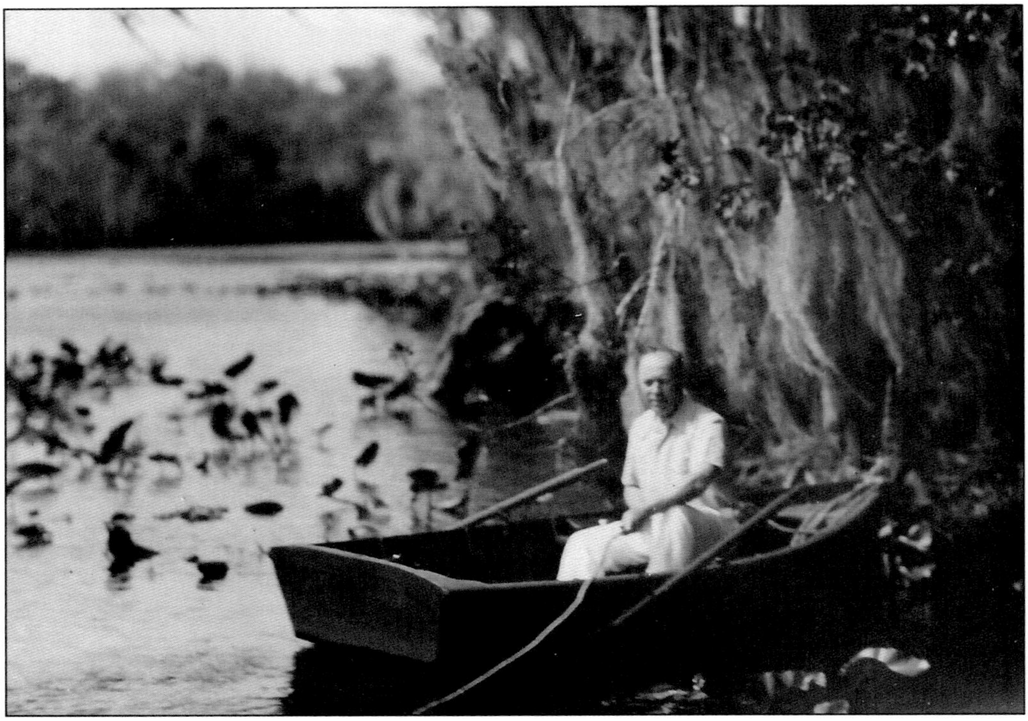

A man fishes with a makeshift fishing rod near "The Island" on Lake Mary in March 1940. For years, the lake was regularly stocked with fish to help keep it clean and environmentally healthy. Residents occasionally took advantage of this with some quiet fishing. The area referred to as The Island was particularly good for fishing with its rich vegetation.

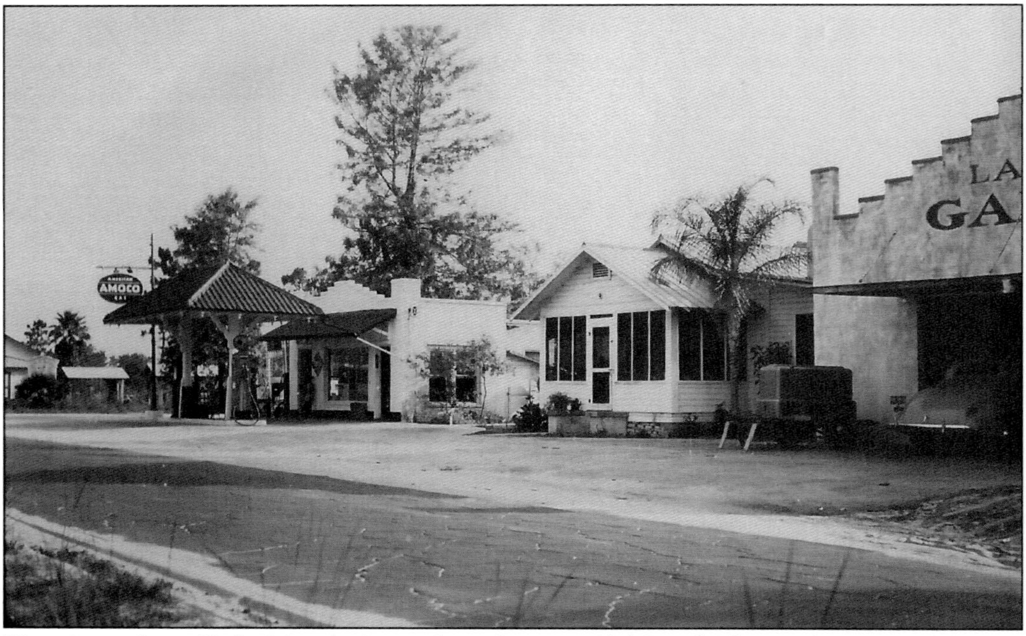

This classic shot of Lake Mary looks south on Country Club Road. This road was one of the first to be paved. Florida's heat and wet summers have apparently damaged this road, which is cracked like a giant jigsaw puzzle.

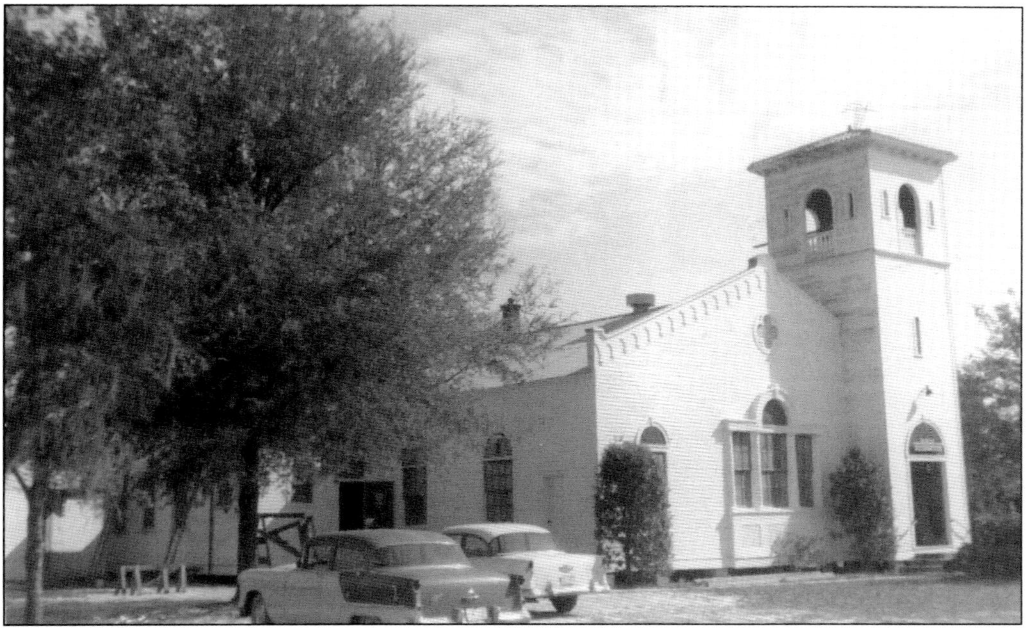

Shown is the First Presbyterian Church in 1959, formerly known as the Community Church. Church attendance was still the norm in Lake Mary and throughout America in the 1950s. In September 1959, President Eisenhower even invited Soviet leader Nikita Khrushchev to church in a move to help smooth cold war relations. Khrushchev turned him down.

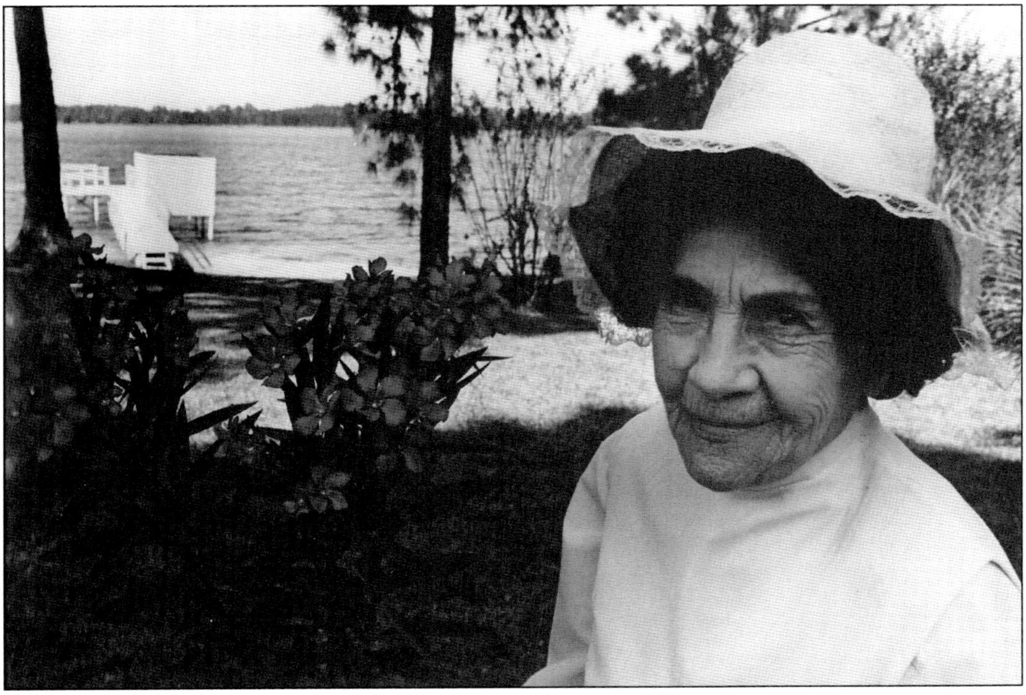

In this photograph, a woman takes a break from working on her garden to enjoy the lake in her backyard. Most Lake Mary residents did not live along the lake itself. In the early years, several families built houses near or between Lake Mary and Crystal Lake. As the town matured to a city, more and more single-family houses grew out of carefully planned neighborhoods.

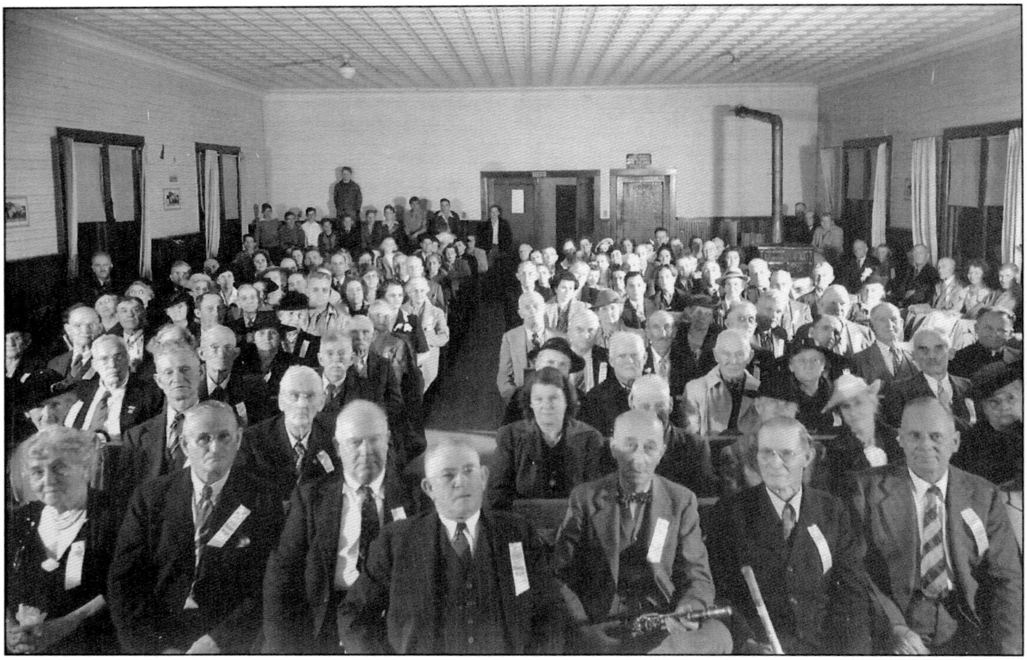

Pictured are two scenes from Pioneer Night at the Community Building. Pioneer Nights commemorated veterans of the Spanish-American War. American policy to no longer tolerate European colonization of the Americas eventually bloomed into all-out war with Spain in the late 1800s. Spain's defeat caused irreparable damage to its empire, and gave America control over lands most Americans had never heard of, including Puerto Rico, Guam, and the Philippines. This war has since been overshadowed by the Civil War and World War I. Patriotic Lake Mary residents recognized this and started these Pioneer Nights in the late 1920s.

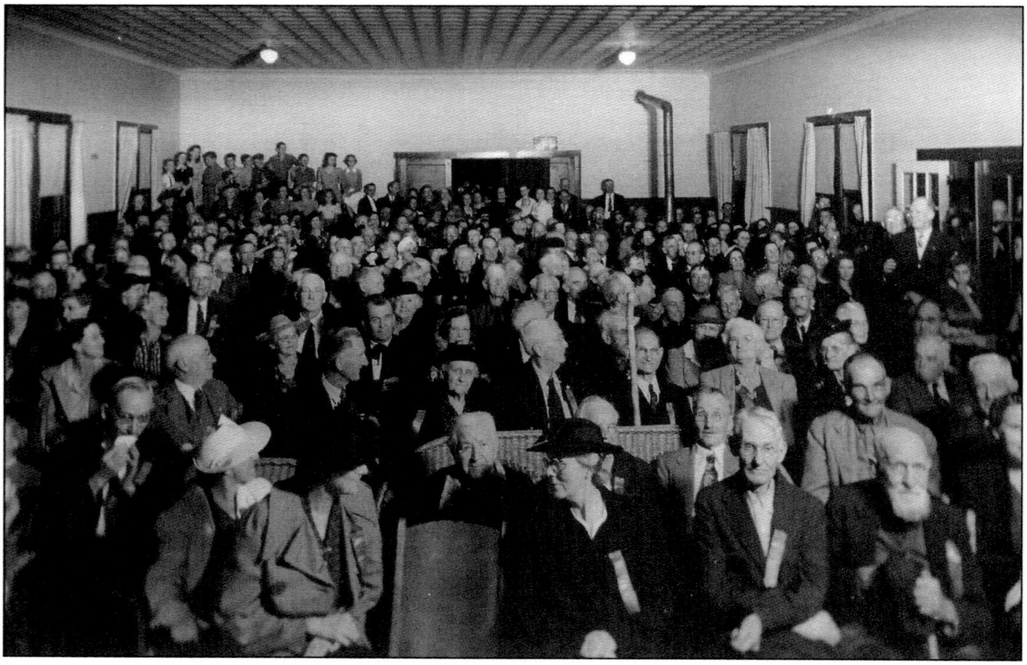

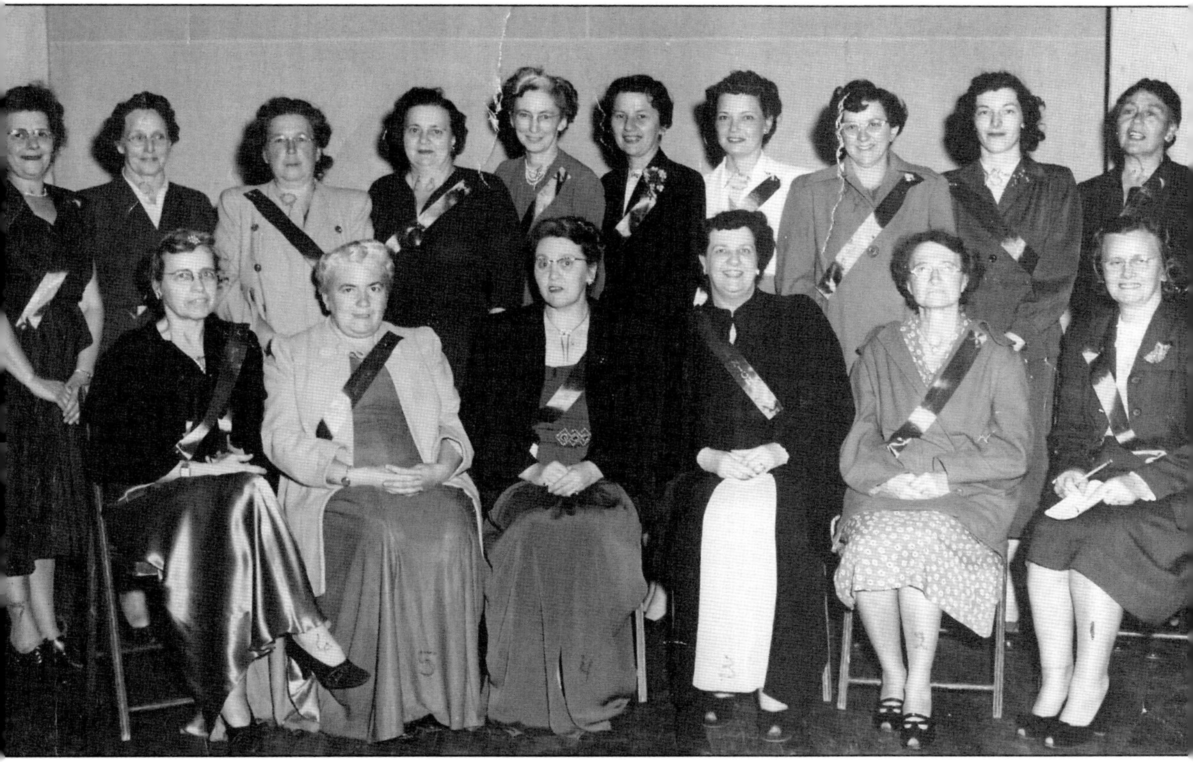

This picture shows the wives of the chamber of commerce members acting as hostesses on Pioneer Night. Note "Pioneer Night" on the banners worn by the ladies. The events were well attended and veterans often came from all areas of central Florida. They met in the Community Building, which today houses the Lake Mary Historical Society.

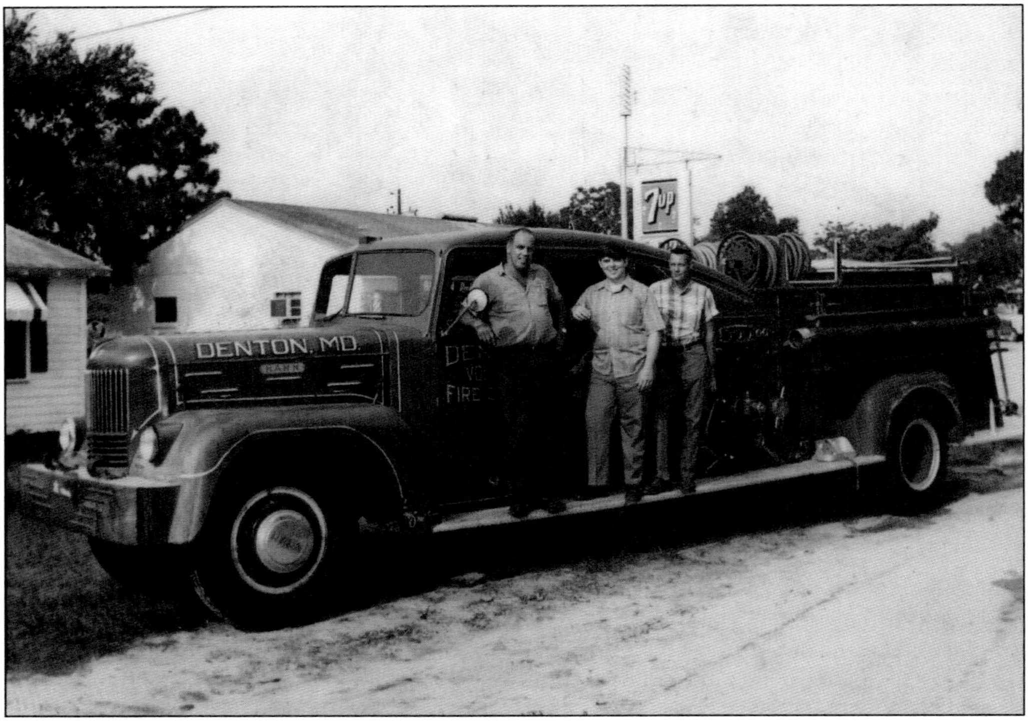

The Lake Mary Volunteer Fire Department often acquired old equipment from various departments in neighboring communities or elsewhere. In this photograph, a few volunteers show off a recently purchased fire truck all the way from Denton, Maryland, an equally small town more than 900 miles away.

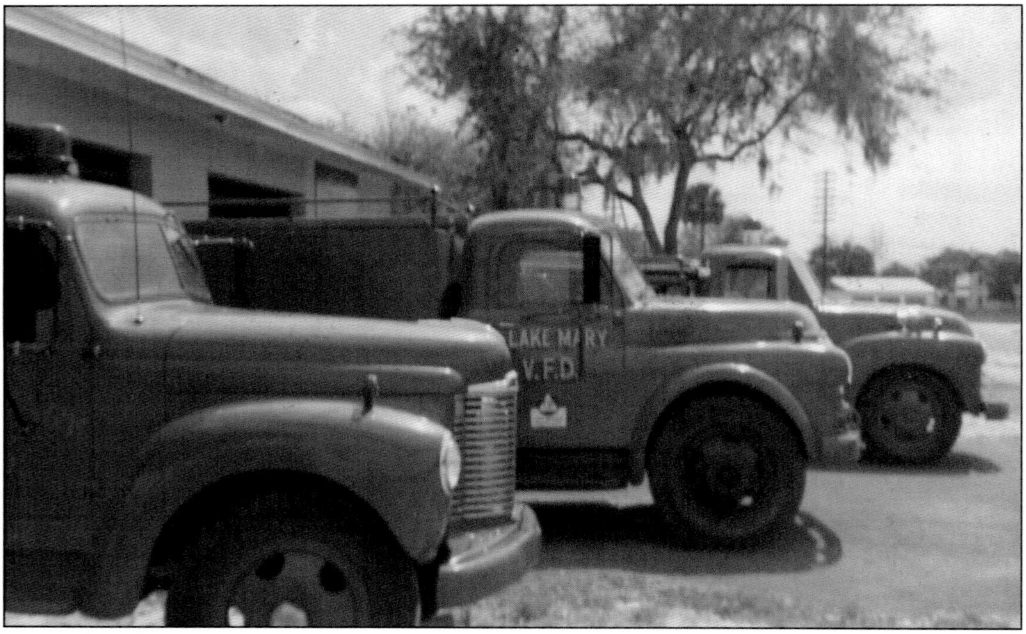

Pictured is a lineup of trucks from the Lake Mary Fire Department in 1963. Volunteers protected Lake Mary and the surrounding areas until 1990, when full-time, salaried personnel were put into place.

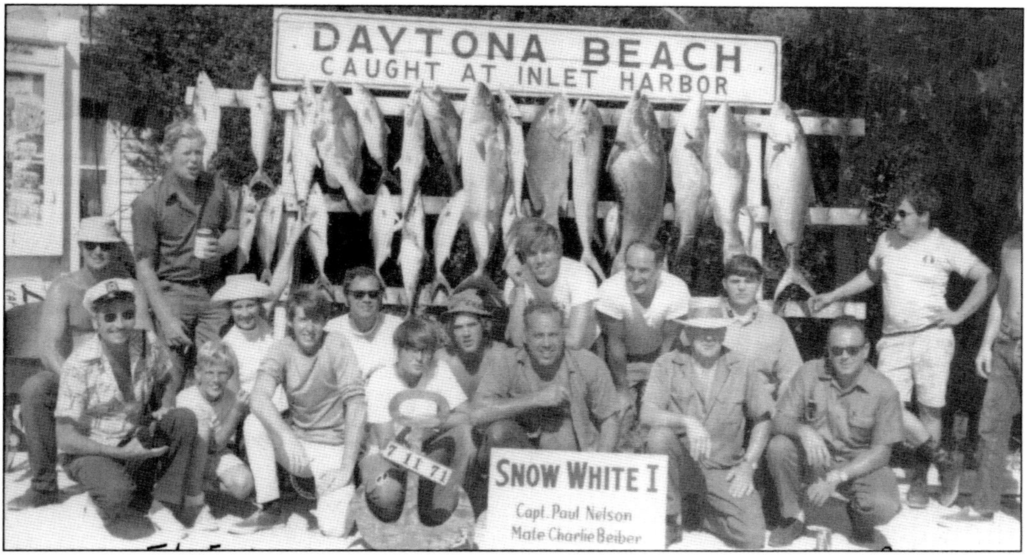

To maintain morale and camaraderie among the volunteers, Lake Mary's Volunteer Fire Department held occasional getaways like this Daytona Beach fishing trip, which yielded quite a catch. The volunteers treated trips like this as family outings, and in this case they brought along their sons for a good father-son bonding experience. After driving home to Lake Mary, even the painstaking chore of scaling and cleaning the fish was a team-building event. Below, the group huddles around sheets of wood that doubled as makeshift tables and prepares for the upcoming feast.

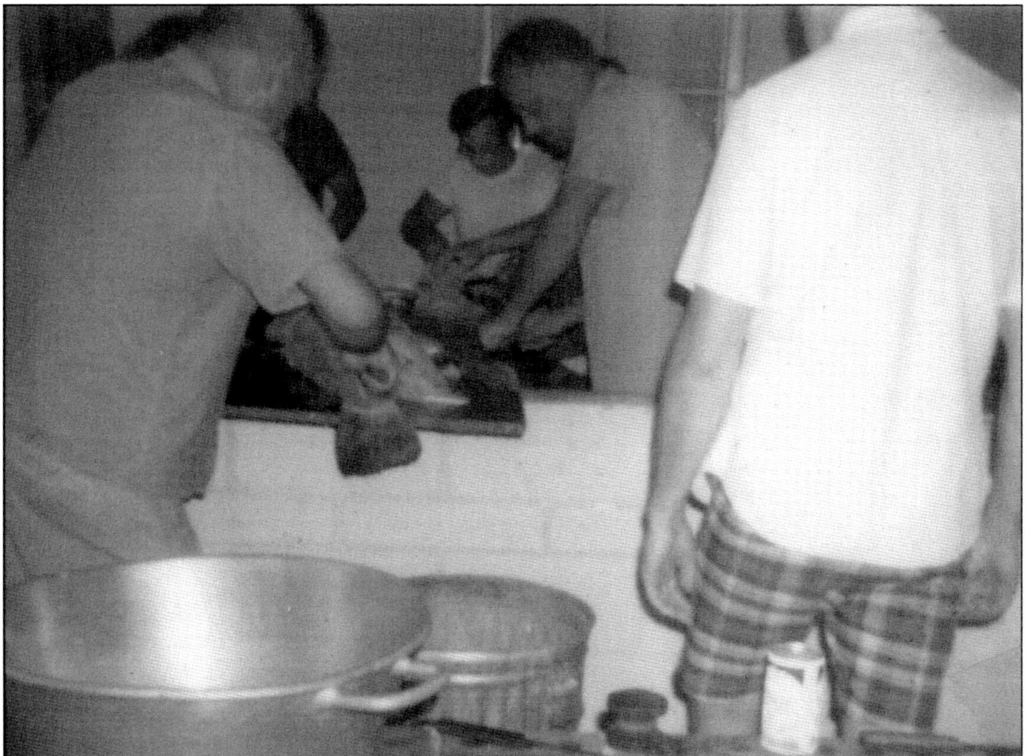

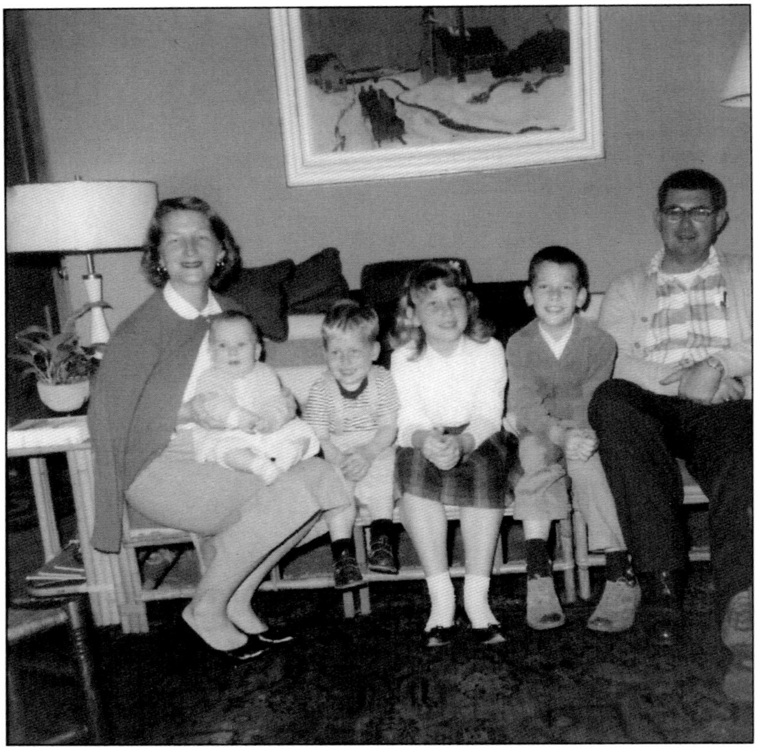

Pictured is a typical Lake Mary family in the late 1950s. The styles shown in this photograph were fairly common to all American families at that time, with the possible exception of the very Floridian wicker furniture. When the Heywood Chair Manufacturing Company invented machines that weaved wicker seats together in the early 1900s, furniture could be produced cheaply, making it widely available.

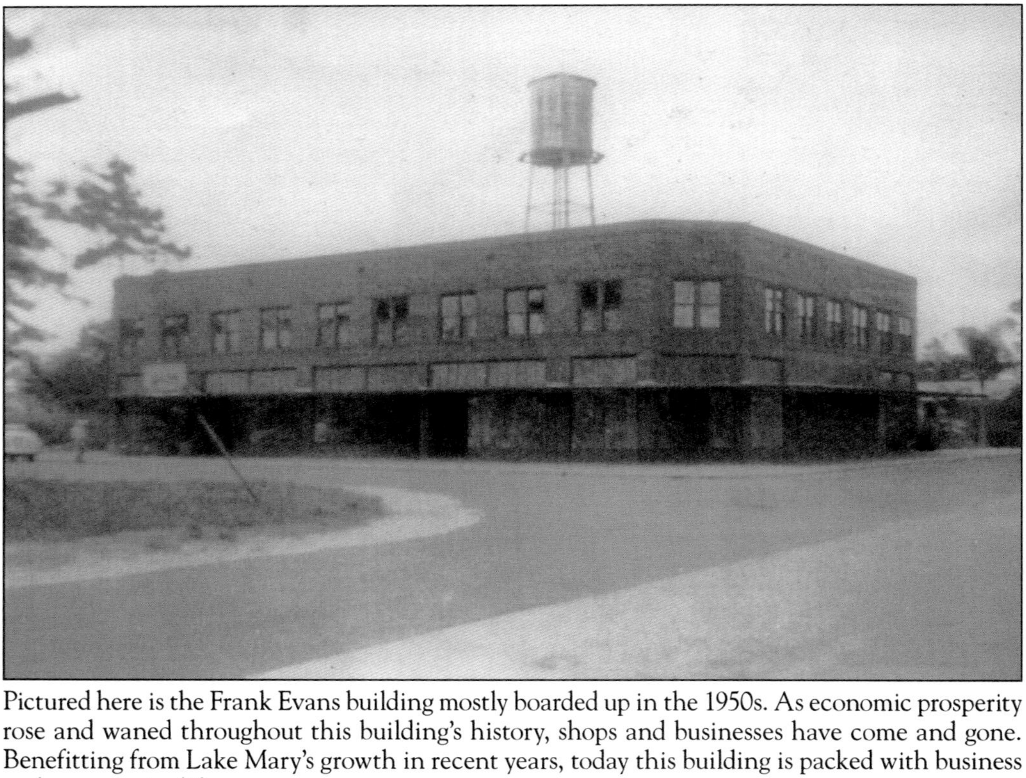

Pictured here is the Frank Evans building mostly boarded up in the 1950s. As economic prosperity rose and waned throughout this building's history, shops and businesses have come and gone. Benefitting from Lake Mary's growth in recent years, today this building is packed with business and community life.

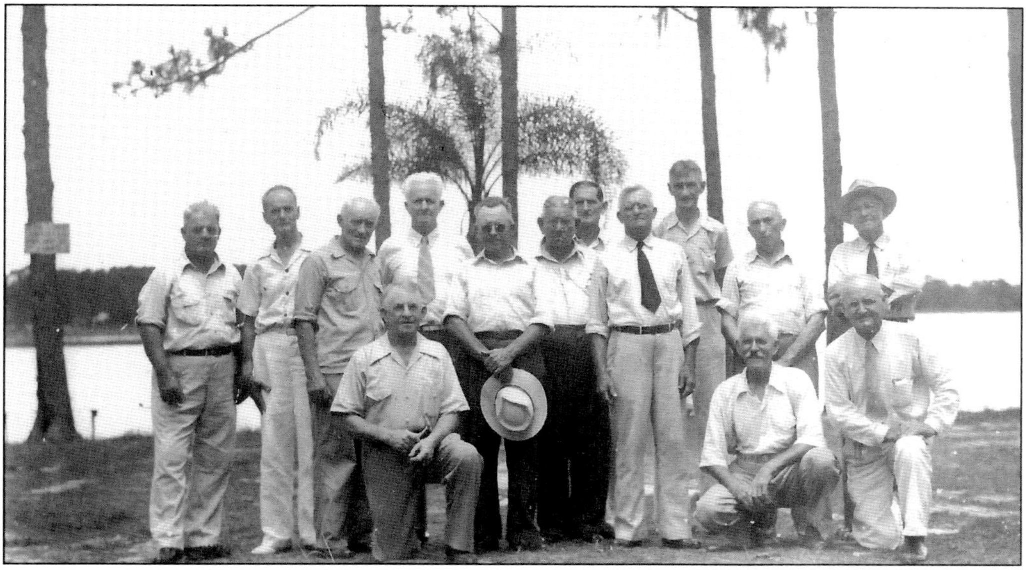

In these two photographs, Frank Evans and fellow residents gather to celebrate various occasions. Pictured above are Spanish-American War veterans in Evansdale Park. Below are friends and family at the Evans house celebrating a wedding. Throughout his life, Evans remained at the center of Lake Mary events, during good and bad. A popular story relates that a boy from town accidently shot his toy gun into the eye of an out-of-town visitor. Not wishing to give his home a bad name, Evans grabbed his hammer, walked from house to house, and smashed every toy gun in town.

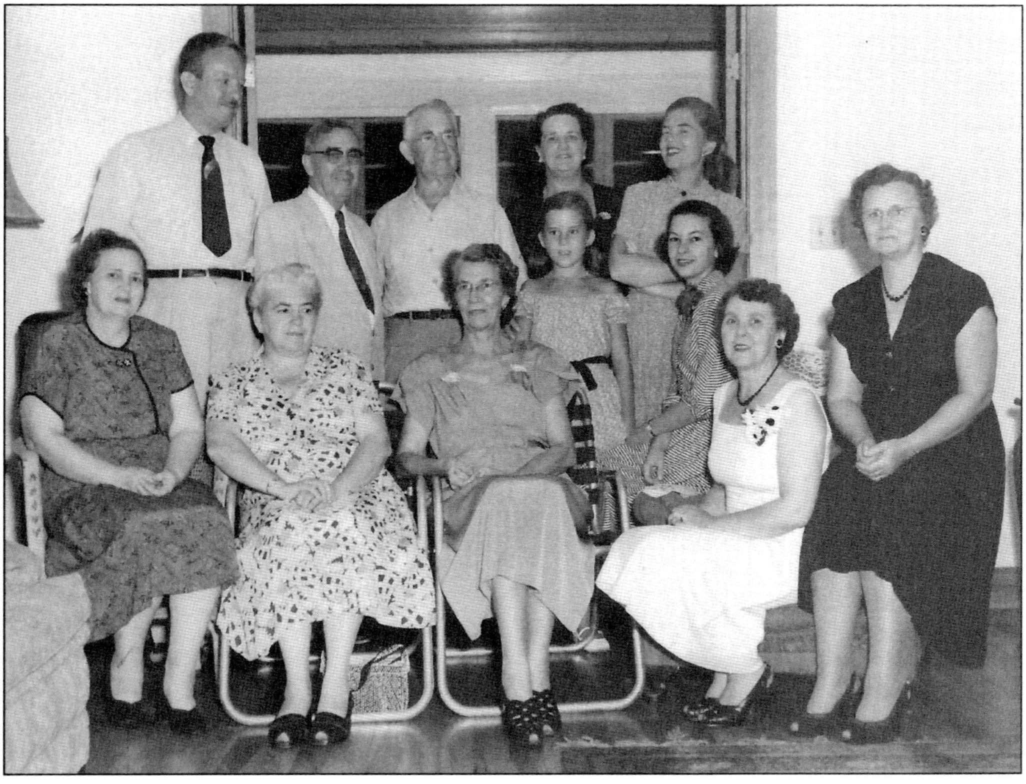

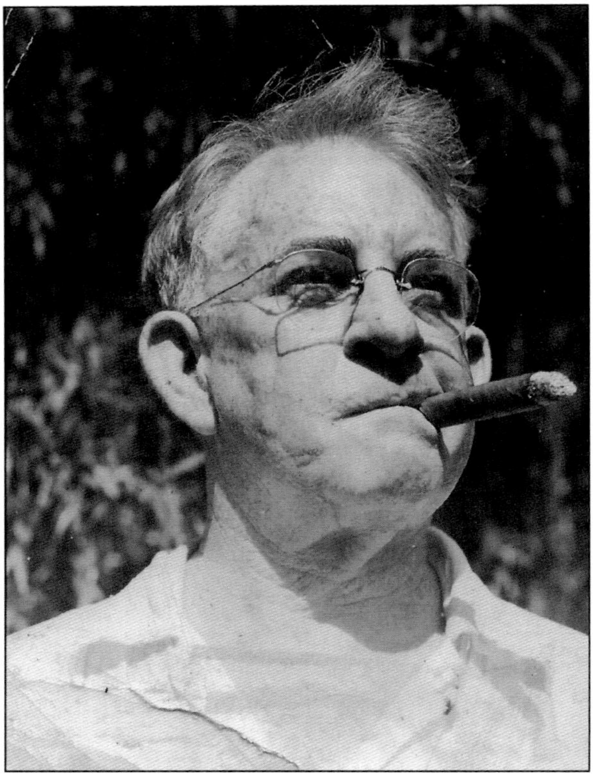

Frank Evans continued to be a major influence in the development of Lake Mary throughout his lifetime. When the eye wall of Hurricane Donna passed through Lake Mary in 1960, the town had to pull together to clear away the fallen trees and repair the damaged houses. During the cleanup, Evans passed away from a heart attack.

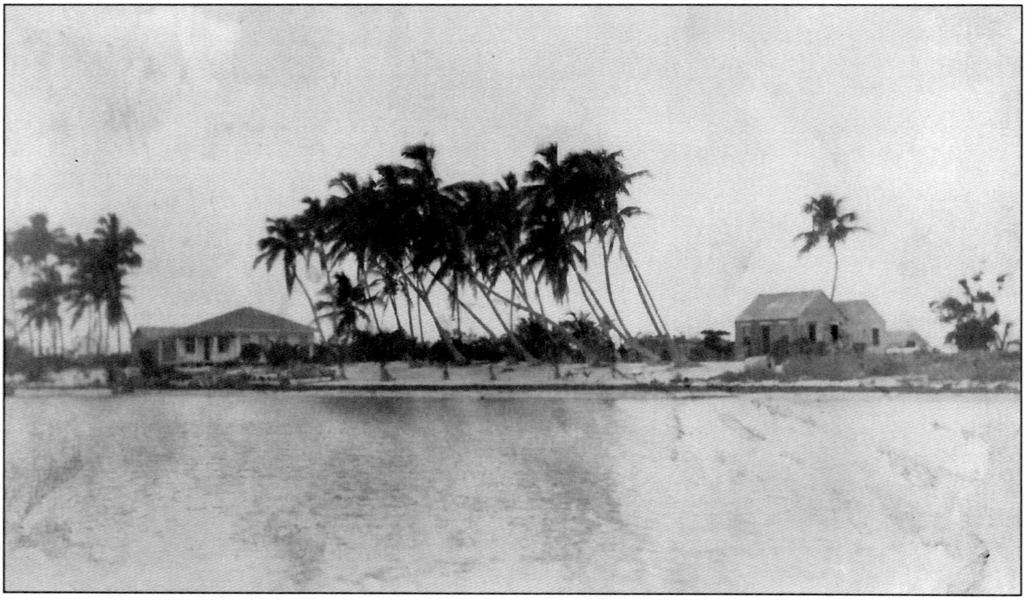

A line of palm trees lean to one side as the result of the harsh winds Lake Mary had to endure during Hurricane Donna. Deformation of trees like this is common following severe tropical storms. Florida is more prone to hurricanes than any other state. Prior to weather satellites and other modern technology that helps predict where the storms will strike, storms could be particularly lethal. Hurricane Donna's estimated fatalities numbered up to 364, compared to more recent storms like Hurricane Charley of 2004, which had about 20 deaths.

Five

Paving of Lake Mary and I-4 Interchange

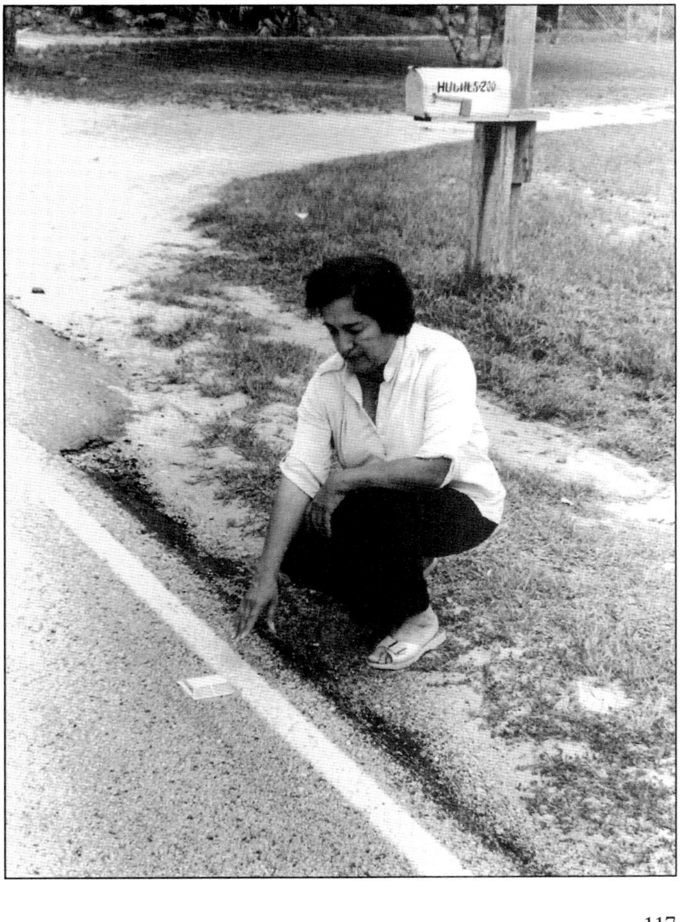

This chapter shows how the community's strength enabled it to springboard from small town to city. Lake Mary's incorporation was a major hallmark in its history, the result of strategic planning and solid, unified objectives. The most visual signs of this work were the paving of Lake Mary streets and the construction of a major interchange.

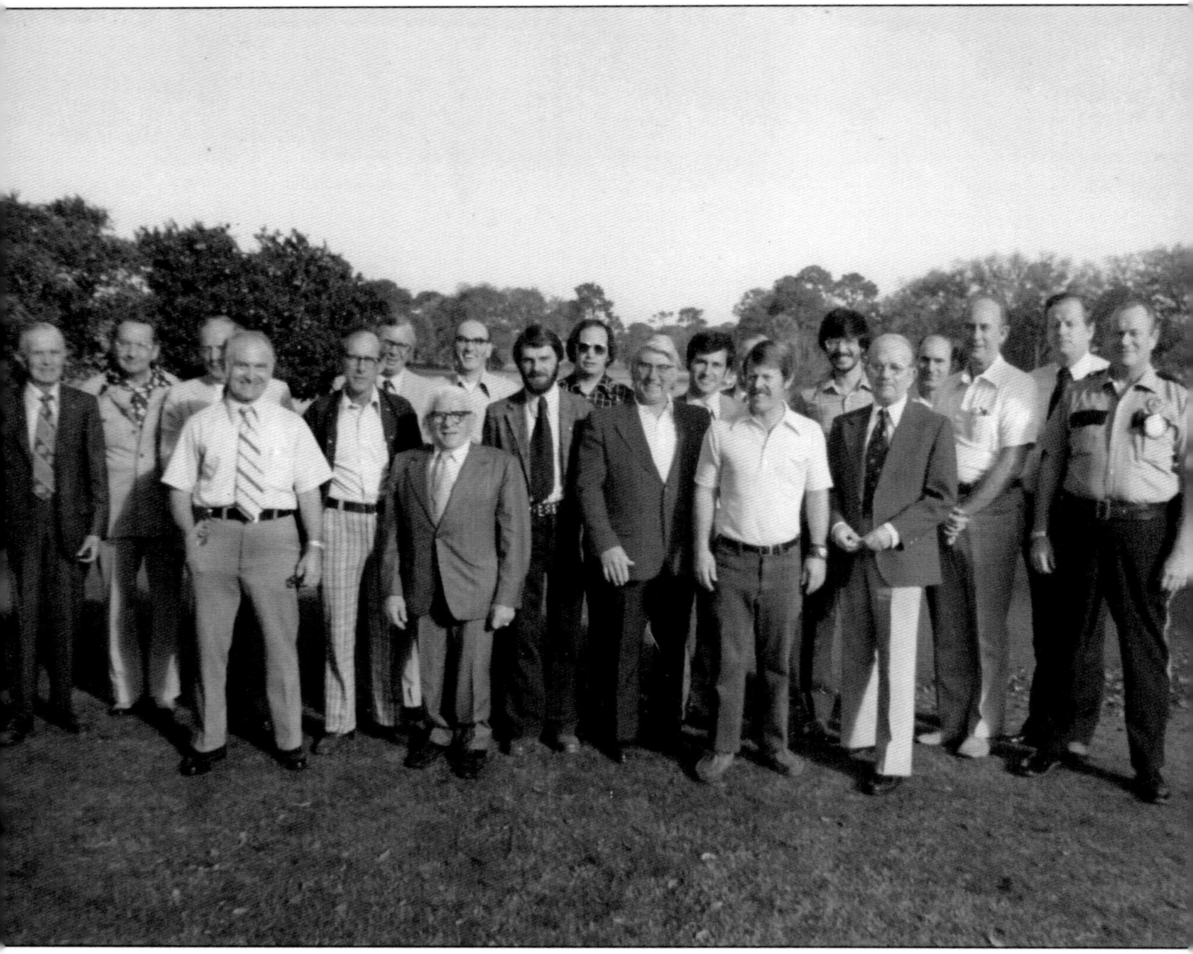

Members of the Lake Mary Chamber of Commerce laid the framework to allow small-town Lake Mary to grow into a prosperous city. The chamber consisted of business and political leaders, as well as the chief of police. At the center of the crowd with white hair, glasses, and a suit with no tie stands Lake Mary's first mayor, Don Jackson, appointed in 1973. Others pictured include Raymond Ball, commissioner Harry Percy, postmaster John Norden, commissioner Marty Bacon, future mayor Walt Sorenson, Errol Greene, and police chief Benson.

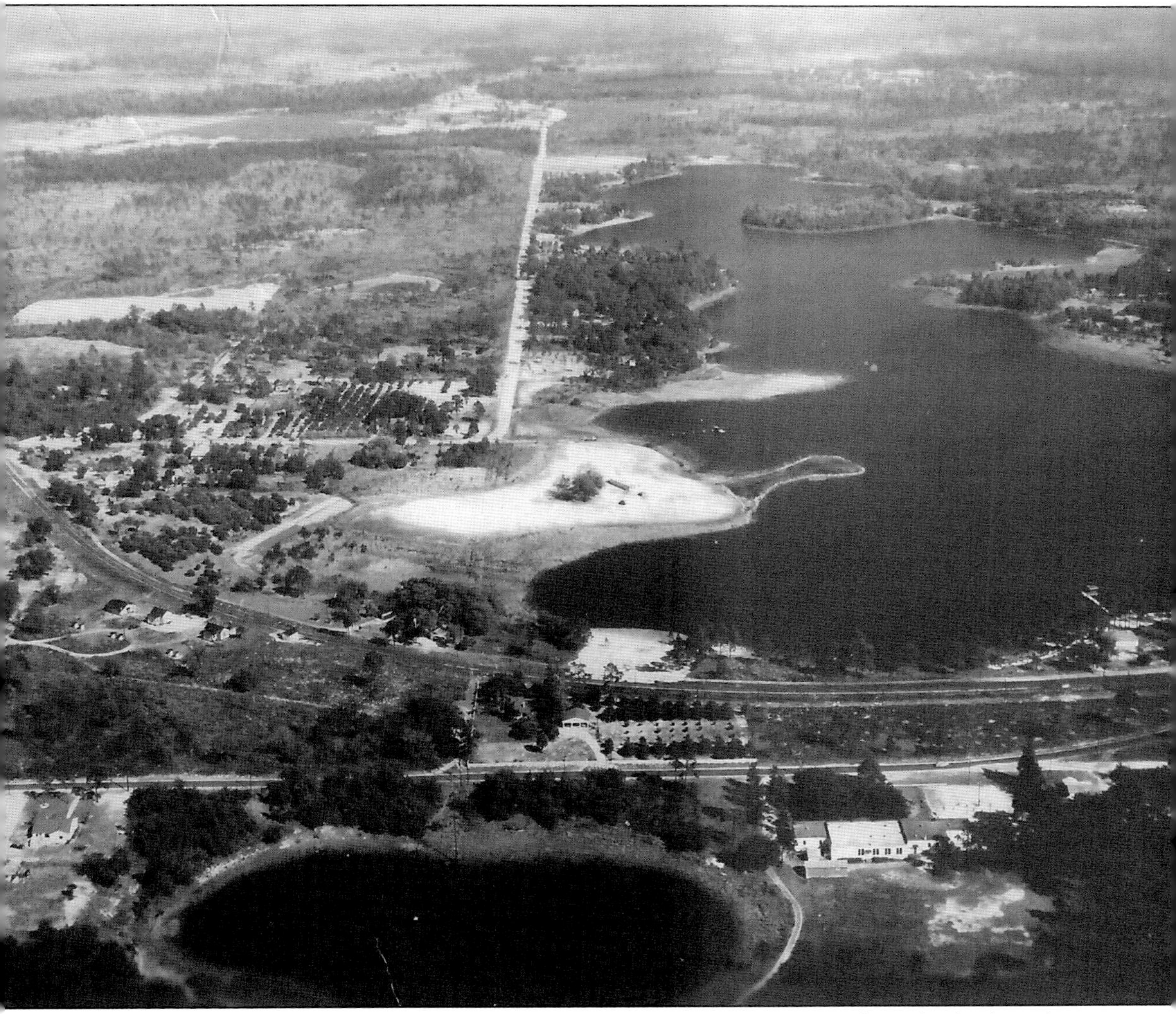

This is an aerial view of Lake Mary prior to the paving of Lake Mary Boulevard, which is the white vertical line at top center. The paving of the road transformed this landscape, cutting a line down the middle of the oval pond at the bottom of the photograph as Lake Mary Boulevard was extended west toward the newly constructed Interstate 4 interchange. The wide curving railroad line pictured here, as well as Country Club Road, which intersects it just out of frame at bottom right, still exist today in roughly the same form.

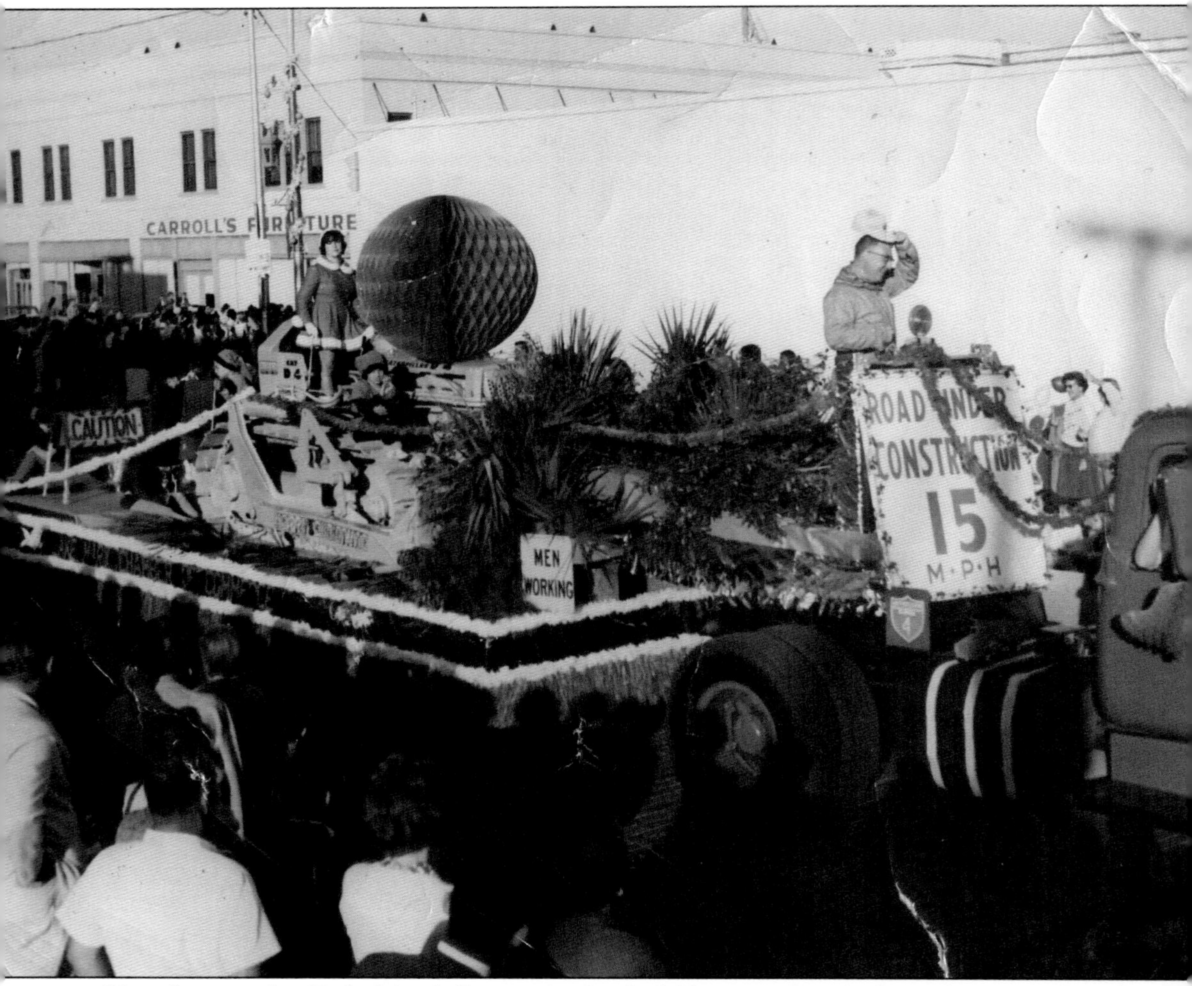

This photograph of Lake Mary's float in the Sanford Christmas Parade shows the town's shared initiative for road paving, which was intended to help spur commerce and lay the foundations for future growth.

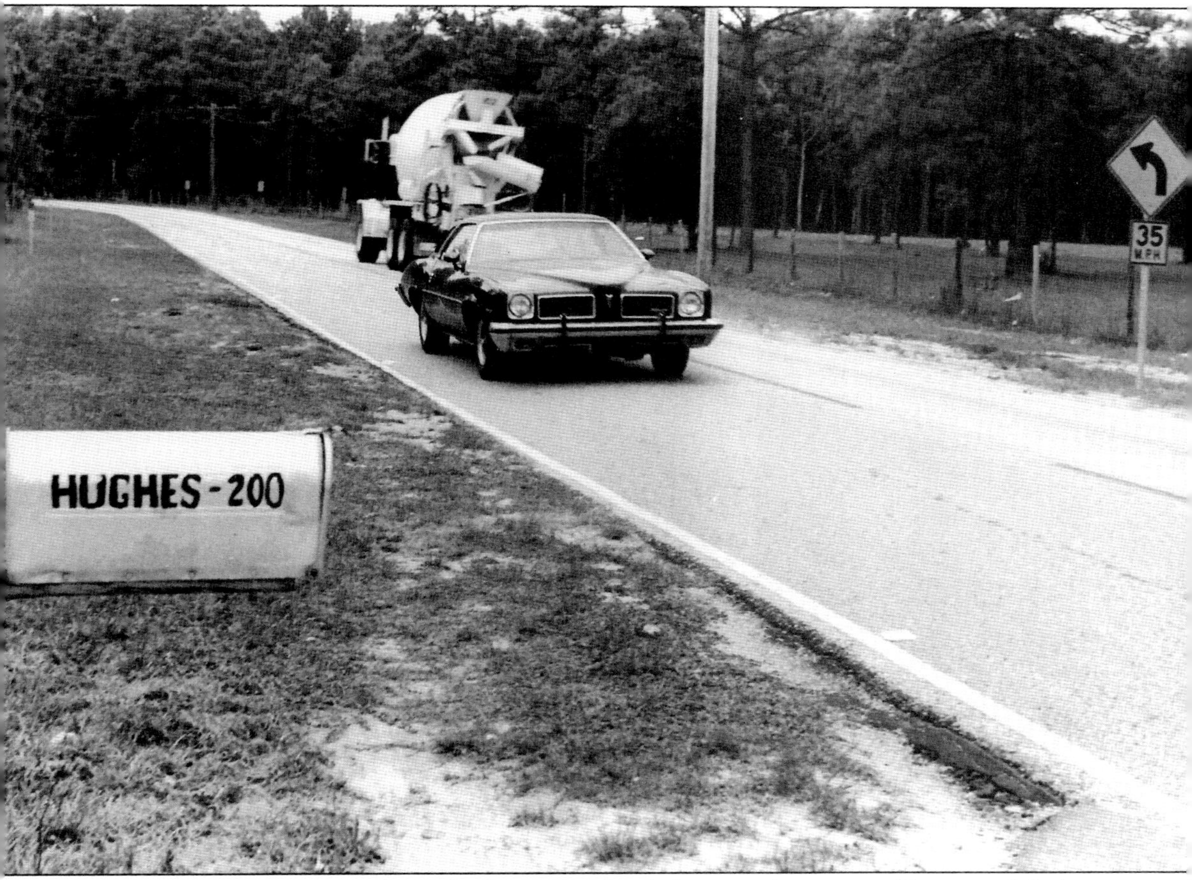

Pictured is a freshly paved road outside the Hughes family home at the corner of Longwood–Lake Mary Road and Washington Avenue, the future home of the River Oaks Church. A little thing like paving roads had a huge effect on this small town. No longer was the community as isolated as it once was. The residents were now well connected.

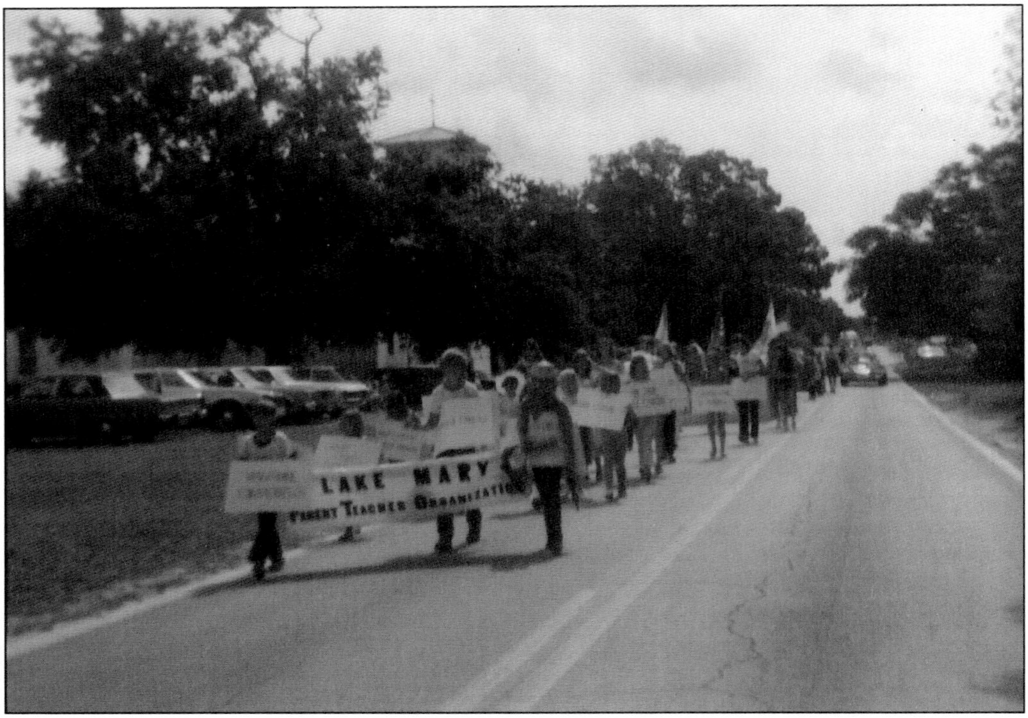

A parade of residents marches through town in these two photographs. Even amidst Lake Mary's growth, local events like this reminded residents of the importance of community. Parades are one of the oldest forms of organized celebrations, dating back as far as 3000 B.C. American celebrations typically observe historical events, holidays, and sports. The parade pictured here was in celebration of Lake Mary Day.

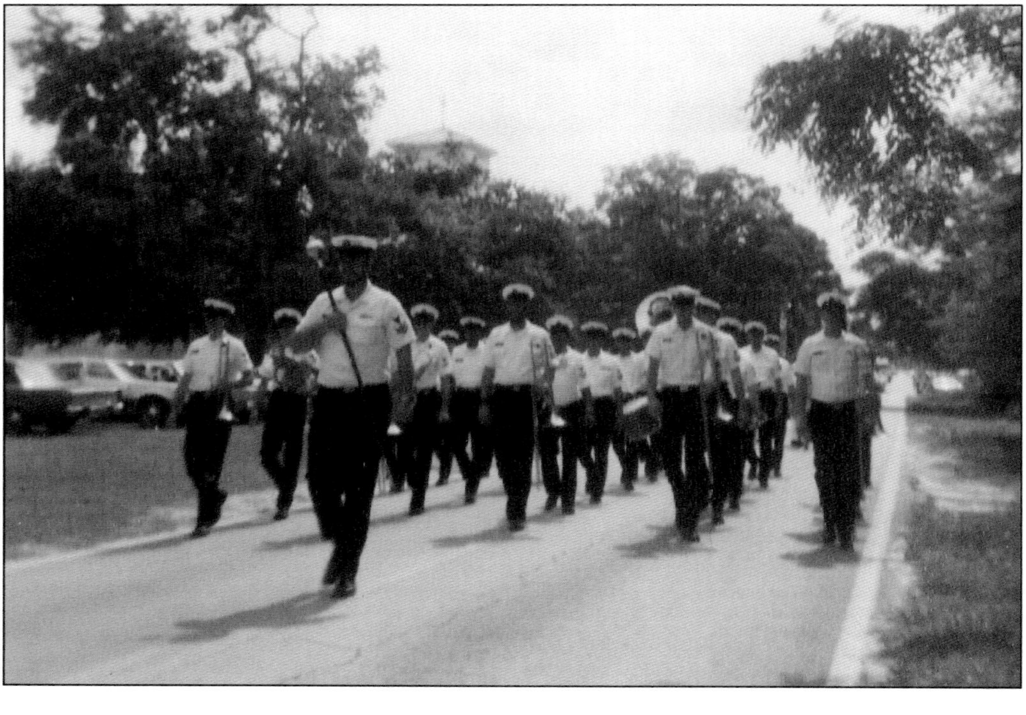

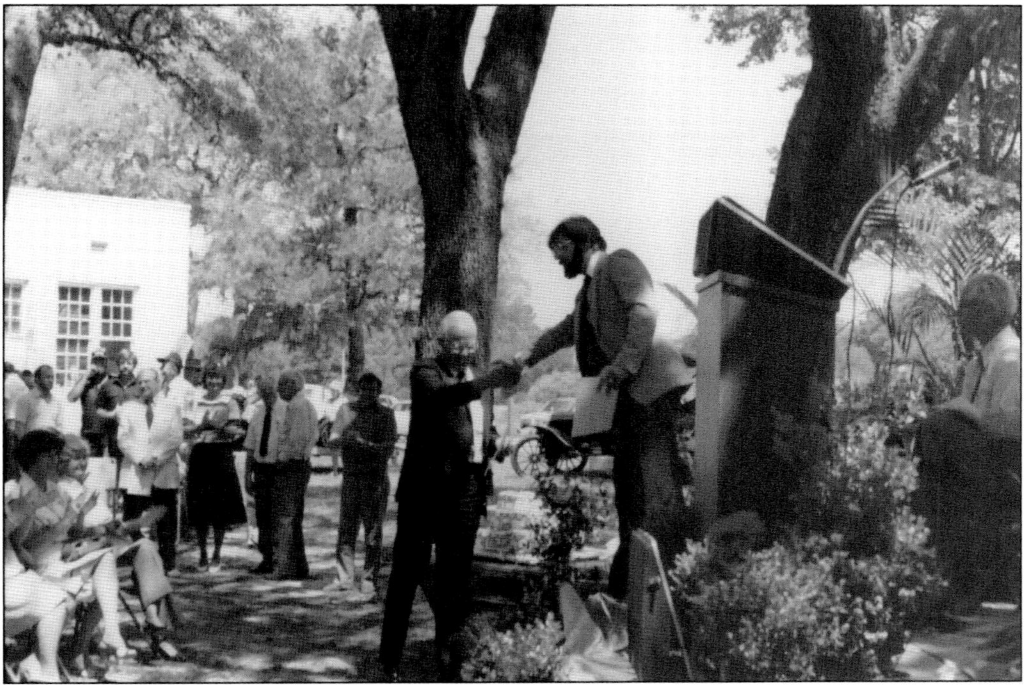

Pictured is the bicentennial celebration of 1976. Lake Mary mayor Walt Sorenson is seen at the center greeting John Polk. Among his many other accomplishments, Sorenson helped champion a building ban within a 208-foot-wide zone along Lake Mary Boulevard in order to allow for road beautification and to preserve the town's natural splendor.

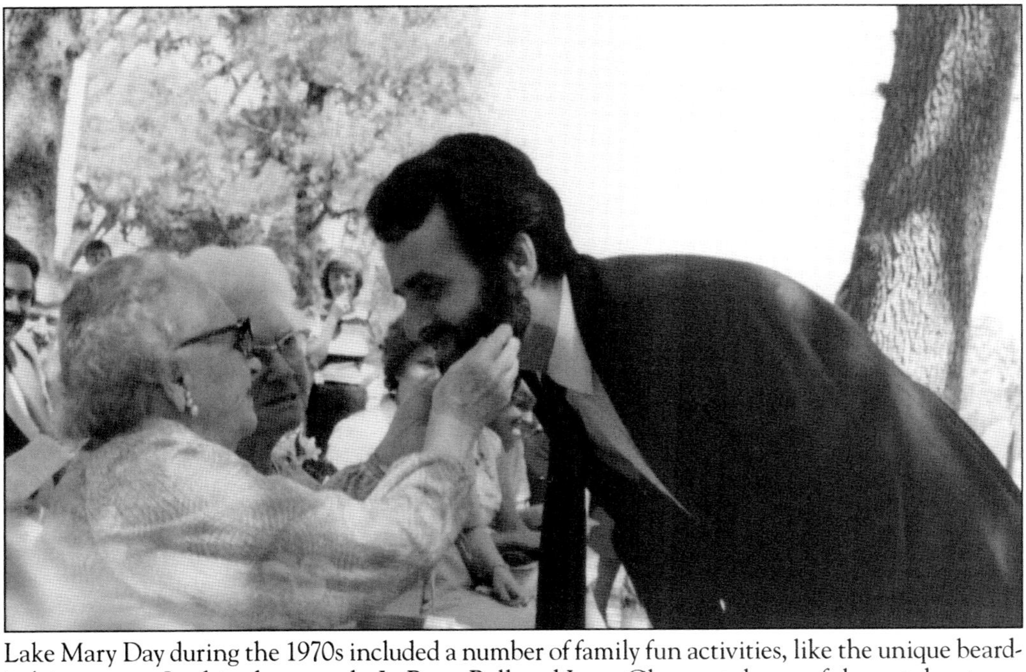

Lake Mary Day during the 1970s included a number of family fun activities, like the unique beard-judging event. In this photograph, LuRene Ball and Lena Gleason take careful mental notes as they judge Dick Fess's beard.

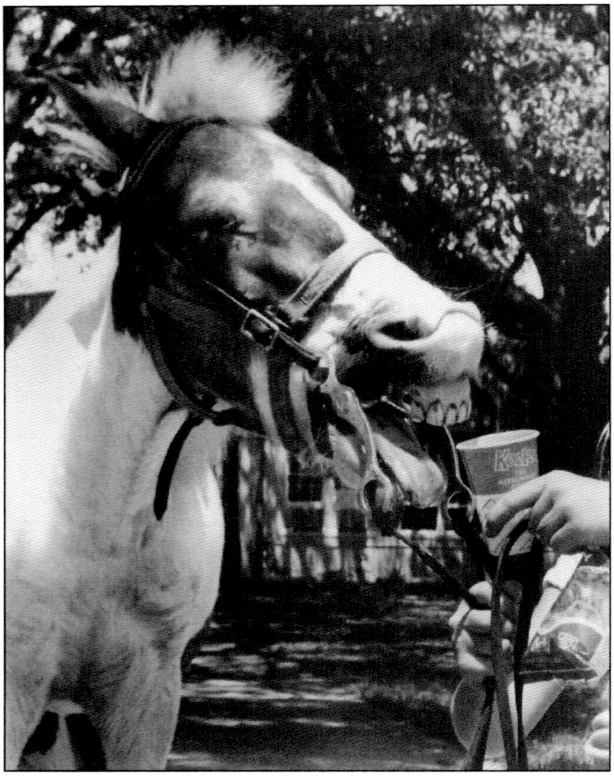

Horses still viewed Lake Mary as their home in the 1970s. The photograph at left shows residents allowing their horse to drink from a paper cup. The photograph below is of Tonka the Beer Drinking Horse, one of Lake Mary's most famous horses. Tonka gained a reputation for drinking a bellyful of alcohol and stumbling around town while he enjoyed the after effects. Locals contributed to the horse's drinking by buying him rounds at happy hour.

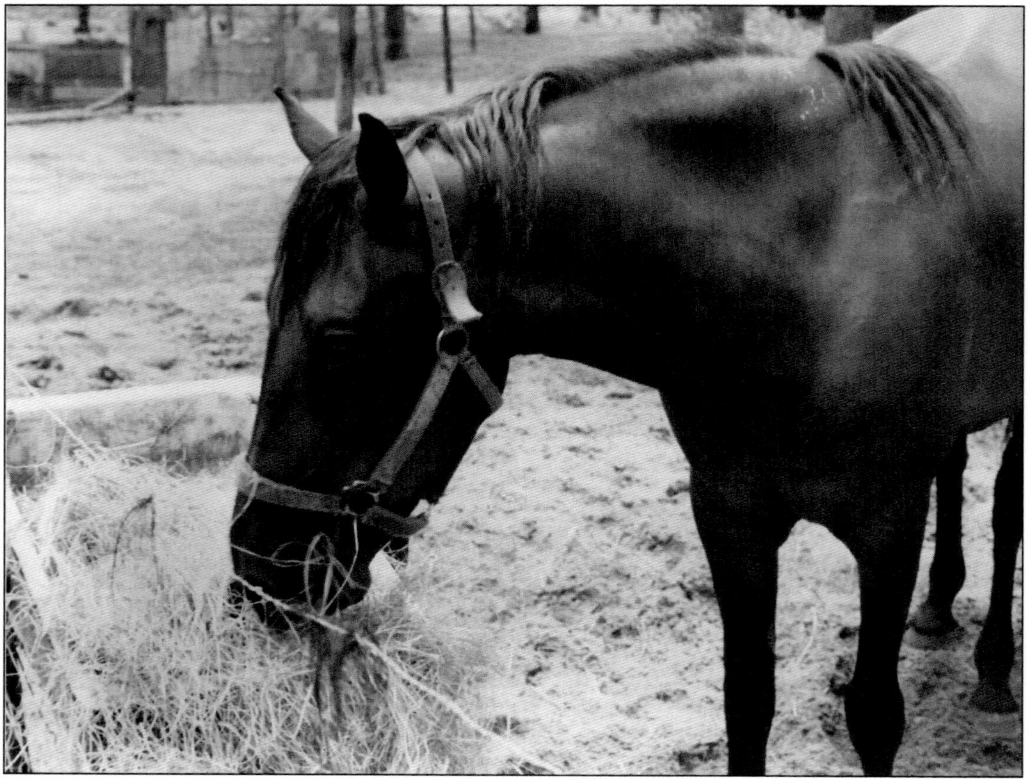

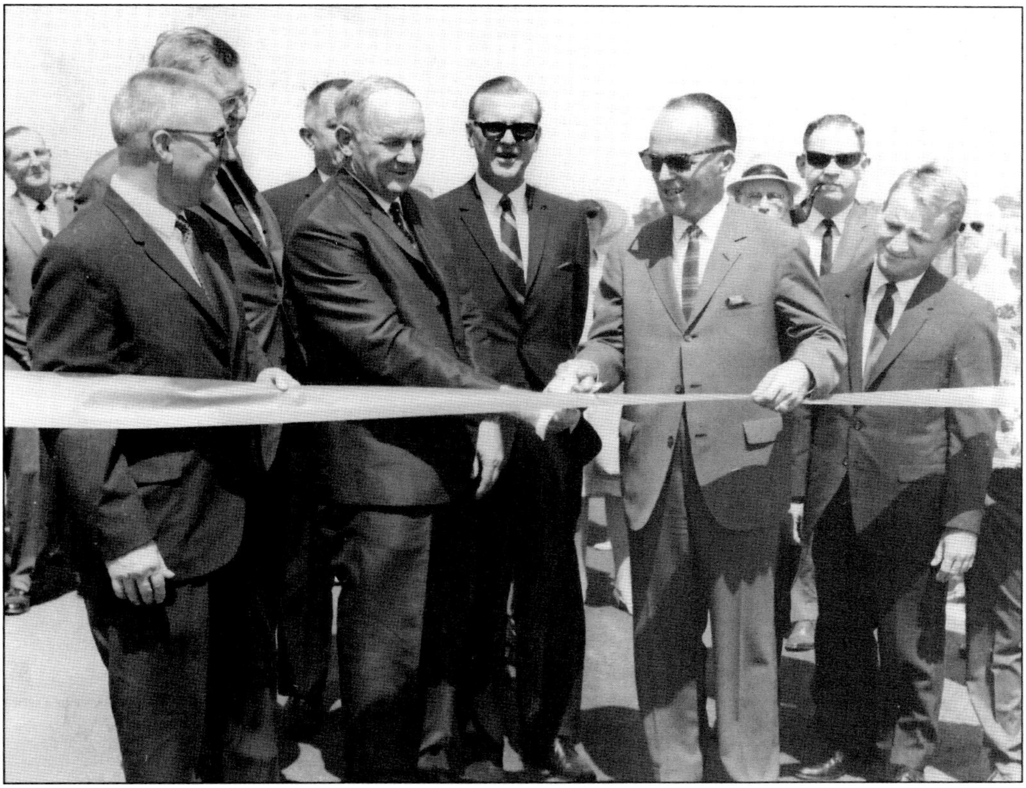

The dedication of the new Interstate 4 interchange was a big deal in Lake Mary. The original segments of Interstate 4 were completed as early as 1959 and were the first interstate highways built in Florida. Construction reached Lake Mary in the mid-1960s. The new access point to the city meant more connections, literally paving the way for its growing commerce. And in true Lake Mary tradition, no ceremony would be complete without some homemade baked items and punch, shown at right.

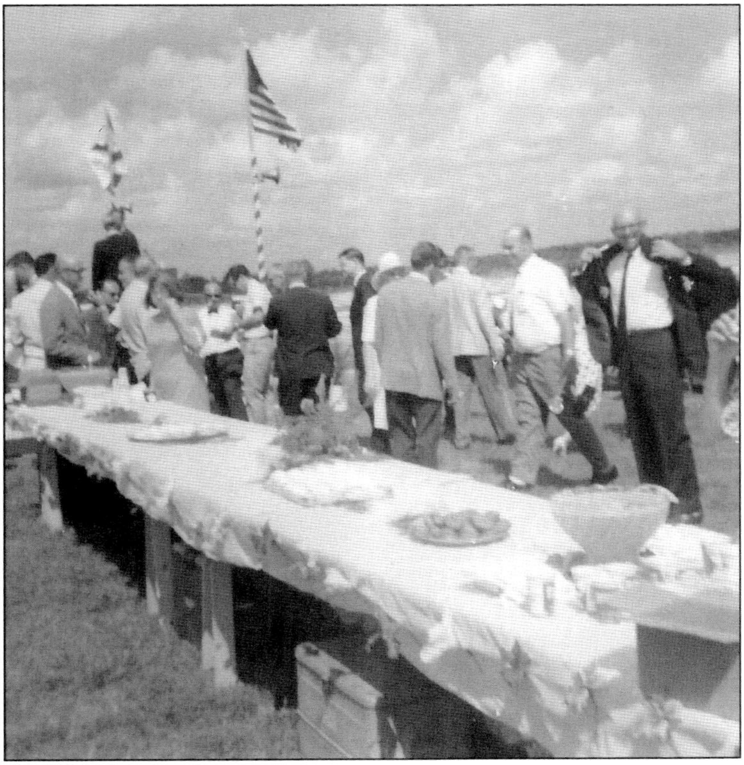

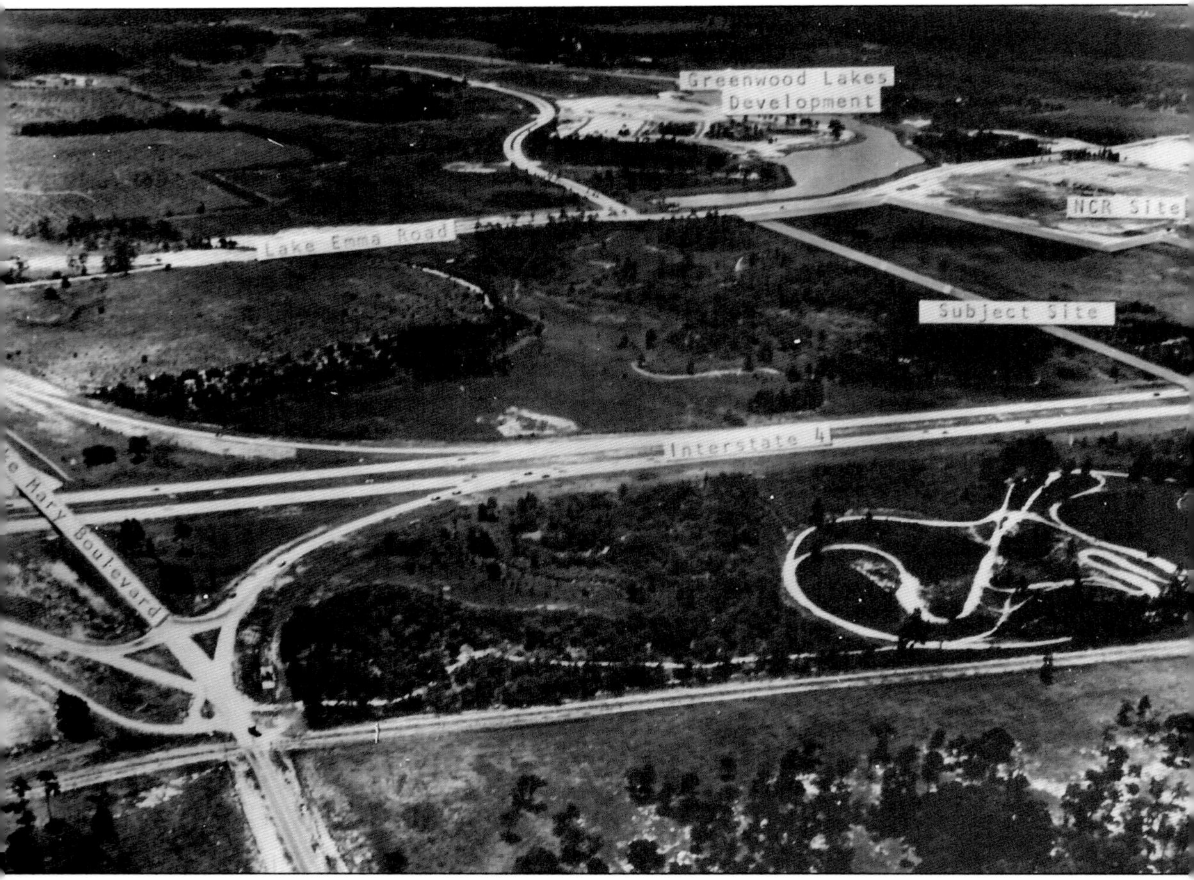

Pictured is the Interstate 4 interchange, looking southeast toward the Greenwood Lakes Development, which was under construction at the time. Although miles west of the traditional downtown Lake Mary, the chamber of commerce was integral in its design and development. Their planning has paid off with a bustling Interstate 4/Lake Mary Boulevard area today.

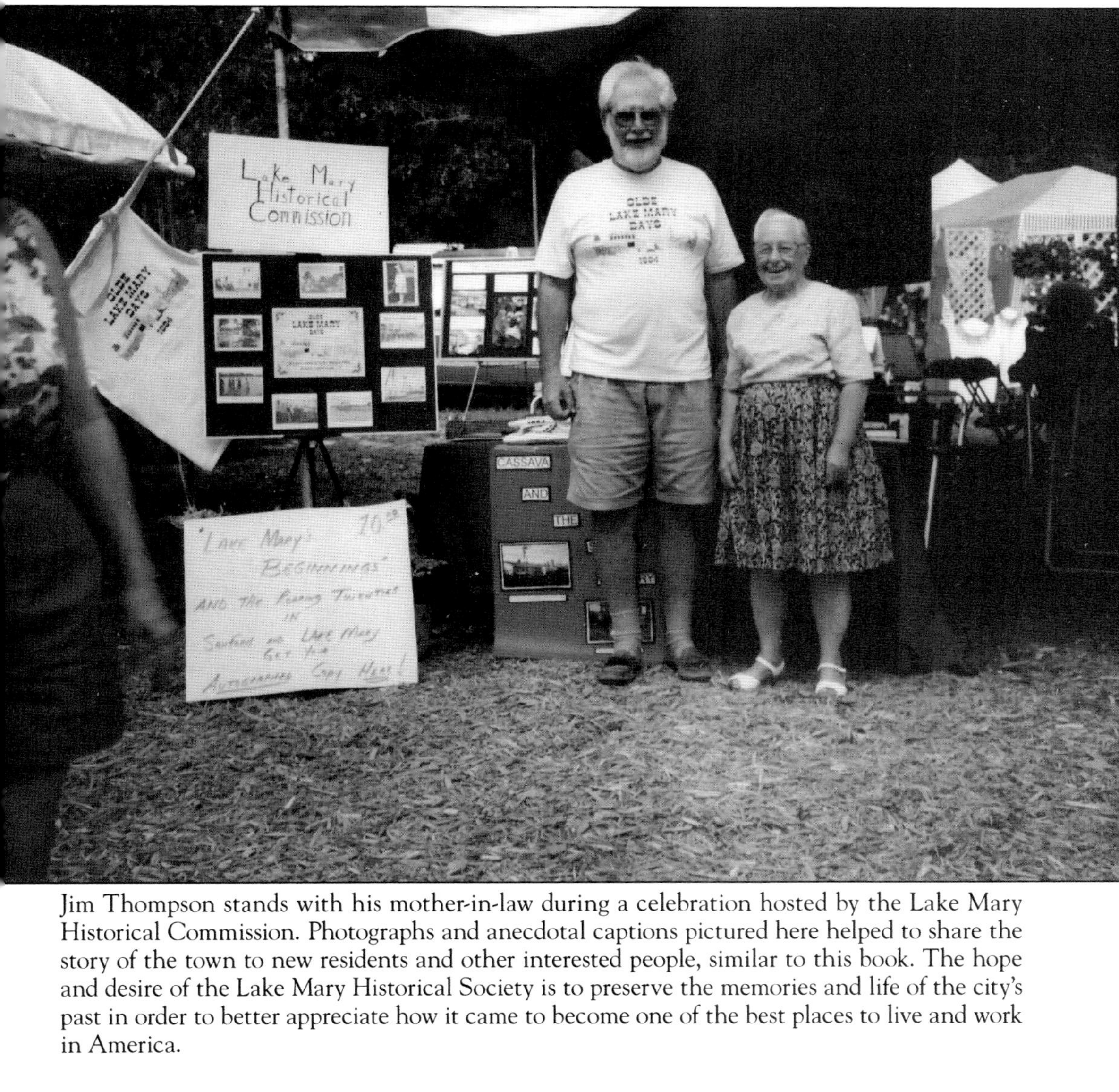

Jim Thompson stands with his mother-in-law during a celebration hosted by the Lake Mary Historical Commission. Photographs and anecdotal captions pictured here helped to share the story of the town to new residents and other interested people, similar to this book. The hope and desire of the Lake Mary Historical Society is to preserve the memories and life of the city's past in order to better appreciate how it came to become one of the best places to live and work in America.

DISCOVER THOUSANDS OF LOCAL HISTORY BOOKS FEATURING MILLIONS OF VINTAGE IMAGES

Arcadia Publishing, the leading local history publisher in the United States, is committed to making history accessible and meaningful through publishing books that celebrate and preserve the heritage of America's people and places.

Find more books like this at
www.arcadiapublishing.com

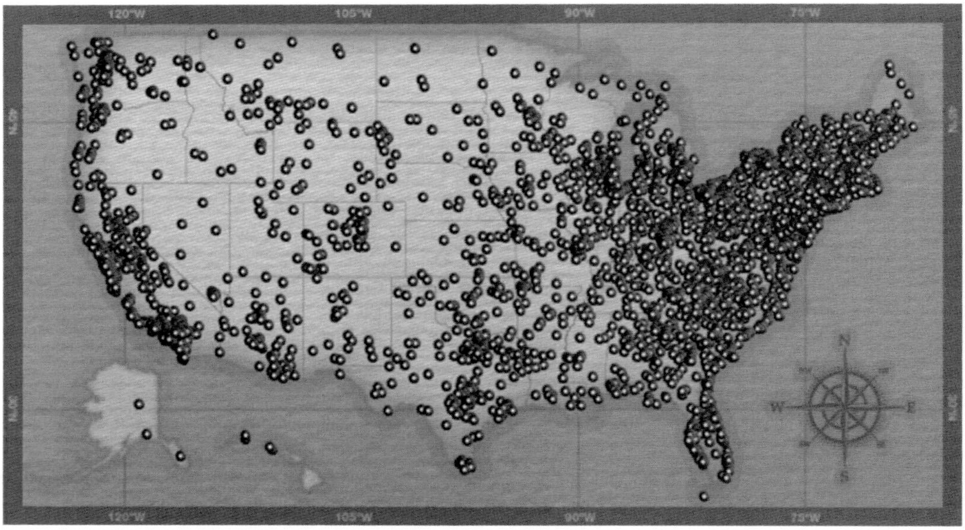

Search for your hometown history, your old stomping grounds, and even your favorite sports team.

Consistent with our mission to preserve history on a local level, this book was printed in South Carolina on American-made paper and manufactured entirely in the United States. Products carrying the accredited Forest Stewardship Council (FSC) label are printed on 100 percent FSC-certified paper.

MADE IN THE USA